WALKING THE MUNROS & TOPS

THE MUNROS AND TOPS

A record-setting walk in the Scottish Highlands

CHRIS TOWNSEND

MAINSTREAM
PUBLISHING

EDINBURGH AND LONDON

The moral right of the author has been asserted

First published in Great Britain in 1997 by
MAINSTREAM PUBLISHING COMPANY (EDINBURGH) LTD
7 Albany Street
Edinburgh EH1 3UG

ISBN 1 85158 986 4

A catalogue record for this book is available from the British Library

Typeset in 11 on 13pt Berkeley
Printed and bound in Great Britain by Butler and Tanner Ltd, Frome

Contents

Acknowledgements

The walk could not have taken place without support and help from many people. In particular I must thank my partner Denise Thorn for giving up so much time to sort out my supplies and then drive thousands of miles to bring them to me. She also co-ordinated rendezvous points with those coming out to walk with me and dealt with my mail and phone calls. Her encouragement and confidence in my ability to complete the walk were invaluable. Finally, she carefully checked the manuscript for the book, correcting errors and making many useful suggestions. I cannot thank her enough. My thanks also to my step-daughter Hazel Walsh for accepting my absence for the summer and coming on many long car journeys to meet me briefly in remote spots.

I am grateful to Andy and Jane Smith for the essential support they gave to the support team.

Stephen Laycock and Perseverance Mills, makers of Pertex fabric, provided sponsorship and Pertex clothing was provided by Rab, Sprayway and Buffalo. Carlton Reid of Front Page Creations handled publicity, ensuring good coverage of the walk in Scottish newspapers and even a few mentions in papers south of the border.

As always John Traynor gave me enthusiastic support and came up with many suggestions for sponsorship and publicity.

The Brasher Boot Company generously provided me with Brasher Boots. Aarn Tate supplied me with three packs to test. Other equipment was supplied specially for the walk by Mountain and Wildlife Ventures (Hilleberg tent), Lowe Alpine (pack), Field & Trek (Arc'teryx pack), Coleman (Micro stoves), Lyon Equipment (Ortlieb waterbag), the Dry Walker Shop (Bothy Boots) and Saracen Cycles (Rufftrax mountain bike). Alastair Forsyth of the Forsyth Cycle Shop in Grantown-on-Spey gave useful advice on bikes.

Those friends who joined me on the walk greatly contributed to its success. In particular I thank Chris Ainsworth and Paul Riley for their essential assistance on the Cuillin Ridge, Andy Hicks for staying with me for a week of mostly bad weather and Chris Brasher and Cameron McNeish for making the last day especially memorable. Thanks also to Bill Wallace, John Manning, Jan Dulla and Katarina Tomcanyova for their company. John Manning took the photograph of me which is used on the jacket of this book.

Ronnie Cann and Robert Bradford, Vicki Stonebridge and Tom and Liz Forrest all let me stay with them during the walk, for which I am grateful.

Author's Note

A Note on Measurements, Nomenclature and Location
Munros and Tops are summits over 3,000 feet high which is slightly more than 914 metres. Nobody would make a list, or climb, hills of 914 metres and above so I've stuck with the traditional feet. For the sake of consistency I've used imperial measures elsewhere too.

There are several different ways of spelling many of the names of the hills. As it is the 'official' list I've used the spellings as are given in *Munro's Tables*.

Many of the hills are not named on the Ordnance Survey maps and in some places it can be hard to identify the exact position of the summit, especially with Tops. To ensure I reached the right summits I highlighted each one on the maps, using the grid reference given in the *Tables*.

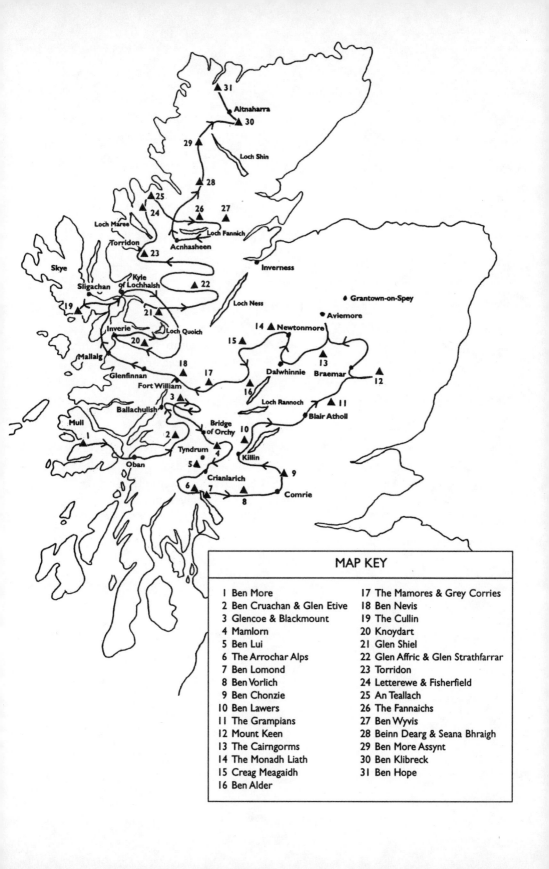

MAP KEY

1 Ben More	17 The Mamores & Grey Corries
2 Ben Cruachan & Glen Etive	18 Ben Nevis
3 Glencoe & Blackmount	19 The Cuillin
4 Mamlorn	20 Knoydart
5 Ben Lui	21 Glen Shiel
6 The Arrochar Alps	22 Glen Affric & Glen Strathfarrar
7 Ben Lomond	23 Torridon
8 Ben Vorlich	24 Letterewe & Fisherfield
9 Ben Chonzie	25 An Teallach
10 Ben Lawers	26 The Fannaichs
11 The Grampians	27 Ben Wyvis
12 Mount Keen	28 Beinn Dearg & Seana Bhraigh
13 The Cairngorms	29 Ben More Assynt
14 The Monadh Liath	30 Ben Klibreck
15 Creag Meagaidh	31 Ben Hope
16 Ben Alder	

Before The Walk:
Inspiration & Preparation

'It is interesting and almost strange that no one has yet attempted all the Munros and Tops in a single expedition.'

Andrew Dempster
The Munro Phenomenon

The sentence flew off the page and grabbed my imagination. A familiar sensation swept over me, a feeling of inspiration and excitement, and I knew immediately that I wanted to attempt such a trip. It had been three years since I'd last done a summer long walk and I was looking for a new challenge, a new excuse to spend a summer in the wilds. I didn't want to roam too far from home though. I had a new partner and a step-daughter from whom I didn't want to be parted for long. Also, having lived in the Scottish Highlands for seven years I felt that a long walk through my adopted home would be a good way to learn about it more intimately and perhaps to clarify some of the thoughts and feelings that had developed since I moved there. I know of no better way really to get to know a place than by walking through it day after day, week after week, month after month. I had anyway been considering a walk over the Munros for many years though I'd never thought of including the Tops as well.

On my first round of the Munros – completed on Sgurr nan Gillean on Skye back in 1981 – I'd barely noticed the Tops. Some I'd done inadvertently because they lay between two Munros, others I'd avoided in favour of a traverse along their sides, most I'd simply passed by, not even aware they were there. Most books on the Munros don't even mention the Tops.

To find out what the tops are we need to go back to 1891 when Sir Hugh Munro published his *Tables of Heights over 3,000 Feet* in the *Scottish*

Mountaineering Club Journal. Without explaining the criteria on which he based his definitions, Munro divided the summits in his list into 'Separate Mountains' (now known as Munros) and 'Subsidiary Tops', writing in his introduction that 'the exact number cannot be determined, owing to the impossibility of deciding what should be considered distinct mountains'. The description 'Top' covers all the hills in the list as well as being used for the Subsidiary Tops so all the Munros are Tops, but not all the Tops are Munros!

At the time of the walk the revised list, published in *Munro's Tables,* contained 277 Munros and 240 Tops, 517 summits in total. A year after my walk, and just before this book went to press, a new edition of the *Tables* was published in which eight Tops are promoted to Munro status. There are also various changes to the Tops, with 15 deletions and 9 new ones, resulting in a total list of 511 summits. If I'd waited a year I would have had six less peaks to climb! The new Munros are Stob Coire Raineach on Buachaille Etive Beag, Stob na Broige on Buchaille Etive Mor, Stob Coire Sgreamhach on Bidean nam Bian, Spidean Coire nan Clach on Beinn Eighe, Tom na Gruagaich on Ben Alligin, An Stuc in the Ben Lawers group, Sgurr na Carnach on the Five Sisters of Kintail and Sgor an Lochain Uaine in the Cairngorms. One Munro, Sgor an Iubhair in the Mamores, has been demoted to a Top. This means there are now 284 Munros. I climbed all these peaks of course. However, those who dash up and down just the Munros will now have to go back and dash up eight more! The new revision does rationalise the *Tables* a little but begs the question as to how far the list can be changed and still be called *Munro's Tables.*

Climbing hills should be about enjoyment not list ticking however. A reason for climbing the Tops is that many of them lie on ridges or spurs far from the parent Munro and are often fine peaks in their own right. Sgurr na Lapaich above Glen Affric is one example. This knowledge alone made me want to see what other Tops were like. And that's a good reason for collecting summits, whether Munros, Tops, Corbetts (peaks in Scotland between 2,500 and 3,000 feet) or whatever.

This knowledge alone made me want to see what other Tops were like. And that's a good reason for collecting summits, whether Munros, Tops, Corbetts (peaks in Scotland between 2,500 and 3,000 feet) or whatever.

Most Munroists climb the hills as day walks, many by the shortest, quickest route. However, I've always felt that the best way to experience the mountains is on long walks where I sleep out in the wilds at night, where I live in the hills 24 hours a day, week after week. That way moving and living in wild country becomes what I do and the experience is far more intense and satisfying than just being out for a day or even a week.

That the inspiration for this walk came first from a book is not unusual. The nature, the wildness, of the land comes first but the idea for a specific walk has often come from the writings of others. Books have always been central to my outdoor wanderings, a seemingly contradictory statement but true. My first long distance walk, from Land's End to John O'Groats in 1978, was inspired by John Hillaby's *Journey Through Britain*. On that trip I discovered for the first time the glorious wild lands of the West and North Highlands, an area I longed to explore more closely. Soon after that End to End walk I read Hamish Brown's superb *Hamish's Mountain Walk* about the first continuous round of the Munros. Ever since I'd wanted to walk the Munros in one trip but had somehow never got round to doing so. However, between 1979 and 1993 I did manage two 500 plus-mile walks over 147 Munros plus seven coast to coast crossings of Scotland which included 185 Munros and Corbetts, which gave me a good idea what a continuous round would be like. Also, inspired by other landscapes, other writings, I ventured further afield, walking the 2,600 mile Pacific Crest Trail and the 3,000 mile Continental Divide Trail in the Western USA, then heading north into Canada to make the first ever walk, 1,600 miles in total, along the length of the Canadian Rockies and a 1,000 mile walk through the Yukon Territory. More recently I came closer to home and walked 1,300 miles through the mountains of Norway and Sweden. This wealth of wilderness wandering was good preparation for a solo round of the Munros and Tops.

Always I had this thought that one day I would climb the Munros in one journey. While I thought about it others followed in Hamish's footsteps. By 1995 16 people had completed continuous rounds, some extending the venture to include the 3,000 foot peaks of the rest of Britain. Craig Caldwell even took in all 221 Corbetts in a 13 month epic, described in his book *Climb Every Mountain*. In the 1980s those tackling the round were walkers, in the 1990s runners got involved and time became an important factor. By using bicycles for road sections Andrew Johnstone and Rory Gibson set a record of 51 days in 1992. The record for a trip solely on foot, 66 days 7 hours, was set by Mike Cudahy in 1994. Running ventures rely on good back-up with support crews being essential. Although I've tried hill running I'm a walker at heart and for me the best way to appreciate wild land is by walking through it and camping out in it. Hamish Brown's long walk remained my inspiration rather than the fast times of the runners.

13

The thought of doing something not done before is challenging and gives an edge of excitement and adventure to a walk. The heart of any backpacking trip is the spending of weeks at a time living in wild country though, not the completing of a route. Although it is the great pleasure and satisfaction of doing this that has me going back again and again I do find that a goal gives a walk a focus and an overall shape as well of course as a beginning and an end.

As always I wanted to do the walk as soon as possible. Planning, however, takes time. Fortunately the initial burst of inspiration occurred too late in the summer to set out that year so I had the whole of the next autumn and winter to plan the walk. That I would go alone was never in doubt. All my previous long walks had been solo ones. On the practical level it is so much easier not to have to share decision making. If I wanted to walk for 12 hours I could. If I wanted to stay in bed all morning I could do that too. For me that freedom is an essential part of a long trip. There are other, deeper reasons for walking solo however. Only by being alone could I be open to all the subtleties of the mountain world, could I hope to find that heightened awareness of nature, that joy in creation, which I'd experienced on previous walks and which is a main reason I keep going back.

Of course I expected and hoped that friends would join me occasionally for one or more days. Indeed, I needed support for the Cuillin of Skye as some of the peaks there require rock climbing skills and I am not a climber. Arranging for competent friends to join me there was an essential part of the planning and was, in the end, to play a crucial part in the overall form of the walk.

That initial buzz of excitement when the idea of the walk first leapt to mind eventually gave way to a more sober assessment of just what was involved. This is the point at which ventures come closest to being abandoned! The planning often seems a more daunting task than the actual walk but once I begin I find I actually enjoy it.

After many hours spent poring over maps my rough estimates were for at least 500,000 feet of climbing and 1,600 miles of walking. How long the walk would take would depend in part on the weather but my initial plan was for 110 days, including ten rest days. I'd averaged around 16 miles a day on other long walks so it seemed reasonable to assume I could do so again. Although early April would have been the best time to start, so I could avoid both the midge and stalking seasons, I would still be working as a Nordic ski tour leader then. Mid-May was the earliest I could begin which meant a finish around late August. I would just have to cope with the midges and avoid the deer stalkers. I knew though that this rough plan would be amended on a day to day, week to week basis and that the final journey could turn out to be very different.

One reason for this was the route. Day walks up the Munros from the nearest car park are well documented in several guidebooks but there are, thankfully, no detailed descriptions of multi-day routes nor much in the way of information on climbing the Tops. Indeed, most guidebooks ignore the latter, only Irvine Butterfield's *The High Mountains of Britain and Ireland* giving brief information on them. Planning the route involved working through a pile of maps and plotting a cat's cradle of a route as I tried to link the 517 summits by the easiest and quickest way, which was often not the same. Apart from a pile of maps, the essential reference work was *Munro's Tables* of course but I also used *Hamish's Mountain Walk* and *The High Mountains of Britain and Ireland*. I also found Bartholomew's *Munro Map*, a wall chart showing all the Munros and Tops, very useful for giving an overview of the whole route. It ended up pinned to a wall in the hall at home so my progress could be plotted on it by my partner Denise and seven-year-old Hazel.

All the other long walks I've done have been point to point journeys where the day to day route could be altered if the weather was bad or the terrain difficult. However a round of the Munros and Tops doesn't allow for alternative routes. If the weather was so bad that I couldn't reach a summit then I would just have to wait until it improved. There was some choice of route between the different groups of hills of course and the major part of the planning was working out a detailed route both over and between the summits. The main problem lay with those hills that lie far from others such as Ben Wyvis, Ben Chonzie, Ben Hope, Ben More on Mull and the Cuillin of Skye. These could only be reached by long road journeys. I hate road walking and had no desire to spend days slogging along tarmac. The answer was to do what Hamish Brown did and use a bicycle as this didn't break my self-imposed rule of a completely self-propelled journey. The bike itself would be brought out when needed by Denise.

Starting with one of the outlying hills was also a way to cut down on the total distance and the amount of time needed to travel between groups of hills so, like Hamish Brown, I chose Ben More on the island of Mull as my first summit. After that I planned on heading south and east through the Southern Highlands then north into the Cairngorms, back west over Ben Alder and the Mamores to Ben Nevis, east again over the Grey Corries to the Monadh Liath and over Creag Meagaidh to the Great Glen. Next it would be out to the far west and Knoydart and Skye before turning north to Glen Shiel and a zigzag route through the Northern

Highlands to Ben Hope. Overall it was a daunting prospect, but then the challenge was one reason for going.

Fitness is of course needed for a strenuous mountain walk. Here my skiing would be important. For much of the four months preceding the walk I would be leading ski tours in Norway, culminating in a two week ski camping expedition to Spitsbergen in the April. That, I hoped, would see me fit enough.

Resupplying with food is a key logistical problem on any extended backpacking trip. I knew that I would need at least 2lb of dried food a day. In the remote wildernesses of northern Canada I've carried up to 17 days' worth of food at a time, which, with the gear needed for such places, led to pack weights of 70lb and more. But on those walks I mostly walked through the mountains not over them. Climbing four and more summits a day, with anything from 3,000 to 10,000 feet of ascent, meant I wouldn't be able to carry anything like that weight. Nowhere in the Highlands is anywhere near as remote as the Northern Rockies or the Yukon however so careful planning should mean I didn't have to carry more than a few days' food at a time for most of the walk. Where there were local shops I would use them but most of the food was packed up into boxes to be sent to post offices or other places or else brought out to road crossings by Denise, who was to be my main support. Denise is also a keen hill-walker and during the preparations for the walk we planned for her to climb some of the summits with me. We also arranged for her to walk in with supplies in some places. However, unforeseen difficulties with child care arrangements meant these plans had to be abandoned. My greatest regret of the walk was that Denise hadn't been with me on any of the summits.

Planning the walk took time and energy and there was always the danger that the actual adventure itself could vanish in a welter of lists and logistics, maps and food. This was only temporary of course. I knew that when the walk actually began, when I took the first step, all the organisation would fade into the background. Then it would just be me and the hills, for a summer at least.

Chapter 1

STORMS IN THE SOUTH-WEST

18 – 31 MAY MULL TO INVERORAN 167 MILES 42 SUMMITS

'The majority of hillwalking is done in less than satisfactory weather, and somehow, no matter how foul and inclement it is, you cannot wait to get back up the hills and do it again.'

Muriel Gray
The First Fifty

A rush of final preparations; a checking of gear, maps, food, supply points; a tidying up of bits of work, letters that hadn't been written, people who hadn't been contacted, marked the last fortnight before the walk was to start. On returning from the Spitsbergen ski tour, where we'd camped in temperatures of –25°C, I'd hoped to be able to unwind from the ski season and then mentally prepare myself for the long summer ahead. Instead I was flying round in a state of tension unable to believe I could tie up all the loose ends.

Relief came on the morning of 18 May, 1996, when I left home with Denise and Hazel and headed for Mull. If anything hadn't been done now it would have to wait, possibly for ever. I couldn't wait any longer even though, after two weeks of sunny weather, winter had returned for a last fling and the forecast for the next few days was not promising.

Snow was falling and the sky was thick with dark cloud as we passed by the invisible Cairngorms but to the west the sky was clearer. The sun was out as we went by Loch Linnhe, its shores bright with the green of spring, to the Corran and Lochaline ferries. Denise and Hazel were staying in a B&B but I wanted to camp this first night. The tent was pitched on the bright green sheep-cropped grass close to Loch na Keal. I bundled some gear into the pack, said farewell to Denise and Hazel, and, at 3.15 in the afternoon, set off up Ben More. The walk had begun.

I'd been up the peak once before, 15 years earlier, on my only previous visit to Mull, a day trip from Oban. Then I'd traversed the peak from south to north in thick mist and heavy rain, an inadvertent route as I'd intended to descend the way I'd ascended but was led astray by a wrong compass bearing on the summit, not knowing that the rocks there are magnetic. On the way down I hadn't checked the compass until I began to wonder about the unfamiliarity of the scenery. By then it made sense to continue down even though it meant hitch-hiking back to the ferry rather than catching the bus.

That had been a hasty trip on which I'd seen little so I was pleased now to climb Ben More in sunshine though a stiff and cold north-east wind rather detracted from the feel of summer. Because of the unseasonably cold wind I was wearing thick stretch fleece tights, taken at the last minute, along with a top of the same material. I was only a short way up Gleann na Beinne Fada and admiring some nice little waterfalls and the rocky slopes and ridges of A'Chioch and Ben More when I felt a cold draught around my nether regions. The tights had split from waist to crotch! Shorts did until I reached the ridge above but there the wind was so strong and cold that over-trousers were required. This was a harbinger of the future – strong winds were to be a major feature of the walk.

A'Chioch, a fine pointed rocky hill though not a Top as it's below 3,000 feet, gave a bit of scrambling both up and down. More easy scrambling along a narrow pinnacled ridge led to the summit of Ben More. The view was extensive and splendid – a vast spread of sea and islands sparkling in the sun out to the west though there was cloud inland. As it was the first summit I set up the tripod and took some self-portraits. I sat beside the cairn a while, trying to feel a sense of beginning, a sense of something significant but nothing came. All I could really feel was the chill of the wind. I headed down. The walk had started though it seemed like a day out. I wasn't even carrying a full pack.

Back at the tent the only sounds were the cries of oyster-catchers, the calling of lambs and the gurgling of a nearby stream. I sat and watched the sunset over supper, feeling content. Camping is an essential part of a mountain walk for me and it was here at my first camp that I really felt I had begun rather than on the first summit. The knowledge that I had a summer of such nights to come filled me with delight.

The alarm on my watch woke me at 6.30 a.m. I had a long day ahead, cycling to Bridge of Awe. My first full day of the walk would be spent on a bike! The wind had gone and the morning was chilly, only a few degrees above freezing. Denise and Hazel had left the bike with me as their B&B was some five miles away. I had therefore to cycle with a full pack which

I soon found uncomfortable and tiring. Happily, Denise had guessed this would be so and I met them after a couple of miles driving out to meet me. Without the pack I could look round and enjoy the rich green island landscape. I had a rest and a coffee at the B&B while Denise and Hazel breakfasted then set off for Craignure and the ferry. The wind had returned, bringing light showers, so I was wearing my rain gear. Bright yellow gorse and rich green pastures lined the road, their colours a welcome contrast to the grey sky.

The ferry crossing was dull with low cloud hiding the views and the rain becoming heavier and steadier. The only point of interest was a chance meeting with Sue, a friend from years gone by who brought back memories of weekend dashes from Tyneside, where I'd lived for a few years before moving north, with Tyneside Loipers cross-country ski club to ski tour in Glen Shee and other areas.

Oban was crowded and wet. Leaving the bike chained to car park railings I joined Denise and Hazel in a packed café for lunch. Here Denise repaired my torn pants and the sleeve of my stretch fleece top, the seam of which was also splitting. I could have done it myself but I have to admit that Denise was far faster and much neater than I would have been. My sewing kit hadn't seen daylight for some time and I hadn't bothered checking it before the trip. I should have done for the needles were rusty.

An hour and a half on the bike in further rain and gloomy weather saw me to Bridge of Awe and a camp site mostly filled with caravans. After about 33 miles of cycling, more than I'd done in one day in years, my backside felt somewhat sore and I was glad I'd be walking again the next day. The bike was loaded into the car and I said farewell to Denise and Hazel who were returning home. For the next few weeks I'd be in the hills that lay farthest from home and also in an area with several post offices so I wasn't due to see them again for three weeks. Watching them drive away made the walk seem more real. I was on my own now.

With five probably unwashed days in the hills ahead I paid 20 pence for a shower but the instructions were so complicated my six minutes were almost up before I had hot water. It was a bit cool for wet hair anyway.

With cycle rides, ferries and car support I didn't yet feel as if I was beginning a long mountain walk. The next few days would change that. My plan for the first full mountain backpacking day was to traverse the five Tops and two Munros that make up Ben Cruachan, a huge and magnificent mountain whose south slopes rise steeply above the Pass of Brander, then cross Glen Noe and climb two more Munros, Beinn

19

a'Chochuill and Beinn Eunaich, before descending to Glen Kinglass to camp. This seemed like an ambitious first day but I had done most of it before, all bar two outlying Tops in fact, in nine and a half hours and with a full pack. However, as I was to learn, outlying Tops could add several hours and much effort to a day or even make a planned day simply too long and too hard to complete.

Even more important was the weather. On my previous ascent of these hills it had been dry and calm. On this occasion the day was cold, overcast and wet as I started very steeply straight up the hillside south of the Allt Gruiniche. At a height of about 2,000 feet I entered dense cloud and heavy rain began to fall. On the first Top, Stob Dearg (often called the Taynuilt Peak), it was snowing and the south-east wind was bitter. To save weight I hadn't bothered with gloves, a decision I cursed now as my hands were soon frozen. Socks were the answer, a ploy I'd last used at the end of a long walk through the Canadian Rockies when my mitts proved inadequate in temperatures of −20° and below. As I had done then I pulled a pair of socks over my hands. They were soon sodden but being wool still gave some warmth. A rocky ridge edged with big snow banks to the north led to Cruachan itself. A few snow buntings, a bird I'd last seen a few weeks before on Spitsbergen, darted about the summit, oblivious to the lashing sleet and snow. I cowered behind the summit cairn for a quick snack then left the pack while I set off for the first outlier from the ridge, Meall Cuanail. As with many Tops, and in some places even Munros, that lay out on spurs well off the main route the difficulty wasn't climbing it but the return ascent. In this case the col between the two hills was at about 2,750 feet, only 250 feet or so below Meall Cuanail but with a 950 foot climb back to Cruachan.

As I descended the weather worsened with stronger gusts of wind and driving sleet. The rocks were slick with wet snow and I had to tread carefully. I never like leaving my pack for long but I knew that it would often be essential on this walk unless I wanted it to be much harder than necessary. Today however I wasn't far below Cruachan's summit before I became worried, frightened even, that I mightn't be able to find the pack again or that I would need something in it. In this weather even being quarter of an hour from my shelter, food and warm clothing seemed unwise so I went back up and collected the pack. Standing on the summit was now difficult. As I descended to the col again the feeling grew that going on was not sensible. Following my instincts in the mountains has often been the wisest course so I decided to drop down into Coire Cruachan and find somewhere to camp. I did nip up Meall Cuanail first but by mid afternoon I was camped in the slight shelter of a small bank a little above the Cruachan Reservoir. Outside the tent the rain hammered down.

Although relieved to be out of the storm I felt despondent. My first full day and I'd only climbed three summits instead of the nine planned. By the time I was dry and warm and full of coffee and soup the weather had improved a little and I could see the ridge above the camp. I suddenly realised I could go out again. Unlike all the other long walks I'd done this wasn't a simple A to B one. In what order or by what route I did all the hills didn't matter. So at 5.45 p.m. I set off to do the last four summits of the Cruachan group, starting with a direct ascent of Drochaid Glas. The light pack made it much easier and I moved fast to keep warm in the still cold and strong wind. It was dry now though and there were bits of views as the clouds came and went. Distant hills shone in the sun and there seemed to be lochs everywhere. One snowy peak to the north stood out. Bidean nam Bian in Glencoe I guessed. Stob Diamh, the other Munro, and Sron an Isean were soon done then it was over Stob Garbh and a steep descent back to the tent. My legs felt a little weary as I trudged through the last peat hags to camp. This wasn't surprising, I'd done 7,765 feet of ascent. With seven summits done I felt much better though I had a problem for the next day as I was still the wrong side of Cruachan.

The rain returned and kept up all night and into the next day, making me glad I'd seized the brief let-up in the storm to finish the Cruachan peaks. Rather than cross the main ridge, I skirted round the east side of the mountain via the Allt Coire Ghlais glen then went up the Allt Mhoille glen to the Lairig Noe, a pass below Beinn a'Chochuill. This peak and Beinn Eunaich were both in cloud and blasted by sleet and hail so I was over them quickly, briefly greeting four hooded figures on the last summit – the first people I'd seen on the summits – before hurrying down north-east to Glen Kinglass where I camped in birch woods on the floor of the glen. Bursts of heavy rain continued. Everything was damp, my boots and socks sodden. Now a day behind schedule I spent the evening revising my plans. As throughout the walk the key was where and when the next supply point was. I didn't have a rendezvous arranged so the time of arrival didn't matter but I did want to get to Ballachulish, where there should be a parcel for me at the post office, before my food ran out. This would mean missing out some summits and climbing them from Glencoe. Which ones, and how many, would depend on the weather, which showed no sign of improving.

Slugs filled the tent porch at dawn. Thick black ones and slim light brown ones, with eyes on stalks and moving slowly, examining each blade of grass. Outside birds were singing and two cuckoos were calling. But the rain still fell. It was to be a third day of cold, wet, misty and very windy summits.

On the track up Glen Kinglass a four-wheel drive vehicle stopped. I was asked where I'd come from and where I was going. I vaguely indicated the hills to the south and said I'd camped 'up that way'. 'That's why I didn't see you when I drove up earlier,' came the reply, making me glad I'd been out of sight of the track. I was told to ignore any barking I heard as a party were out with foxhounds combing the hillside for a fox's earth as some lambs had been killed. I heard nothing and fervently hoped the foxes escaped. Sheep are one of the most destructive domestic animals, cropping vegetation down to the ground and preventing any regeneration of trees or shrubs. Not for nothing did the great conservationist John Muir call them 'hooved locusts' after seeing the damage they did in Yosemite in California. For the Great Wood of Caledon, which once covered much of the Highlands but which is now reduced to a pitiful one per cent of its former coverage, to recover some of its former glory overgrazing by sheep (and deer) has to be ended. During the walk I was to become increasingly disturbed at the degraded nature of the land in the glens and on the lower slopes of the hills, a 'wet desert' caused by grazing and deforestation.

Up in the mist Beinn nan Aighenan, Meall Cruidh and Ben Starav came and went. I noticed little bar compass bearings until the descent from the latter when a narrow rocky arête was followed by two parallel ridges of sloping pinnacles like the teeth of a monster shark fading in and out of the mist. At the col with Glas Bheinn Mhor I left the pack and hurried up and down the peak. I had intended going on to two more summits but it was too wet, windswept and late (7p.m.) and I was too tired to go on so I descended quickly to the Allt Mheuran glen where a narrow path led down past some impressive waterslides and falls, all white with rain. The last of these plunged into a dark, narrow gorge. This is known as the Eas nam Meirlaach or Robbers' Waterfall, so called, apparently, because cattle thieves used to hide their stolen herds in the gorge. Camp was down in Glen Etive where at least the wind was somewhat subdued though the rain poured on.

During the night the wind gusted strongly again, waking me several times as it shook the tent. I felt resigned to the rain, which showed no sign of stopping, but I wasn't looking forward to a fourth day spent staggering about in the mist on compass bearings looking for summits while the wind tried to blow me off the mountains. Some of the gusts of wind were so strong down in the glen I worried that it might even be too windy high up to climb any hills safely.

'A much better day!' The first journal entry for that evening shows my concerns were unneeded. It wasn't just the eventual clearing of the skies that made it a better day though. I'd sloshed down Glen Etive in heavy rain to where a post office was marked on the map. There wasn't one but there was, as I'd hoped, a phone box. I rang Denise. It was a relief to hear her voice and know she was okay. Not long before the walk started she'd found she had to go into hospital to have a potentially serious problem investigated. Yesterday had been the day and now she was recovering from the anaesthetic at a friend's house. It could be two weeks before the results came through but the doctor was hopeful there was no real problem. I felt immensely relieved just at this news. I'd been having to keep a tight control over my thoughts to keep worries over Denise's health from overwhelming me. When this problem arose I'd thought of giving up the walk but Denise wouldn't consider the idea, pointing out that if there was nothing very wrong with her, as was more likely than not, it would then be too late to do the walk that year and I'd have wasted all the planning and preparation.

I plodded back up the glen in the rain and then turned into the dark conifer plantations filling Gleann Charnan. I was heading for the three widely spaced and awkwardly placed Munros plus a Top that lie between Glen Etive and Glen Creran. The rain started to lessen and when I came out of the trees into the upper corrie the clouds began to break up and the hills to appear. I climbed steep grassy slopes to the col between Stob an Fhuarain and Sgor na h-Ulaidh then left the pack for the easy ascent of the first. To the north-east the impressive steep and craggy south-west face of Bidean nam Bian spread out before me, sharp and clear in the post-storm light. It was a joy to have a good view, actually to see the hills I was climbing.

The pack regained, I traversed Sgor na h-Ulaidh as the clouds continued to dissipate, though Cruachan away to the south and Beinn a'Bheithir to the north-west remained cloud capped all day and Ben Starav only appeared briefly late in the afternoon. The terrain was rough and bumpy, typical of west coast hills, and there was a steep and entertaining climb, linking rakes and gullies to bypass small cliffs, up the east end of Beinn Fhionnlaidh.

The complex and rugged terrain made for slow progress and it was a good four miles from Fhionnlaidh to the next peak, Beinn Sgulaird, too far for what remained of the day. I made it to the base of the hill though and camped just west of Airigh nan Lochan at the head of Glen Ure. It was unusual and a great pleasure to be able to lie in the tent with the door open watching thick white cumulus clouds racing past in the blue sky. I was even able to air out some damp gear.

It wasn't to last and I woke to rain and thick low cloud covering the hills. As I was heading north from here and Beinn Sgulaird lay to the south I left the tent and camping gear in place and set off with a light pack. The river Ure was knee-deep with swirling dark rain run-off. I removed my dry socks then emptied out my boots on the far bank. On my return I would just slosh straight across, boots and socks totally sodden again. The ascent was along a rough and bumpy ridge with lots of little knolls and dips, an interesting place but not one for fast travel. Lashing rain and sleet detracted from the enjoyment somewhat however. Above 2,500 feet fresh snow covered the ground. The summit, amazingly, was clear of cloud though the views were minimal.

Back at the tent I had lunch under cover then packed up and headed down Glen Ure to Glen Creran and an uneventful and uninspiring walk mostly through spruce plantations over to Ballachulish, where I needed to be that night as I was now totally out of food. The rain kept up and there were no views so I went at a fast pace, my mind on the thought of the wonderful pleasures I hoped were to be had in Ballachulish, namely a dry bed and a hot bath. I had been going to camp but felt a great desire to be somewhere dry and warm for a night. I arrived just too late for the post office and then found all the B&Bs full or else only open to families. My offers to pay the family rate were refused. I had forgotten it was the spring bank holiday weekend. After trudging the streets for a couple of hours, trying every guest house, B&B and hotel I could find, I ended up in the luxurious Isles of Glencoe hotel, not somewhere I could really afford but I no longer cared about the cost. Tired and not altogether cheerful as I was several days behind schedule I decided I had to have a rest day so I checked in for two nights. My first week was over and I'd climbed 19 peaks, which was fine except that I'd planned on climbing 28.

A good meal and a hot bath made me feel better and the next morning I was even more cheerful as Denise rang up and offered to drive over the next day. Apparently the night before I'd sounded so gloomy she'd decided to come and see me. My main complaint had been about the discomfort my pack was causing me so she was bringing me a new pack. In the one I had the lightweight frame bars, an experiment with a new material, were distorting and pressing painfully into my back. That's one of the problems with using unproven gear on a long walk, not something I would normally do. On this walk though I could change gear quite quickly if I had problems so I'd been prepared to try a few new items.

The post office held parcels containing food supplies, paperback books, camera film and stretch fleece garments to replace those that had split. In Glencoe village I bought some odds and ends in the Glencoe Guides and Gear Mountain Shop and chatted to the proprietor, mountaineer Paul Moores, whom I'd first met in the Austrian Alps a few years earlier at a press event organised by a footwear company.

Back at the hotel I had a reading/gear sorting/clothes washing/note writing afternoon, fairly normal on a day off from a long walk. The next morning I left my slightly unreal bubble of luxury and walked round to the National Trust for Scotland camp-site in Glencoe. Unsurprisingly this was quite busy but it's a spacious site and I was able to find a reasonably quiet spot. Denise turned up mid-morning with lots of bits and pieces including two packs, both of which I loaded up and hauled round the site before settling on one. Reminding me that a friend was coming up to join me in six days' time, Denise left after a few hours and I set off back to Ballachulish and Beinn a'Bheithir, one of the hills I hadn't done the first week and which held two Munros and one Top.

On a brilliant January day 16 years earlier I had climbed this fine horseshoe-shaped mountain, which rises high above the meeting of Lochs Leven and Linnhe. Returning triggered many memories as that first ascent had been done with a good friend, Reggie Love, who had died in a mountaineering accident in the Alps a few years later. Reggie, who was from Galloway, had introduced me to winter hill-walking in the Highlands and we'd had a number of great days out together. I'd never before returned to any of the hills I'd climbed with Reggie as I knew that to do so could not just be a casual visit. On those hills I would always remember him and the days we had together. Climbing Beinn a'Bheithir brought him back as if he was still alive and I half expected to hear his voice round every corner. Bitter-sweet is an apt description of how I felt.

The day on Beinn a'Bheithir with Reggie had been near perfect. I remember especially cramponing up a crisp white curving snow arête to one of the summits, from where the view was tremendous. The weather was not so good this time with rain and wind though the clouds stayed above the Tops. Some scrambling along the narrow top of the north ridge of Sgorr Bhan enlivened the long ascent. Next came the curving arête again, still impressive without the snow, leading to Sgorr Dhearg. After a short drop an easy ascent led to the second Munro, Sgorr Dhonuill. As I

25

left this summit I could see dense mist rolling in from the sea. I hurried down westwards searching for a way north off the ridge. Just as the mist closed in I found a wet slippery scree gully that led down into Gleann a'Chaolais. Although I didn't remember it at the time Reggie and I had descended the same gully, though with somewhat more difficulty according to my notes which say we front pointed down it and that one of my crampons snapped in two and fell off, something I cannot remember at all.

The north side of Beinn a'Bheithir is sullied by dense spruce plantations which hamper access and give the lower slopes of the mountain a dark, dreary feel. The straight sided blocks of trees look horribly artificial from above too. Much of this timber factory had been recently clearcut making the descent through the tangle of mud and torn branches left behind difficult until I reached a forestry road. Then it was just a trudge back to the camp-site where there were many camp-fires burning and I could hear people celebrating the bank holiday late into the night.

I felt like celebrating the next morning when I woke to sunshine streaming through the tent door. A fine day at last. Before moving on I wanted to do the Aonach Eagach, that spectacular narrow rocky spine (the name means 'the notched ridge') that forms the north wall of Glencoe and involves some exposed scrambling. I'd traversed it several times before and knew that some of the scrambling was difficult, at least mentally, because of the drops involved. I really didn't want to attempt it in a storm so this good weather had come at just the right time.

The steep, rough path beside the Clachaig Gully, the standard route at the west end of the ridge for many years, isn't a good way up these days as it is now very eroded and loose. Instead I made a direct ascent from the road up steep grass to the first Munro, Sgor nam Fiannaidh (there are two Munros and two Tops on the Aonach Eagach). There was a sharp breeze and the air was crystal clear, making for magnificent views. Across the glen the snow-streaked rocky peaks of Stob Coire nam Beith and Bidean nam Bian soared above the deep blue of Loch Achtriochtan and the bright white-washed walls of Achnambeithach farm, a wonderful alpine scene. Northwards the great bulk of Ben Nevis rose beyond the long undulating line of the Mamores. Ahead the rocky crest of the Aonach Eagach twisted away into the distance. On it I could see groups of colourful figures, most heading towards me as it is reckoned to be slightly easier to do the walk east to west. However I'd wanted to get high up early on in case the weather changed again. I'd rather be walking down the glen in rain than scrambling along the ridge. Given the good weather, the holiday weekend and the fact that Glencoe is a popular hill-walking destination it wasn't surprising that this was the first day on which I met many people, 25 or more in total.

From Sgorr nam Fiannaidh it's just a walk to Stob Coire Leith, the first Top, but soon afterwards the scrambling starts for between this summit and Meall Dearg, the second Munro, lie the Crazy Pinnacles, a series of contorted rock towers. In places paths traverse below the pinnacles though these are often more exposed than the climb along the crest and have less security as there are no handholds. Parts of the ridge are very narrow indeed and there were a couple of airy moves where I took the opportunity of passing my pack ahead to people coming the other way before attempting them as I was concerned that it would push me out from the rock. Overall, as I wrote in my journal that night, 'most of the scrambling was just on the right side of frightening'.

Further scrambling led to a final steep climb up outward sloping slabs, which I remember being quite intimidating when coming the other way, to the last Top, Am Bodach. Here a group of walkers were sitting enjoying the sun and the view. They were just doing this peak as most of them felt too inexperienced to do the whole ridge though one woman had done it before, in both summer and winter.

The descent was steep but easy and I was soon heading back down Glencoe, using the old road wherever possible, the A82 when I had to. Above, the huge massif of Bidean nam Bian glowed in the low evening sun. The weather had been perfect but after dark a halo appeared round the moon and dark clouds started to fill the sky from the west.

There followed the wettest day yet. I woke to lashing rain and clouds racing overhead on a south-west wind. 'Becoming brighter this afternoon' was the forecast so I lingered in camp over a long breakfast and several cups of coffee. After another stroll up the A82 and a quick look round the NTS Visitor Centre, really an excuse to get out of the rain and have a coffee, I set off up Stob Coire nam Beith. My plan had been to do both Bidean nam Bian and Buachaille Etive Beag but by this time all I hoped was that I could do the six summits of Bidean. I did manage this but they were all done in dense mist, driving rain and a gusty wind that would have blown me over at times but for the trekking poles which I clung to with my head down during the strongest blasts. After Stob Coire nam Beith came Bidean itself followed by a diversion out on a spur to the north to Stob Coire nan Lochan. Then it was a long haul out to Stob Coire Sgreamhach before turning north again to the two Tops of Beinn Fhada.

Patches of old hard snow still lay on the ridges and big drifts were packed into the heads of the corries to either side. I had some fun reaching Beinn Fhada as the initial descent from Stob Coire Sgreamhach took me down a rock buttress that became steeper and steeper. Unable to see what lay below I eventually turned back. I had to lift the pack up onto one ledge I'd slid down before I could haul myself onto it, having come close to breaking the rule that you shouldn't descend anything you can't climb back up. Once on easier ground again I traversed below the crest of the buttress on its east side, a route that was itself very steep, loose and slippery. Looking back from where I rejoined the ridge I could see no way down the steep end of the buttress.

The ridge of Beinn Fhada was also fairly narrow but it was easy after what had gone before. Both Tops done, I descended directly east into the Lairig Eilde. It was well into the evening and I'd had enough of the stormy weather so I decided to make camp. First though I had to find a site. Everywhere was waterlogged, the hillside covered with tiny streams bursting their banks and pools lying on every flat spot. I wandered a good half mile down the glen before I found a half-dry boggy knoll just big enough for the tent high above the thrashing white water of the Allt Lairig Eilde, a river I had to ford the next day. The tent up I stripped off my wet boots, socks and waterproofs, pulled on my dry fleece top and snuggled into the sleeping bag. Outside the rain fell steadily. I wrung out my saturated socks and draped them over a guyline where the rain could wash off some of the mud.

By morning the rain had ceased though the strong wind still blew and clouds were racing across the sky from the south. Occasional spots of sunlight gave me hope it might clear but it remained dull though at least the summits were clear of cloud. The river had gone down though it still looked deep, fast and rough. The path up the glen forded it not far from where I was camped and as I packed up I watched several walkers look at the ford then turn away and continue up the same side of the valley. They probably didn't want to get their boots wet as the ford wasn't difficult. Indeed, I found I could cross by stepping from rock to rock, not that there was any point in trying to keep the river out of my waterlogged boots.

Above lay the long bulky ridge of Buachaille Etive Beag. I aimed for the lowest point on the skyline and left my pack there while I went out to the summits, Stob Coire Raineach, a Top when I did the walk but promoted to Munro status in the 1997 changes to the *Tables*, at the northerly end and Stob Dubh, the original Munro, at the southern. After collecting the pack I dropped straight down into the deep trench of the Lairig Gartain where I had lunch by the river before climbing up steep slopes, with a little easy scrambling at one point, to the Buachaille Etive Mor. This is one of the great hills of Scotland, the cliffs of the massive east face rising dramatically above Rannoch Moor and the A82 as it comes round the Blackmount, guarding the entrance to Glencoe. These cliffs are a major climbing area, especially in winter. I've done little winter climbing but I did do one gully and ridge climb here many years ago on a beautiful winter's day and I can still remember the sense of bursting out into a vast white mountain world that came when we climbed out of the dark cold confines onto the crest of Curved Ridge, a scrambling route in summer. The Buachaille Etive Mor is a big hill too, almost five miles long. At the time it had three Tops and a Munro, Stob Dearg, but the 1997 changes made Stob na Broige a Munro as well. This change is for the good if only because the walk along the ridge is excellent. Leaving the pack again I first went south-east to Stob Coire Altruim and Stob na Broige. Then it was back north-west over Stob na Doire to Stob Dearg, perched right on the edge of the eastern cliffs. The view from here can be superb but this time it was dull and hazy though I could see the distinctive cone of Schiehallion far across Rannoch Moor. It would be three weeks before I was there. Back at the pack I realised that I had walked the length of both Buachailles twice though I hadn't taken the pack to a single summit.

To the south lay the Blackmount hills, a large range with ten Tops, all of which I was hoping to do the next day. To have any chance of this I needed to camp fairly high. First though I had to drop down into Glen Etive and ford the river there. The long sides of the Buachaille are steep but not very craggy so I went straight down the hillside into the glen. The river was still high and fast with brown rainwater run-off. The map showed a bridge a half mile or so downstream. I walked down the road to it only to find that the far side was barred by a high and ugly metal gate topped with barbed wire. Rolls of barbed wire jutted out into the river too to prevent anyone trying to climb round the edge of the gate. Clearly visitors weren't welcome. I prospected carefully along the river looking for a ford. A hundred yards above the bridge a wide stony section looked passable. My boots now being half-dry I changed into my sandals and waded in. The water was thigh deep in places and I moved slowly and carefully, feeling ahead with my trekking poles and facing upstream so the current couldn't make my knees buckle. I retreated once from a swirling dark pool that seemed too deep and strong to risk venturing into but eventually I found a safe way across.

29

Walking briskly to warm up from the ford I headed up into the Blackmount hills beside the Allt a'Chaorainn. At a confluence of two streams I came to a slightly sloping but dry patch of grass that looked quite a good site, especially as it was reasonably sheltered from the strong south-west wind that had been blowing all day. It was only at 600 feet but I'd had a strenuous day (over 7,000 feet of ascent) and knew that this might be the last sheltered site I found so I made camp.

Each time there was a storm I felt that the weather couldn't get any worse yet somehow it did. The next day was no exception. The rain returned overnight though the wind had lessened and I was reasonably optimistic about the day as I climbed to the Bealach Euar-chathaidh which divides the Blackmount hills from the Stob Gabhar group to the south. My plan was to leave the pack there and go out and back to the four northern summits then carry the load over the rest.

As I climbed the slopes of Clach Leathad, one of the two Tops in this group, the rain became heavier and the wind started to strengthen. The long traverse over Creise, a Munro, to the northernmost and lowest summit, Stob a'Ghlais Choire, and back was quite exhilarating and somewhat alarming as I staggered about over boulder fields in thick mist buffeted by the now very strong wind and lashed by the torrential rain which was interspersed with bursts of hail. I did dip out of the mist on the little rock cone of Stob a'Ghlais Choire to see a view across the silver pool and lake-dotted dark expanse of Rannoch Moor and to the south the snow-streaked corrie walls below invisible Meall a'Bhuiridh. To reach this peak I had to return over Creise to where a narrow ridge led down to a col and broader stony slopes that led to the summit. Detritus from the alpine ski resort that lies on the northern slopes of this summit decorated the cairn.

On the descent back to the pack from Clach Leathad the wind was frighteningly strong. Even with the poles I had trouble keeping my feet. The appearance of the pack, leaning against a rock, was a relief. I'd been away for three-and-three-quarter hours which in these conditions was far too long for comfort. Due to the wind, the strongest I'd experienced, I decided it would be sensible not to go on so instead I descended south into Coireach a'Ba and sloshed through interminable bogs to join the West Highland Way.

Here it follows the old road across the Blackmount and so has a hard surface, which I followed down to Victoria Bridge and the Inveroran Hotel. All the rooms were full, this being a major staging post on the West Highland Way, Scotland's most popular long distance footpath, so I pitched my tent by the bridge then returned to the bar for a meal in the warm. 'It's more sheltered just across the way,' said the barman. As the wind was still increasing I took his advice and moved camp to a large patch of grass almost opposite the hotel and sheltered from the south and west by a large bank. Even here the wind shook the tent, each gust coming with an incredibly loud roar. I had two pints of 80/- ale which I hoped would help me sleep. The forecast on the television in the bar was for severe gales and the chart showed a deep depression west of Scotland.

A wild night followed. Many times I was woken by the tent thrashing in the wind and the hammering of the torrential rain on the flysheet. Morning came with no change so I abandoned any thoughts of returning to the summits I'd missed and decided instead to walk over to Bridge of Orchy, a little under two miles away, and collect my supply parcel from the post office. The West Highland Way goes this way so the path was a good one making the walking easy even with the hail showers and storm-force winds. The post office was a little cubby-hole on the railway station, warmed by a calor gas heater. Other walkers were on the station, grim-faced West Highland Wayfarers who'd had enough and were going home, defeated by the weather. Others were waiting in Bridge of Orchy for a bus or else trying to thumb a lift. There not being much room in the tiny post office I sheltered under a railway bridge to transfer my supplies to the pack. The parcel contained four days' food, two paperbacks, a map and four camera films along with a letter from Denise and a note with a 20 pence piece sellotaped to it from Hazel. These last two items cheered me up enormously.

Back at the tent the wind seemed stronger. The forecast was for showery, windy weather for the next few days. I'd been out for two weeks now and had done 42 peaks, eight fewer than I'd planned. Going on in the rain wasn't a cheerful thought but I was to have a companion for the next week. Andy Hicks was driving up from Yorkshire that day and should arrive during the evening. A keen long distance hill runner who the year before had completed the Bob Graham Round (42 summits, 72 miles and 25,000 feet of ascent in under 24 hours in the English Lake District) and had also done innumerable two-day mountain marathons and Long Distance Walkers' Association Hundred Mile events, Andy seemed an ideal person to keep me going.

Chapter 2

A WEEK OF COMPANY

1 – 7 JUNE INVERORAN TO CRIANLARICH 91 MILES 30 SUMMITS

*'What more evocative sight could there be than a curtain of windblown rain
sweeping horizontally across a hillside beneath scuttling black clouds?'*

Ralph Storer
The Joy of Hillwalking

June began with another night of wind and rain. Andy hadn't turned up
until 11 p.m. the previous evening. We'd then sat in the bar discussing
plans over a pint so it had been a late night. Everyone else in the bar
seemed to be walking the West Highland Way and we gathered from the
barman that such walkers were the main customers of the hotel. Indeed,
a minibus service was available so that walkers who wanted to stay here
two nights could walk the next section then be brought back here and
ferried out again the next day.

Before leaving the Blackmount area I had eight summits still to climb,
two of them the ones I'd missed ten days earlier because of the storm on
Ben Starav. It would make for a long day but they could be linked with
the ones I'd skipped yesterday. However two extra days at Inveroran
meant extra supplies were needed and as it was still very stormy we began
the next day by driving in Andy's car to the nearest shop, which was in
Tyndrum. There I stocked up on dried fruit, chocolate, coffee, sugar,
cheese, muesli and an extra dried meal. I also bought a copy of *The
Scotsman* which said that the previous day had seen 70 m.p.h. winds in
the Highlands and that a coach had been blown over on the Slochd
summit on the A9. The storm was moving away now though and the
forecast was for lessening wind with sunshine and showers for the next
few days.

As the wind was still from the south-west and the rain was still pouring
down, when we returned to Inveroran we headed west on the wet and

boggy track beside the Abhainn Shira first so that we would have the storm at least partly at our backs as we headed back east over the hills. Plantations line both sides of the river for the first couple of miles making for dull walking. The path runs on the north side of the river at first but as the plantations come to an end it crosses to the south bank. The Shira was deep and fast here which made for an exciting crossing of the old rickety bridge, which was missing several planks and had others that moved alarmingly when trodden on. Once past Loch Dochard – where a tent was pitched, the first one I'd seen away from roadside camp-sites – we turned north, intending to climb into Coire Chaorach. However the flat land beyond the loch was a maze of bogs and streams which took some time and one knee-deep ford to thread a way through. Negotiating these wetlands pushed us westwards so we ended up climbing into Coire nam Ban and onto the south-east ridge of Stob Coir'an Albannaich. Near the mist-shrouded summit we met two women coming up from Glen Etive, the only other walkers we saw all day.

A tortuous route now led eastwards over the other seven summits. We contoured round Meall Tarsuinn, a minor summit, on the way to Meall nan Eun, this was going to be a long enough day without adding any extra hills. The clouds were lifting now and the rain showers were less frequent though the wind still blew. Beyond Meall nan Eun there was a steep drop followed by a steep climb onto the long easy-angled ridge that stretched over Stob a'Bhruaich to Stob Gabhar. We cut north below the summit cone of the latter to the northernmost Top of the group, Sron nan Giubhas, then came back to the summit. A painful, stinging hail shower blasted in here so we hurried on down a little rocky arête to Aonach Eagach. Beyond this Top lay the last col of the day followed by a final pull up the last summit, Stob a'Choire Odhair, where we were again greeted by hail. Keen to get out of the weather, which was worsening rapidly with heavy rain and low cloud, we quickly descended the south ridge into Coire Toaig where we joined the path that led down to the Abhainn Shira.

In the bar that evening I felt content. It had been a long day but I could now move on without leaving any hills still to climb behind me. This was my third night at Inveroran, somewhere I'd never intended to stay at all – Bridge of Orchy for one night had been the original plan – and whilst having a warm bar to repair to at night was pleasant I was keen to return to camping in the hills and moving on each day. Andy again slept in his car, keeping his tent dry and packed. Ahead lay the mass of hills east of Bridge of Orchy that surround Glens Lyon and Lochay. These are mostly grassy, rounded tops, less rocky and rugged than those farther west, so I hoped to make better time even if the weather remained stormy.

For the first time since leaving Glencoe I had an unbroken night's sleep, the wind having dropped to a mere breeze. In the morning I walked over to Bridge of Orchy again, meeting Andy at the station where he was leaving his car. Used to fell running rather than backpacking, Andy was dressed for fast movement in ultralight, studded fell running shoes. His pack was small too, at least to my eyes. For him it was a heavier load than he'd carried in years. From the station we headed up the muddy, eroded path into Coire Dothaidh to the col between Beinn Dorain and Beinn an Dothaidh where we left the packs while we went up the latter. The clouds were broken and high but the actual summit was still just in the mist, a pity as it's a fine viewpoint. It's a fine mountain too, a huge steep pyramid when seen from the A82, and the southern end of a curving wall of hills that spreads north and then north-east, towering above Rannoch Moor and the railway line which runs at its foot. We were now to walk the whole of this range with one diversion east to a couple of outlying summits. There were a few people around on Dorain and Dothaidh but once we headed north we saw only one other walker.

The skies continued to clear and the showers ceased so for the first time in six days I walked without my waterproof jacket on. The wind was cold though so my windshirt and even at times a hat were needed. Packs back on again, we climbed Beinn an Dothaidh which gave good views west to the hills of yesterday. Skirting east of the main ridge we picked up a narrow but regularly used path that led across the hillside and down to the col north-west of the outliers, Beinn a'Chuirn and Beinn Mhanach. Again we left the packs while we climbed this pair. Great masses of cloud rose into the sky and little squalls of rain blew past but there were also bright shafts of sunlight in places making for some dramatic lighting with rainbows appearing against the dark sky.

Loaded up again we set off up the steep slopes of Beinn Achaladair. Andy quickly pulled ahead. I plodded slowly after him, suddenly feeling very tired and with no energy at all. I paused to eat an energy bar then hauled myself upwards. I suspect that if I'd been alone I might well have camped at this point but Andy encouraged me on. By the time we reached the summit my energy had returned and for the rest of the day I felt fine. The views probably helped for the evening light was magical as we walked along the long ridge of Beinn Achaladair with its two summits and over Meall Buidhe to Beinn a'Chrechais. The distant hills were layered shades of grey while below the waters of Loch Tulla and the many lochs and pools out on Rannoch Moor sparkled against the dark land. We could see from the Blackmount hills round over the Glencoe tops to the Mamores and the bulk of Ben Nevis while to the south the twin pyramids of Ben More and Stob Binnein and the notched top of Ben Lui stood out with further west the amazingly steep and sharp twin peaks of Ben Cruachan. Eastwards we could see straight down Loch Ericht though Ben Alder looked an unimpressive flat bump. Far in the distance lay the indistinct snow-splashed Cairngorms. The light changed constantly as the sun went in and out of the clouds though the sky was slowly deepening to red. It was a glorious evening and I was glad for once to be high in the hills so late.

There was no view from Beinn a'Chreachain however as clouds had swirled in round the summit as we approached. The wind was now very cold so we headed straight off down the north-east ridge. The descent was easy at first but we soon came to very steep and craggy slopes above Coire Dubh Mor, in which we wanted to camp. Finding a way off looked difficult. We skirted the edge looking for a safe route. Eventually Andy suggested we descend the gully down which the Allt Learg Mheuran, the stream that drains the corrie, tumbled. It did seem the easiest option so we started carefully down. The gully was steep and loose but not very difficult, just a slither down unstable wet rock and loose earth covered in places with slimy moss. The light was fading now as we hadn't left Bridge of Orchy until 1.30 p.m. so we were glad to find a dry and only slightly bumpy camp-site beside the stream at the foot of the corrie. It was half past midnight before I'd finished cooking and eating and Andy was up until 2 a.m.

Yet again the clearance in the weather was short-lived and we woke to a steady downpour and a gusty south wind. To the east of us lay a mass of rounded, undistinguished, grassy hills lying between Glen Lyon and Loch Rannoch. Unfortunately the highest of these dull mounds, Meall Buidhe, reaches 3,054 feet and is therefore a Munro. The name itself is a giveaway. 'Meall' is usually applied to rounded hills (though there are exceptions like Meall Buidhe in Knoydart). 'Buidhe' means yellow, a reference to the colour of the dried grasses found on the hills. Peter Drummond in *Scottish Hill and Mountain Names* says there are at least 28 Meall Buidhes. He points out that the Glen Lyon Meall Buidhe is grassy and therefore paler than the dark heather of the surrounding moorland.

The reason for the name is much more interesting than the hill itself, especially when the weather is wet. Climbing the hill from the west is a long and tedious way to do it too. An ascent from the south is probably easiest. We traversed, contoured and slogged over tussocks and through peat bogs for around eight miles to the summit, passing another Meall Buidhe en route. It was very, very wet and very, very windy again. The only point of interest was a good view of a large, dark, hill fox loping across the slopes. On the summit we had to turn straight into the driving, stinging rain to descend the southern slopes to the reservoir of Loch an Daimh. Here we camped just below the dam beside the remnants of the burn. After two long days it was nice to stop early.

Sunshine in the morning was a surprise as it had been a stormy night with strong gusts of wind shaking the tents and bursts of heavy rain rattling on the flysheets. The day began with a stiff climb up Sron Chona Choirein to the south from where it was an easy walk to the fine little peak of Stuchd an Lochain whose summit cairn perches on the edge of some broken crags above little Lochan nan Cat. Kept moving by the cold wind, we descended directly south beside the Allt Cashlie into Glen Lyon where we found a sheltered lunch spot in the lee of a conifer plantation. Another steep climb led up to the col west of Meall Ghaordaidh. On the way up Andy's bob-hat was blown off but he was able to race after it and grab it before it disappeared forever. I wasn't so lucky. Feeling hot I removed my hat and tucked it down the front of my windshirt. Later I found it had vanished. Leaving the packs at the col we were blown up to the summit by the now extremely strong wind. Meall Ghaordaidh is described by Butterfield as 'quite the dullest hill in the Southern Highlands'. Maybe so, but it can be quite exciting when you can barely stand up in the wind! At the summit we sheltered in the large cairn that surrounds the trig point and discovered we both had the same idea, or rather desire, and that was to get off the mountain as quickly as possible. Our original plan had been to head west to Beinn Heasgarnich, a long high level walk. However the wind was too strong to stay on the tops so we decided to descend south into Glen Lochay and then walk up the glen and find somewhere to camp.

Once we were out of the wind the descent beside the Allt Ghaordaidh was quite enjoyable. After the faded brown of the tops the lush green of the boulder-dotted glen was refreshing. In places we passed the lichen and moss-covered stone walls of old shielings. Glen Lochay was rich and fertile and we walked up it past birch and alder woods interspersed with grassy meadows full of cattle and sheep. Deer were wandering beside the river and the monotonous call of cuckoos rang out from the trees while black and white orange-beaked oyster-catchers yelped excitedly and flew up and down the river banks as we passed. Two orange tents were pitched at the end of the public road. A school minibus was parked nearby. The upper glen was bleaker and wilder. The wind was stronger here too. I really didn't want another disturbed night so I was pleased when we found a well-sheltered site just to the east of a thick spruce plantation. As we intended staying here two nights while we climbed the peaks either side of the glen a good site was important. There was a lot of cow dung around but no sign of the cows and the site was flat and calm. The cattle had been wallowing in the trickle of a burn that ran nearby but by following it into the dense spruces we were able to find some water that we hoped wasn't contaminated. A few midges, the first of the walk, fluttered sluggishly around the tent. I lit a mosquito coil in the porch just in case they became more active.

South of our camp lay two hills, each with a Munro and a Top, while to the north lay two more Munros and another Top. Along with Meall Ghaordaidh and Ben Challum, which lies further west, they make up part of the ancient deer forest of Mamlorn and form a horseshoe of hills round the head of Glen Lochay. Those to the south are rolling, rounded, featureless hills so we went that way first, leaving the more interesting summits to the north for later in the day when the cloud that covered the hills might have cleared. After crossing the river Lochay by the bridge below the cottage at Badour we climbed straight up steep grassy slopes to Meall Glas. Steady rain was falling and the summit was misty with a strong wind blowing so we were quickly round to Beinn Cheathaich then down steeply to the col west of Meall a'Churain. The cloud lifted as we went up the latter then headed south to Sgiath Chuil, though other tops remained hidden. Returning northwards we descended to the bulldozed hydro track beside Lubchurran Burn that led back to Glen Lochay.

After lunch in the shelter of the tents we set off up the glen to Batavaime above which we followed a hydro track that traversed the hillside round to a very steep, craggy ridge which led to the neat rocky summit of Stob nan Clach from where easy slopes curved round the steep headwall of Coire-cheathaich to cloud-capped Creag Mhor. With steep craggy corries and long rock-strewn ridges this hill had a bit of character compared with the fairly dull lumps we'd been on for the last few days and the walking was enjoyable despite the strong wind. The descent north-east from the summit was steep with lots of little crags to be rounded. Then it was just a long ascent up easy slopes to Beinn Heasgarnich in wind now so strong it made walking difficult. Open slopes led south back to the camp. It had been a long though unspectacular day with the most ascent I'd yet done – 8,880 feet. My legs had registered this and I'd had a dull, tight ache in my right calf during

37

the afternoon. I tried not to be alarmed at this. One of my biggest fears throughout the walk was that an injury of some sort would force me to stop. This was the first problem I'd had and all I could do was hope it wouldn't get any worse.

Another, less serious, problem was that the stove kept cutting out. It started again if I shook it but the flame died away in a few minutes. This made cooking a lengthy and frustrating process. I could unblock the jet with a tiny pricker but I couldn't clean the fuel line which is where I guessed the blockage must be. No gas cartridge stoves are field maintainable, one reason I'd never used them on previous long walks, which had mostly been in remote areas where reliability was very important. They are, however, the lightest stoves which is why I was using one on this walk, knowing that if I had problems it would only be for a few days. As it was Andy was using an older model of the same stove which he offered to loan me when he returned home.

The rain faded away during the night and we woke to clearing skies and sunshine, the best weather since I'd been on the Aonach Eagach ten days earlier. It actually began to feel hot as we walked up the glen to Lochan Chailein and beyond it the col south of Ben Challum, which was in view early on, dominating the head of Glen Lochay. Leaving the packs we climbed up to the South Top and then the summit. Only a thin thermal top was needed though I tied my windshirt round my waist just in case. The sense of freedom in not being bundled up in fleece and waterproofs was very welcome. The views from the summit were superb. As well as the hills of the last few days with Ben Lawers beyond them to the east we could see the steep pyramids of Ben More and Stob Binnein, the far cone of Ben Lomond and the rugged outline of the Arrochar Alps, the sweeping curves of Ben Lui, where I was headed next, the twin horns of Ben Cruachan and away to the north the bulky shape of Ben Nevis. After all the days and summits in cloud and storm it was a great pleasure to be able to sit and take in this splendid scene.

Good weather is relaxing, especially after days of storm. So far our navigation and route selection had been very accurate. It had to be, given the conditions. But now, feeling relaxed and carefree, we made a mistake. Our destination was Crianlarich, in itself a puzzle as Tyndrum was much nearer both to Ben Challum and Ben Lui. I couldn't imagine why I wasn't going there. It was too late to change this now though as I had supplies waiting at the post office in Crianlarich. We decided to contour south from the col then descend directly to Crianlarich. There were two things wrong with this route. The first was that the traverse was across wet, boggy ground covered with tussocks of thick grass which made for slow and arduous walking. Then, when we finally got down into Strath Fillan we were faced with the wide, deep river Fillan which barred the way to the town, frustratingly visible just across the water. At this point I remembered why my original plan had been to descend to Inverhaggernie, 1½ miles from Crianlarich. There was a bridge there. We debated crossing the railway viaduct into the town but decided this wasn't really a good idea so we reluctantly set off for the bridge. However half a mile or so upstream the river speeded up round a big gravel bank and for a short distance looked no more than knee deep. It wasn't and we were soon on the far bank. Downstream, Ben More, Stob Binnein and Cruach Ardrain rose into a deep blue sky above the green woodlands of the strath.

Our short-cut meant the post office was closed when we arrived in Crianlarich. There isn't a camp-site in the town so we searched for a B&B and found the pleasant and comfortable Glenardran Guest House. I rang Denise to discover that much would be happening in the next 24 hours. To start with Chris Brasher was hoping to arrive the following evening and have a day or two out on the hills with me. He was ringing that evening to confirm this and check I'd made it to Crianlarich. I'd met Chris several times before at promotional weekends for his walking boots and at outdoor trade shows. He'd got in touch after reading an article about the walk I'd written in *TGO* (*The Great Outdoors*) magazine. He'd enthused about the walk then said he'd like to join me for a few days somewhere. I was delighted at this and hoped very much we could arrange something. Although probably best known to the general public as an Olympic gold medal winner, founder of the London Marathon and sports journalist and to the walking world as the designer of excellent boots (which I was wearing on this walk) Chris Brasher is an important figure in the conservation movement in Scotland, being involved in the purchase and management of several estates by conservation trusts, often in part with money donated by the Brasher Boot Company. Unsurprisingly he is a very busy man so setting up a meeting proved quite difficult and over the summer he had many phone calls with Denise, sometimes from places like Munich or Paris.

Also due to arrive in Crianlarich was Carlton Reid, a mountain biker and journalist I'd known for many years and whose company Front Page Creations handled public relations for Pertex, the company which was my main sponsor. He'd set up a live Radio 5 interview for the morning after next and was hoping to get some other publicity for me. This meant

39

I would have to stay there for a day. I didn't mind this as my calf had been sore again making a rest day probably a good thing.

The sunny weather continued and Andy headed off for Ben More and Stob Binnein. I was tempted to go with him but decided resting my leg was a better idea so instead I spent the day doing chores.

Chris Brasher had confirmed he was coming so I'd booked him into the guest house. He turned up mid-evening, having driven down from Fort Augustus after attending a meeting of the management committee for the West Affric estate. This had recently been taken over by the National Trust for Scotland and is managed jointly by the NTS, Trees for Life and the Chris Brasher Trust. I wouldn't be there until mid-August. Chris was unsure about walking with me the next day. One of his passions is racing and he owns a number of horses, one of which, Master Boots, was running at Haydock the next afternoon. As the trainer and his assistant were in the USA, Chris thought he really ought to be at the race himself. He still hadn't made up his mind when we went off to our beds.

Chapter 3

THE DEEP SOUTH

8 – 15 JUNE CRIANLARICH TO COMRIE 117 MILES 25 SUMMITS

'There is a lot to be learned from climbing mountains, more than you might think.'

David Brower
Let the Mountains Talk, Let the Rivers Run

A strange day, beginning with people and ending alone for the first time since Andy had arrived, saw the walk recommence. Chris Brasher announced he was going to Haydock to see his horse run but hoped to join me later in the summer. Over a cooked breakfast, most unusual for me, we discussed my itinerary and made tentative plans to meet in Glen Feshie in about a month.

Then Radio 5 Live rang up and I stood in the guest house hallway being interviewed for a few minutes, linked in after a piece on tee-shirts for the Euro'96 football competition – 'Scotland have a mountain to climb in England now here's an Englishman with mountains to climb in Scotland'. It felt very unreal, talking to an unseen audience who would undoubtedly have forgotten all about it within a few minutes. This surreal episode over I packed up and walked round the corner to the Tea House, a café on the railway station, where I met Carlton and his girlfriend Jude who were hoping a newspaper journalist they'd contacted might turn up. We waited until midday over endless cups of coffee. No journalist. I didn't mind, the walk was becoming a private affair and I'd felt detached from the people, the conversation, the speed of events that had occurred since reaching Crianlarich. I was quite happy to play my part, it was just that I didn't feel involved. Instead my mind was faraway, high in the hills, wondering about what was to come. After three weeks being in the hills had become reality, a way of life, and everything else seemed unreal.

It might seem to those who know the Scottish hills that the obvious route from the Mamlorn hills was east to Ben Lawers and so it would have been if it wasn't for the hills that lie around Loch Lomond. I would reach these via the Ben Lui group and the outlier of Beinn Bhuidhe and then head east along the hills to the south of Crianlarich. First though I had to head north-west which I did along the West Highland Way, which here runs through the plantations in Strath Fillan, a mostly dull and viewless route. The night before Chris Brasher had said it should be called the West Lowland Way as it avoids all the hills along the route. After half an hour Carlton and Jude turned up for a photography session. I posed patiently on some rocks while Carlton darted round changing angles and lenses. The photos he took were later to appear in several newspaper reports. Then it was off on my own along the WHW to the track up Glen Cononish on which I met up with Andy. He'd caught the train to Bridge of Orchy earlier in the day to collect his car which he'd now left at Tyndrum. A keen football fan, he had a ticket for a Euro'96 match in Leeds the next day and so was driving back that night. Before then he had time to come up a final hill with me, Ben Lui (or, more correctly, Beinn Laoigh), one of the finest and most distinctive mountains in the Southern Highlands. The view of its twin peaks soaring above the depths of Coire Gaothaich, whose gullies are popular with winter climbers, is a classic one. Ben Lui (whose curved summit ridge has a Munro at one end and a Top at the other) and the three other Munros in the group are rough, rocky western peaks and I was looking forward to them after the grass plodding on the hills to the east.

This was another mountain I'd climbed with Reggie Love and had never returned to since and again his memory, his presence, were tangible throughout the day. On that first ascent, 17 years earlier, it had been a perfect winter's day, now it was cloudy and the light was dull and flat though occasional flashes of sunlight hinted of better things. We climbed Beinn Dubhchraig and Ben Oss first, summits I'd also done with Reggie. There were people on Beinn Dubhchraig, the first on a summit since the Aonach Eagach, 12 days before. They complained about the popularity of the hills, blaming, in a way that was humorous but suggested something a little more serious behind it, Hamish Brown and the SMC and the various guidebook writers. I, however, was already surprised at how few people I'd met. Obviously the bad weather was a factor but I'd still expected to meet far more people than I had. In the last week Andy and I had only seen two or three other walkers apart from those on Beinn Dorain the day we'd left Bridge of Orchy. That had been a Sunday and today was a Saturday. Maybe it was too early in the season for many walkers to be out mid-week, I wondered. Whilst a plausible idea this was belied by the dozens of people I'd met walking the West Highland Way at Inveroran.

From Ben Oss we rounded the precipitous slopes of Coire Laoigh and climbed Ben Lui. I said farewell to Andy here and watched him speed off down towards Tyndrum, hoping to get there before the hotel stopped serving food. I watched him for some time then turned and set off in the other direction, alone again. It had been good to have company, especially as Andy had pushed me to keep going in bad conditions when it was hard to force myself on. That third week had been a crucial one. Now I had done too much to consider stopping. I had also adapted fully to life as a full time hill-walker. On every long walk I'd found there was an initial breaking-in period during which I had to adjust to living in the wilds. During this time worries always arose about fitness, motivation, the route, gear, food and other matters though these were a cover for my real concerns, which were about the walk as a whole and whether I could do it and, even more importantly, whether I would enjoy it. On this walk the bad weather had made this initial period harder than usual and also longer. But now I couldn't imagine doing anything other than climbing hills and sleeping in a tent. The questions in my mind were no longer whether I could go on, whether I would find somewhere to camp or whether my food would run out but rather what would the views be like from the next summit, where could I find a camp-site with a good view and what was the most interesting way up the next hill. Slowly I was letting living in the present dominate over worrying about the future. To put it another way, I was beginning to enjoy myself.

From the NW Top of Ben Lui I descended to the col with Beinn a'Chleidh then nipped up and down this peak without the pack before descending into Coire Annaich, where I found a reasonable camp-site beside the Allt nan Caorainn though a line of electricity pylons marching across the landscape rather spoilt the view. Gentle rain began as I was pitching the tent. By morning the rain was heavier and low cloud shrouded all the hills. I set off down the narrow, steep-sided, straight-as-an-arrow slot of Glen Fyne, first on a footpath then on a wide vehicle track. At the cottage of Inverchorachan I left the pack and headed up an intermittent path towards the isolated Munro of Beinn Bhuidhe that walls the west side of the glen. Two walkers were ahead of me with two more pairs not far behind but I soon lost sight of all of them as dense mist enveloped me at around 2,500 feet. A very strong gusty south-west wind was driving the rain along now and driving me on as well. I was on the

43

summit in an hour and a quarter and back at the pack 50 minutes later.

Further down Glen Fyne mixed deciduous woodland lined the track with huge banks of bluebells brightening the dull weather. Earlier I'd noticed the yellow flowers of tormentil and the nodding purple butterwort on the hillsides, tiny splashes of colour amongst the grey-brown grasses. Details such as this can enliven even the dullest day. Nature is never boring.

At the end of Glen Fyne lies Loch Fyne and the A83 road which, unfortunately, I had to follow for a while. Picking up speed – as always I wanted to get the road walking over with as quickly as possible – I was soon in the tiny village of Cairndow where I sheltered from the rain for an hour over a baked potato and a coffee in the bar of the Stagecoach Hotel. I rang Denise and discovered that my support team for the Cuillin ridge, essential for getting me over the more difficult sections, could only be there during the last week in July. I'd planned on cycling there from Glen Shiel, the nearest I would be to Skye on the mainland, but I was now so far behind my original schedule that it was very unlikely I could get there in time. Denise suggested I should cycle there from South Laggan in the Great Glen instead. This was five or six weeks away but I would have to make a decision soon. I promised to think about it.

To reach the Arrochar Alps I had to walk up Glen Kinglas. The remains of the old road run just below the new highway so I followed this most of the way up the glen which at least kept me away from the smell of the traffic and the risk of being knocked down, though the noise was still loud. At Butterbridge I crossed Kinglas Water on the old bridge and camped on the edge of the plantations that line this side of the glen. It was as far away from the road as I could get. Two other tents were pitched next to the old bridge. The heavy rain continued and I was soon zipped into the tent with no intention of re-emerging before morning. The ideal camp is one where you can sit outside the tent, or at least in the open doorway, and watch the world outside, watch the play of light as clouds pass over the sun, the flight of birds, the activities of animals (tents make good hides), even the meanderings of insects. In stormy weather this isn't possible unless you want to get cold and wet so all too often on this walk so far I'd spent my evenings lying inside my green nylon shelter. If it had been a very long day I usually went to sleep straight after dinner, on others like this one, when I'd been walking for 9½ hours, I read a book. My present paperback was a Tom Sharpe novel. His savage humour matched the savage weather though the story was nothing to do with the outdoors.

The Arrochar Alps are a compact group of steep, rough, rugged hills lying east of Loch Lomond. The name comes from the village of Arrochar to the south-east at the end of Loch Long. The most famous and distinctive of these hills is The Cobbler, which, at 2,900 feet doesn't reach Munro level, but which is still far finer and more of a mountain than many hills well above 3,000 feet. Easily accessible from Glasgow it played a major part in the development of rock climbing in Scotland as there are some large cliffs below the summit.

The Cobbler, along with many other Corbetts and indeed some peaks below Corbett height, gives the lie to the idea that height is the most important factor in defining a mountain. It may be if you want to reduce mountains to pure figures but aesthetically the height of a mountain is irrelevant. What matters is its shape, its ruggedness, its steepness, its corries and cliffs, its ridges and gullies, all those things that make up the essence of a mountain, that come closest to the idea of the 'perfect' mountain. A real mountain, a mountain that feels like a mountain, is exciting, stimulating, challenging and frightening. A real mountain makes you pause, makes you realise that this is not a mere bump to be rushed up and down but a complex structure that requires thought and care and skill. The Cobbler is a real mountain. Grassy bumps like some of those I'd climbed with Andy the week before are not mountains. Hills yes, but mountains no. This may seem to beg the question as to why I was doing this walk. Well, in part to think, or perhaps more accurately, to feel more deeply about, and perhaps to understand better, issues such as the nature of mountains.

Because I'd walked over all those rounded hills the fulfilment I'd felt on climbing Ben Lui and was now feeling as I approached the Arrochar Alps was stronger and clearer. The rain, constant all night, stopped during the ascent of the highest of the Arrochar hills, Beinn Ime, though the summit was in mist. The Arrochar Alps are all separate mountains with deep cols between them and no high-level linking ridges so the round of them all, although not long, involves a great deal of ascent. By the end of the day I would have climbed 7,875 feet in just over ten miles and been out for over ten hours. From Beinn Ime I descended to the broad Bealach a'Mhaim where I left the pack while I went up and down Beinn Narnain, from which four walkers were descending. The cloud had lifted now and there were good views of the nearby spiky summit ridge of The Cobbler and further away the cone of Ben Lomond. The light was flat and dull though and all the summits to the north were hidden in cloud.

45

From the bealach I descended north-east a short way then contoured below the craggy east face of Beinn Ime to the south-west slopes of Ben Vane. A steep climb up rough ground led to the summit followed by an even steeper descent down gullies and terraces to dammed Loch Sloy. I sat under the bridge below the dam to avoid the rain which had started again and had some food while I tried to summon up the energy for the next ascent. I needed the rest and the food as the climb to Ben Vorlich is steep and unrelenting. This is a long ridge of a mountain, running south–north above Loch Sloy and steep on every side. Back in mist again I went along the ridge over the main summit and the north Top then dropped down the north-east ridge to some very boggy ground that led north to Srath Dubh-uisage. After searching round for a while I found a tiny, almost flat patch of dry ground by a small burn that just held the tent. A line of pylons marred the view again but unlike the previous night I couldn't hear any cars or see a road. The wind had dropped too, which was a relief. The only sounds were the rippling of the water in the burn and the occasional call of a cuckoo. Once a fox yelped loudly.

The calm and quiet didn't last and I woke to, or rather was woken by, lashing rain and a gusty wind. It was my 25th day and it had rained on 19 of them and been very windy on 22. Only three days had been dry and sunny. For a short while I felt totally fed up and full of self-pity. It wasn't supposed to be like this. I wanted to see the hills. I wanted to walk in sunshine listening to the birds and noting the details of flowers, rocks and streams.

I also wanted to be in unspoilt wild country. From the tent I could see power lines strung between monstrous pylons and the straight cut where a bulldozed road ran, while the glen, which should have been rich with oak and pine forest, was a deforested, degraded and desolate swamp. I hated it. I hated the rain, I hated the walk and I hated myself for being there. I was most definitely not at one with the world. Indeed my mood was so foul that if I'd had a companion they'd have gone home.

I managed to pull myself out of this black mood into a merely sullen one in which I felt that I might as well continue as otherwise the effort I'd put in so far would be wasted. I slogged down the glen through the bogs towards the woods above Glen Falloch where I intended turning south and following the West Highland Way to the Inversnaid Hotel to collect a supply parcel that should be waiting for me and from where I would climb Ben Lomond before turning back north.

My dour mood began to lift as I entered the woods, a mix of oak and ash and other deciduous trees and carpeted with bluebells. Although small this was a wild, natural bit of forest in which I couldn't help but feel renewed, couldn't help but feel that sense of awe that old woods always engender in me. This, I felt, was how the world should be. Woods also have an air of waiting, a feeling that something is about to happen, a sense of mystery. I became more alert and walked as silently as I could, avoiding treading on sticks or brushing against bushes. My attention and care was rewarded when I dropped down a bank to the stream. A movement caught my eye and I froze in mid-step. A sleek, dark otter dived into the stream below me, swam up a pool and then ran along some rocks about ten feet in front of me. The magical moment changed my mood completely. It was a highlight of the walk so far.

I'd come down into the stream bed in search of a way across the railway line which barred my way to the A82 road. Just below where I'd seen the otter the railway crossed the stream on a small bridge. I passed under this on a narrow strip of sloping slippery rocks that ran above the water. A steep wooded bank led down to the road. To head south I first had to head north to the bridge over the river Falloch at Inverarnan. Before crossing I sheltered from the rain for an hour or so in the Stagger Inn and it being well before lunchtime, I was the only customer. Outside the rain poured on.

It was still pouring when I arrived at the Inversnaid Hotel two and a half hours after I left the Stagger Inn. Despite the downpour the beautiful woods of oak, birch, rowan and hazel along the West Highland Way were relaxing to walk through. Forests in rain always smell wonderfully earthy and fresh and to this was added in places the sharp, garlic-like smell of ramsons, whose white flowers decorated many banks. There were many other flowers about too which, along with the fresh green of the newly-opened leaves, made the forest bright and cheerful in contrast to the lowering skies. The path however was running with water, in places several inches deep. A few walkers passed me heading north, most heavily bundled up in waterproofs but some in shorts with their heads bare, having decided, it seemed, that they were going to get wet anyway. When I'd first walked this way in 1978, on a Land's End to John O'Groats walk, the path was rough and unclear and I lost it in a few places (there was a path though despite what some guidebooks of the time said). The West Highland Way hadn't been established then and I met no other walkers. Now the path is not only wide and clear but heavily eroded in places by the tens of thousands of walkers who use it every year.

Mostly the walking was easy if wet but around Rob Roy's Cave where a great tangle of boulders falls right down to the loch shore I lost the path and suddenly found myself doing some interesting scrambling. A party of German day walkers watched my antics dubiously as I slid precariously down a steep boulder.

Whether Rob Roy ever used this cave is open to question but after he became an outlaw, when his estates were seized by the Duke of Montrose, Inversnaid and the surrounding land was where he lived. Sir Walter Scott's *Rob Roy*, which I was to read in just a few days time, is set in the area. The east side of Loch Lomond is almost as wild as it was in Scott's day and it's easy to imagine Rob Roy and his men sweeping down from the crags and through the trees.

The hotel had my food parcel, an arrangement made for me by Denise, and could provide dinner, bed and breakfast for £28. Not fancying another wet camp I decided to stay and dry out a little. The only problem was that dinner was at a set time, 6.15 p.m., and I still wanted to climb Ben Lomond. There wasn't time before dinner so I decided on a late start and spent the remainder of the afternoon spreading out gear to dry and soaking in a bath. The room hadn't been fully prepared and I spent some time chatting to the woman sorting out the linen. She'd just come back from a weekend in London. 'The weather's nice down there.' Here, she said, the summer was over mid-August, which was a bit of an exaggeration. My concern was that it didn't seem to have started yet.

The hotel was warm and comfortable making me feel reluctant to go out again into the storm. Oh, the perils of civilisation! However, my will wasn't that weak so at 7.30 p.m. I set off for Ben Lomond in the continuing gloom. The path along the shore south of Inversnaid was a slippery, muddy morass. I crossed the Cailness Burn on a bridge then climbed steep slopes into the burn's upper glen. Here the water was a raging torrent and I had to go upstream for some way before I managed to wade it, keeping my boots on as they were already sodden. Then it was up to the north ridge of Ben Lomond which I followed to the summit, picking up a path up the final steep buttresses. The wind was very strong near the top, threatening to blow me off the ridge at times. Practically crawling the last few yards I arrived on the summit at 10 p.m. and so wasn't surprised to have this very popular peak to myself. (The next time I was to be there would be in the following autumn in the company of a crowd of people at the launch of Cameron McNeish's book *The Munros*. The contrast was enormous.)

The rain had stopped by the time I reached the summit but as the mist was still dense and there were no views I headed straight back down, staying east of the Cailness Burn when back in the upper glen, a mistake as it meant I had to go a long way north of the burn, which tumbles down very steep rocky slopes to the lake, before I could safely descend in the growing darkness back to the West Highland Way. The hillside was steep and slippery and I had to pick a route carefully round small crags and in the lower parts through tall bracken that hid boulders and holes before I reached the now shadowy forest.

Now in total darkness I stumbled, slithered and staggered along the muddy lochshore path, cursing myself for leaving my trekking poles at the hotel. They would have been very useful here. I didn't use my headlamp as I could just see well enough to pick out the path ahead most of the time and I knew that if I switched it on my vision would be limited to its small circle of light. I finally arrived back at the hotel just after midnight. All was in darkness and I had to search around for an unlocked door.

The next day I was feeling quite cheerful as the forecast was for good weather for the next few days though today would be windy and showery. However it was mostly dry with bursts of sunshine for the walk back north along the West Highland Way and there were good views across the loch and of the many waterfalls, still rain-swollen, tumbling down the steep slopes. Rounding one bend in the path I came suddenly on four shaggy-haired wild goats who eyed me suspiciously before continuing their browsing.

A couple of miles from Beinglas farm, which lies on the Way just across Glen Falloch from Inverarnan, I met a couple heading south who asked me how far it was to Inverarnan. I assumed they meant Inversnaid but after a bit of confusion realised they did mean Inverarnan as they were intending catching the bus back from there to Crianlarich where they'd begun. Their only map was an inadequate sketch on a leaflet about the West Highland Way. I showed them on my map where they were and where Inverarnan was. They'd thought it was actually on the path and had somehow missed the clear signposts to it at Beinnglas.

At Beinglas there's a camp-site and some curious-looking wooden tipi-like cabins that can be rented plus a small store where I bought some chocolate bars. Leaving the West Highland Way for the last time I headed east up the path alongside the Ben Glas burn which crashed down in a tremendous waterfall known, according to Louis Stott in his *Waterfalls of Scotland*, as either the Devil's Staircase or the Grey Fox. The fall descends in several branches for some 120 feet and after all the rain was quite spectacular.

I was heading for Beinn Chabhair, the first summit in the long line of

11 rocky peaks that lies south of Crianlarich, not that I thought I could do all or even most of them in what remained of the day. My plan was simply to see how far I could get and then have a high-level camp.

As I plodded slowly up the path the light showers of the morning turned to heavier rain and the wind strengthened from the north-west. Near the summit there were showers of hail and I was only just able to stay upright in the heaviest gusts. Battered by the weather and feeling tired from the day before I decided to camp at the next col. When I reached it though the wind was whistling through. As the gale was from the north-west I dropped south into Coire a'Chuilinn in search of a sheltered site. I had to lose 550 feet of height before I was out of the worst of the wind. The rain was the heaviest it had been and my legs, clad only in thin nylon trail pants, were soaked. The wind was very cold too and when I stopped I started to feel quite chilled. Once in the tent I slid into the sleeping bag then pulled on both my fleece sweaters and my hat and slipped the bivvy bag over my sleeping bag for extra warmth as my legs were quite cold. The stove was on next, providing a touch of warmth as well as hot food and drink. Within an hour I had warmed up.

In the morning the clouds were still rushing across the sky from the north-west and the summits were in cloud. However, according to my altimeter the pressure, which hadn't varied much for the last fortnight, was rising rapidly so I was optimistic about the weather and stayed that way even when it started raining.

My optimism was justified as the day was one of the most enjoyable yet and I climbed all ten summits. These are rough craggy hills with steep sides bitten into by big corries so that the route twisted and turned, making for interesting walking and constantly giving new viewpoints. By the time I reached the first summits the rain had stopped, the clouds had lifted and the wind had dropped to an intermittent though cold breeze. Occasional bursts of sunlight lit up the mountains. I wrote in my journal that evening: 'This is the sort of day I imagined for the walk – linking tops by paths and traverses, and being able to see, before camping high at a scenic spot.' The first summits, An Caisteal and Beinn a'Chroin (which has a Munro and a Top), are rather shapeless, bumpy, craggy hills with no distinctive features. A longish descent then led to a col below Stob Glas. This little knob, the blunt, slightly raised end of a ridge running down from Cruach Ardrain, doesn't reach 3,000 feet so I traversed below the crags of the steep south face then climbed to the col between Beinn Tulaichean and Cruach Ardrain. A few people were about on the latter, which I went out and back to, leaving the pack at the col. It's really just an outlier of Cruach Ardrain rather than a separate mountain though it has Munro status. Cruach Ardrain itself, which came next, is a fine, pointed, rocky hill. The descent was on a steep, slippery scree path on which I caught up a walker wearing large bright green plastic mountaineering boots and a bright orange and blue jacket. He was treading cautiously, his clumsy rigid boots skidding on the loose stones. 'Steep slopes,' he said in a German-sounding accent. With flexible boots that I could easily place flat on the ground and trekking poles I was far more stable and thus able to move much faster.

After passing over Stob Garbh, a Top, I dropped to the col at the head of Benmore Glen and then climbed steep grassy slopes to the Bealach-eadar-dha Beinn which lies between Ben More and Stob Binnein. These were also hills that I'd previously climbed only in winter in the company of Reggie Love. They were the last of the hills I'd climbed with him so as I walked over them I thought of him again, saw his grinning face as he waved his ice axe on reaching the summit, and remembered our long glissade from the bealach down into Benmore Glen, one of those glissades that start out standing but end up as a slide. Farewell, Reggie, I thought, and thank you. I learnt so much from you and your companionship on the hills made for memorable days. Your presence will always be there.

Ben More was done without the pack as my way off lay over Stob Binnein and its two Tops, Stob Coire an Lochain and Meall na Dige. Compared with the hills to the west that I'd climbed earlier in the day these two simple cone-shaped hills are fairly rock and crag free. Their distinctive, classic shape makes them easily identifiable from afar and they're two of the best known hills in the southern Highlands as well as being the highest summits south of the river Tay. The best view of the day was looking back to this pair from Meall na Dige which lies about a mile east of Stob Binnein. From this last peak I descended east into Coire Cheathaich where I camped on the flattish floor of the corrie at a height of 2,180 feet, my highest camp yet. I'd been out ten hours and climbed 8,850 feet but it didn't feel like it as the weather had been calm. It was a joy not to feel under pressure to keep moving or to get down because of the wind and rain. It made camping more enjoyable too as I was able to leave the tent door open for the first time in many days. Another change was that when I took my boots off they were almost dry and my feet didn't look like wrinkled prunes. The site felt wild too, with no pylons, hydro works, roads or plantations visible.

The next hills, Ben Vorlich and Stuc a'Chroin, lay some ten miles to the east though I would have to walk further than that to get round the dense

51

plantations above Strathyre that blocked access from the west. To get there I descended to Monachlye glen, then took the forestry track down to Loch Voil where I walked the road to Balquhidder. The loch was pretty with some attractive trees on its banks but the huge conifer plantations were a bit too dominant, especially as there were many large, ugly, cleared areas where all the trees had been felled to leave a devastated hillside covered with a latticework of grey, torn branches and churned-up soil. These eyesores made a mockery of the notices nailed to many trees: 'Only use downed wood for fires'.

At Balquhidder half a dozen people were photographing Rob Roy's grave. I phoned Denise to hear that she had had the results from her operation and everything was okay. The relief was enormous and I felt amazingly light-hearted. It seemed appropriate that it was a warm, sunny day for once. I even changed to shorts for the walk along the road. I was also happy because I would be seeing Denise the next day as she was driving down with Hazel to stay with friends who lived not too far from the town of Comrie where I was headed. Feeling like celebrating, I had a large lunch of Madras curry and chocolate fudge cake with ice-cream in the Kingshouse Hotel in Strathyre.

From too much previous experience I knew that trying to force a way through closely planted conifers is frustrating, painful and slow and a good way to get hot, sore and scratched as well as bad tempered. To avoid this I walked north from Kingshouse rather than heading directly east towards Ben Vorlich and Stuc a'Chroin through the plantations lining the glen. An abandoned railway line parallels the A84 most of the way so I followed this through peaceful birch woods and long grass, ignoring the occasional 'private' notice and fence. Just before Loch Earn I turned east and followed a minor road to heavily planted Glen Ample where a track led up the glen to Glenample farm. I finally left the road here for a path that led to Ben Vorlich. A man was descending in long strides. His clothing – high topped leather boots with elastic sides, faded denim jeans, an old sweatshirt – plus the battered leather jacket slung through the straps of a small rucksack suggested he wasn't a regular hill-walker but the owner of the motorbike I'd earlier passed by the side of the track. An Australian, he'd set off on the spur of the moment, inspired by the weather, had reached the summit and had a great time.

The climb of Vorlich was easy. From the summit the hills to the west and north were silhouetted against the bright sky. To the south a murky heat haze shimmered over the Lowlands. As I looked across the flat lands it really did feel like the edge of the mountains, the end of one world and the start of another. I was glad I was turning back north. The most dramatic view was nearby, the north ridge of Stuc a'Chroin, looking impressively steep and rocky. As I descended to the col between the two peaks, the Bealach an Dubh Choirein, I studied the ridge carefully, my appreciation of its grandeur given an edge by the knowledge that I would be climbing it shortly. Leaving the pack at the col I headed up. As well as being steep and rocky enough to require hands in places it was very loose and slippery and I was relieved to reach the easier ground just before the summit. Not wanting to descend some of the stuff I'd come up I dropped down to the north-west at the start of the descent and was gratified then to pick up a steep path that cut back to the bealach.

Down in Gleann an Dubh Choirein to the east I soon found a fine dry and flat grassy camp-site near the burn. The gusty and cool west wind which had been blowing on the tops just reached the camp, rustling the tent at times.

A day off from the hills followed. Wearing sandals as it was very warm, I had a pleasant morning walk down the glen to the paved road in Glen Artney. The best views were back along the burn to slowly shrinking Ben Vorlich and Stuc a'Chroin framing the head of the glen. A short way down the road and Denise and Hazel drove up. After three weeks apart I was delighted to see them. I still had further to travel under my own power however so I was soon cycling down the glen to the little town of Comrie, a half hour hilly ride on a narrow road that was quite exciting in places.

From Comrie I was whisked off in the car for the hour's drive to Pool O'Muckart and the house of our friends Ronnie and Robert. Here we had a delightful lunch, prepared by Ronnie, in their beautiful garden, with the civilised elegance of the latter being a great contrast to the wildness of the hills. The meal of fresh orange juice, crusty bread and green salad with a selection of excellent cheeses would have been a pleasure at any time but it was especially enjoyable after all the days on dried food.

After lunch I had work to do as the proofs of a book had arrived at home a few days before and needed checking. First I had a shower, changed into some clean clothes Denise had brought from home and, for the first time on the walk, put my hill clothes into a washing machine. I sat in an appropriately book-lined and quiet study and pored over the proofs, trying to concentrate. For three hours I was absorbed in stories of walks from the past, some of them over hills I would be climbing on this walk.

Ronnie cooked a superb dinner with which we had wine and then afterwards port. Combined with the rather grand and formal surroundings of Ronnie and Robert's house this left me feeling a little distanced from the usual reality of eating a mushy stew from a pan in the tent. The touch of luxury was welcome though.

My attention turned back to the walk early the following day as Denise produced another pack for me and a new stove from Coleman as well as four days' food. From now on she would meet up with me more often and do most of the resupplying. I left the stretch fleece top with her as I hadn't worn it for a week.

Back in Comrie we then walked back to where they'd picked me up the day before so I could be sure the walk was continuous. This may seem pedantic but I felt it was important, not just for ensuring my walk was continuous but also to make sure it stayed so. If I missed even 100 yards it would then be too easy to skip other sections and once I did that the walk would be broken.

I watched Denise and Hazel walk away, glad that it would not be another three weeks before I saw them again, then shouldered the pack and set off through the streets of Comrie.

Chapter 4

EAST TO THE SUN

'These Hielands of ours, as we ca' them, gentlemen, are but a wild kind of warld by themsells, full of heights and howes, woods, caverns, lochs, rivers, and mountains, that it would tire the very deevil's wings to flee to the tap o' them.'
Sir Walter Scott
Rob Roy

North of Comrie lies a solitary Munro, Ben Chonzie, a heathery undistinguished lump that is the highest point of the large area of rolling moorland between Strath Earn and Loch Tay. I left the town on the Circular Walk, a well-maintained path that runs through some lovely mixed woodland in lower Glen Lednock. Below the path the river Lednock runs down a deep, gloomy ravine, at one point crashing down in the waterfall known as the Deil's Caldron. Beyond the woods I joined the road that runs through a mixture of farmland and moorland up Glen Lednock to the Loch Lednock reservoir. The clacking of stonechats and wheatears and the bubbling cries of curlews rang in the air. At the large farm of Invergeldie I left the road for a bulldozed track that climbs high up on the slopes of Ben Chonzie. I dumped the pack just beyond a track junction and was on top within an hour, passing many walkers descending as I climbed. The views were hazy with distant hills invisible and nearer ones shadowy silhouettes. There were masses of hares, a feature of Ben Chonzie noted by many observers.

Back at the pack I continued up Glen Lednock to the reservoir, intending to camp at its head. A gentle humming noise filled the air. By the time I reached the far end of the loch it had turned into a dull but loud rumble and I could see the concrete block of the pumping station responsible. Knowing the noise would keep me awake I continued on up the track, wondering where I would find anywhere to camp or any water

55

to drink on the heather-covered hillsides that lay all around, unpromising terrain for a site. I had just resigned myself to going on for maybe hours more when the track crossed the tiny Allt an Driuchd. A few yards upstream a small patch of flat grass lay right on the edge of the burn. It was just big enough for the tent. I felt relieved. Sometimes such sites appear just when you need them. When they do you never pass them by for it's almost certain that the next site will be a long way further on and probably less comfortable. As it was 9 p.m. I didn't even consider not using this one. Once the tent was up I cooked and ate dinner, scribbled some hasty notes then fell asleep.

It was a nondescript morning, a bit of cloud, a bit of sun, a bit of blue sky. Pleasant but not inspiring. The initial walking was much the same. Not far beyond my camp I crossed the height of the land. Ahead lay the long dark waters of Loch Tay with beyond it the Ben Lawers hills and the very rugged looking Tarmachan ridge, where I was headed. After a short pathless section of high stepping through deep heather I picked up the bulldozed road that led down to another reservoir, Lochan Brealaich, from where a paved road took me quickly down through sombre plantations to the attractive little village of Killin at the head of Loch Tay. Before leaving Killin I shopped for odds and ends – trail mix (dried fruit and Smarties!), chocolate bars, a chunk of cheese, headlamp batteries, a couple of spare films in case the good weather lasted – sent some postcards and had a nondescript lunch in a café. Fine oaks and ashes surrounded the village. The first were bright with new leaves, on the latter the buds were only just starting to open. On the lower hillsides the first fronds of bracken were unfurling while bright little yellow tormentil flowers dotted the turf.

A steep, direct climb led straight up to Creag na Caillich at the western end of the Tarmachan ridge. The Tarmachans are a wonderful group of rugged summits, especially Meall Garbh, a steep pinnacle when seen from the west and with a narrow arête just below the summit. There are a lot of ups and downs on the ridge with many small knolls and bumps as well as the three Tops and one Munro. The most significant point for me was Meall Garbh as it was the hundredth summit of the walk. Suddenly almost a quarter of the walk was over. It didn't feel like it. I still felt as though I was beginning. It was taking far longer to get into the feel of this walk, to feel comfortable with it, than I'd expected. Maybe it was the lack of a linear route, the lack of the simplicity of walking from A to B. Darting here and there to different points, numbered 1 to 517, was a more disjointed and complex process. Most likely though it was the weather and the failure to keep anywhere near my schedule in the first few weeks. Only in the last few days had I started to relax and settle into the day to day immediacy of the walk without the worry and pressure of feeling I had to push on constantly.

To the south Ben Vorlich and Stuc a'Chroin stood out with beyond them the now distant Ben Lomond. To the west and north however the tops were vanishing into thickening cloud. Not far to the west rose the hump of Meall Ghaordaidh. It seemed surprisingly close. It was now 13 days since I'd crossed it with Andy so in my mind it was far away. A strong cold wind swept the summits. I'd changed from shorts and sandals into boots and long pants on the way up and was glad I'd done so.

From Meall nan Tarmachan I descended steep slopes towards Lochan na Lairige, another reservoir. New construction work was going on around the dam and the pipeline below it and I could see a collection of huts, machines, pipes and flapping plastic sheeting lining the glen below the dam. To avoid camping near this detritus I walked south beside the Allt a'Mhoirneas to camp by the burn only a quarter mile or so from the NTS Ben Lawers Visitor Centre.

Next morning I was outside the Visitor Centre long before it opened – not that I wanted to go inside. (In fact I think it's a pity that this centre is here at all as it has encouraged access up Ben Lawers with the provision of a large car park and the path that leads from its front door, a path that is now wide and worn. The centre would be better down in Killin, leaving Ben Lawers to recover.) I was here to start my ascent of the eight summits of the Lawers range. These lie on a twisting ridge that is seven miles long and which never drops below 2,600 feet, making it the largest area of high ground in the southern Highlands. Deep corries bite into the hillsides though there are few crags and the hills are mostly green and rounded. The whole area is a National Nature Reserve because of the wealth of arctic and alpine plants found here, flourishing on the lime-rich calcareous soil, while from the summits south it is owned by the National Trust for Scotland.

I left the tourist path after a short distance to climb to the head of Coire Odhar where I dumped the pack while I went up Meall Corranaich which lay directly above and then out to Meall a'Choire Leith to the north. These rounded Munros, probably the least visited of the Lawers group, give excellent views of the main part of the range especially Beinn Ghlas and Ben Lawers. I cut below the summit of Corranaich on my return then set off up Beinn Ghlas. Just as I did so two walkers appeared on the path that runs below the latter. 'Where've you been?' one of them said, looking confused. I was puzzled too as I was sure I hadn't met them before. I had anyway seen no other walkers that day. It turned out they'd seen me setting off and had assumed I'd been up Ben Lawers, in which case I was now heading in the wrong direction.

They were the first of the many people that, as I expected, I met on Beinn Ghlas and on the eroded path, about a mile long and far too wide, to Ben Lawers. There were 14 people on or near the summit itself. Also as expected, once over the summit the people faded away and I met only two parties, one of two and one of four, the rest of the day. From Creag an Fhithich wind-rippled Lochan nan Cat, which lies in the deep corrie to the east, looked dramatic. There are good camp-sites by this beautiful lochan, which is backed by the steep and rugged south and east faces of Meall Garbh, An Stuc and Ben Lawers, but I wanted to be much farther on at the day's end. The descent from An Stuc was on very steep, very loose and very slippery slopes. I retreated twice before I found a way down with which I was happy. The pack didn't help. I was again using the one I'd found a bit awkward on the Aonach Eagach. Then I'd thought it was my lack of confidence, now I decided it was mainly the pack as it swayed from side to side instead of hugging the body and stuck out too far at the back, catching on rocks.

Beyond An Stuc the terrain became more gentle, rolling moorland rather than stony mountain, making the walk between Meall Garbh and Meall Greigh easy. An eyesore of a new wire fence, already collapsing in places, ran along the ridge here, marking the boundary of the NTS land. To compensate, the ground was dotted in places by the small pink flowers of moss campion, the first I'd seen this summer. From the col between these last two peaks I descended north to the Inverinain Burn with views across Glen Lyon to the hills I hoped to climb the next day. Low down I cut away from the burn and descended towards Invervar, crossing some fences near the farm of Dericambus and eventually reaching the bridge just below the hamlet. A sign nearby said that stalking took place between 1 August and 31 January and that people should stay off the hills then. Such signs make my blood boil. They are unhelpful and antagonistic. I always ignore them as I don't believe that wild land should be 'owned' to the exclusion of others. What is needed is a legal right to roam over open land. The Labour government is pledged to introduce just such a right. Hopefully it will become law soon, perhaps by the time this book is published.

The sporting estates are a Victorian creation, set up as playgrounds for the rich. Anyone with enough money can buy an estate as a plaything, an appalling situation. To justify their existence estates always go on about the jobs they provide and how stalking is needed for the sake of the deer. However conservation can provide many more jobs, as has happened on the Abernethy estate, now owned by the Royal Society for the Protection of Birds (RSPB), while the best thing for the deer would be a drastic reduction in numbers and the restoration of the forest, their natural habitat. But sporting estates are the main obstacle to forest regeneration and also the right of local people to control and work on the land.

Much of the Highlands is a degraded landscape that has been damaged by years of deforestation and over-grazing. I get no pleasure from an empty, desolate, boggy glen when I know that it was once forested. I would rather see farms dotting the glens between large areas of natural woodland than the impoverished scene we have now. Those who wish to see no change say the land is too poor for this. But just look at any stream tumbling down a hillside, its steep banks rich with trees and plants, able to grow because they are out of reach of sheep and deer. Reduce the numbers of the latter and the trees will return.

Energised by these thoughts I stomped up the track beside the Invervar Burn. Dense plantations lined one side and the slopes were steep so I had to climb 1,000 feet before I found a slightly bumpy but dry and grassy camp-site. It was a peaceful, almost secretive spot with the dark forest below to the south and steep-sided grassy hills rising up all around. Dinner eaten and notes written, I lay in the tent looking out at the view, my usual evening activity when the weather allowed. Pink clouds at sunset gave hope for another fine day.

A great curve of high hills forms the skyline above Invervar. On this broad, high, six-mile-long ridge lie the seven tops of this group. These are flat-topped rolling hills, more similar to the Grampians to the east than the closer, more rugged Lawers range to the south. The summits are fairly featureless, just rounded bumps on the ridge. The pleasure is in the walking high above the world, in the big sky and huge horizons. I began at the western end with Carn Gorm and An Sgorr, which give good views of the rest of the range. As I climbed these peaks the dark clouds that had covered the sky at dawn faded away and the sun began to shine though a cold north-east wind marred any feel of summer. Revelling in the easy walking I was quickly over Meall Garbh and Meall a'Bharr, along which there runs an ugly, rusting iron fence, and onto the most impressive hill of the range, Carn Mairg, whose summit is ringed by pale grey shattered rocks. Here I met other walkers for the only time that day, nine in all and most with hoods, hats and gloves because of the wind though many were also in shorts. The two tops at the south-east end of the ridge, Meall Liath and Creag Mhor, were, like those at the other end, done without the pack. Above, the heavens were a varied and interesting mix of white clouds and blue sky. To the north the hills ran away into the distance. A great shadowed whaleback dominated the nearby scene, the south side of Schiehallion, looking totally unlike the usual graceful cone.

Easy slopes led down into Gleann Mor below Schiehallion. The last time I'd been there, some ten years previously, I'd stayed in Glenmore Bothy which I remembered as being in good condition. I walked down the glen to it only to find the door padlocked and a general air of dilapidation. A window was broken and when I peered inside I could see sagging doors. It's sad to see a once useful bothy slowly turning into a ruin.

Further down the glen I camped beside the remains of some old shielings on a patch of violet dotted turf. Orchids, tormentil and other flowers were growing in the heather which was also brightened by the fresh green of new blaeberry leaves. On the slopes higher up the large white flowers of cloudberry rose above fleshy leaves. This wealth of flowers and new growth had appeared in the last few days. Suddenly it seemed summer had finally started.

Schiehallion – Sidh Chaillean, the fairy hill of the Caledonians – is a very distinctive and very popular mountain, well-known to general tourists as well as hill-walkers, and visible from many other hills owing to its isolated situation. Because of easy access from the large car park near the Braes of Foss to the north-east a wide, well-worn and over-cairned path leads up the east ridge. The rest of the mountain is fairly untouched however. I went directly up the south side from my camp, climbing through steep heather and boulders to join the tourist highway not far from the summit. Rays of sunlight shooting through the dark clouds lit up Loch Rannoch, making the black water shine and sparkle. A bright white distant building catching a shaft of light was Blair Castle, my destination the next day. Also visible to the east was the bulk of Beinn A'Ghlo, now quite close. Even the Cairngorms further round to the north looked far larger than they had before. The hills to the south-west however looked small and distant. For the first time I had a real sense of making progress.

The drizzle that greeted me the next morning was the first rain for a week. It came on a cold, gusty, north wind. An hour's brisk walk through heather which was crawling with masses of large, furry, golden caterpillars with black stripes down their backs – the larva of the northern eggar moth – saw me at the Braes of Foss car park where I had a rendezvous with Denise. I sat and read *Rob Roy* until she turned up then it was a two hour bike ride to Blair Atholl. Loch Tummel seemed endless and all uphill. Turning north straight into the strong headwind made the ride through Killiecrankie even harder so I was happy to reach Blair Atholl where I paid £5 to camp between caravans and campavans on the smart, neat and well-organised caravan park in the grounds of Blair Castle. After working through some paperwork in the café and a short stroll together through the beautiful woodlands along the banks of the river Tilt Denise left for home. Our next meeting was planned for four days' time, in Glen Shee. I set up office in the Roundhouse bar and spent the rest of the afternoon sorting out gear and food and writing.

Crossing the A9 seemed significant. I knew it was just a road but it did separate distinct groups of mountains. I had finally finished with the southern Highlands. For the next two-and-a-half weeks I would be in the Grampians (that is, those hills east of the A9 but south of Deeside – I prefer to call them Grampians rather than southern Cairngorms, the other name by which they are known, as they really are a different range) and the Cairngorms. The great straight trench of Glen Tilt that runs north from Blair Atholl splits the south-westernmost of the Grampians into two massifs, Beinn A'Ghlo and the Ring of Tarf and it was to these that I would go first.

Beinn A'Ghlo, a complex and bulky mountain with many broad ridges and deep corries plus three Munros and one Top, is probably the finest mountain in the Grampians apart from Lochnagar. To reach it I first walked up the road to Loch Moraig. A mix of sun and showers made for wonderfully sharp storm light and there were superb views of Carn Liath, the first Munro, and the hills west of Glen Tilt. Steep banks lined the road and these were a mass of colour, replete with the profligacy of spring, the grass thick with the pinks, whites, blues and purples of herb robert, cow parsley, speedwell, forget-me-not and various vetches. In the damp meadows beyond, white and yellow ox-eye daisies and pale pink lady's smock nodded in the breeze while curlews, lapwings and rooks prodded the ground for food then soared into the air calling as they wheeled and dived, suddenly aware of my presence.

Occasional very heavy but very short showers hammered down from the north, drenching me in seconds. Then the hot sun would come out and I would steam dry almost as quickly. However once up on the mountain the cold north wind took over from the sun as the dominant feature of the weather and I was soon clad in rain jacket and pants with my hat on and a pair of socks pulled over my hands as makeshift mittens, something I hadn't done in many weeks. Ironically, it was Midsummer's Day.

Despite the wind I enjoyed the walk along the twisting ridges that ran between the steep-sided, pale scree-covered tops of Beinn A'Ghlo. It was more reminiscent of the Mamores away to the west, and still to come on this walk, than the rest of the Grampians. From Carn Liath onwards the wind made the walking an exhilarating struggle, the strongest gusts almost knocking me down at times. The rain held off however and the clouds stayed broken and high though distant hills were hidden. To the north the dark vee of the Lairig Ghru was clear, flanked by the blunt pyramid of the Devil's Point and the massive flanks of Ben MacDui, the latter rising into the cloud and looking as though they were dusted with new snow. Up and down I went, over Braigh Coire Chruinn-bhalgain and with a diversion out to Airgiod Bheinn, until I reached the last and highest summit, Carn nan Gabhar. Below to the east Loch Loch was shining in the sun and topped with white-capped wind-driven waves. Beyond the water rose the grey scree slopes of Carn an Righ and Carn Iutharn Mhor. Across Glen Tilt the hills looked shapeless lumps except for the tiny pointed peak of Carn a'Chlamain.

After descending Carn nan Gabhar's long north ridge into Glen Tilt I followed the river Tilt upstream to the Falls of Tarf where the Water of Tarf crashes down a narrow rock-walled gorge into a deep pool before running into the river Tilt. As I passed under a craggy bit of hillside raucous screeching echoed above me. I looked up. Two magnificent peregrine falcons scythed through the air. I watched them briefly then moved on, not wishing to disturb them for too long. Thin but loud whistling from the river denoted common sandpipers which I could see bobbing on the stones and flying fast and low over the water. The white rumps of wheatears flashed from bushes.

At the Falls, a favourite spot where I had camped many times before, a bright turquoise tent was pitched right next to the bridge over the Water of Tarf. Two men and a dog were sitting outside. I stopped and stared at their camp, momentarily nonplussed. I wanted to camp here as it was ideally placed for my goal for the next day, the Ring of Tarf hills to the west. However I'd not camped wild near others before and I wasn't sure whether to stay or move on a little way, though I knew I couldn't go far as there were few camp-sites upstream. When wild camping I prefer to keep away from other people. Solitude is after all a main reason for camping far from towns and roads. I tend to assume that others feel the same way though on occasion I have had people come and camp close by even though there were plenty of camp-sites further away. I can only guess that they are so overawed by the immensity of the wilds that being near another human provides some form of security. At the Falls of Tarf there isn't much space for camping as the steep walls of Glen Tilt rise not far back from the river. On the left bank of the Tilt opposite the falls there is a series of grassy terraces so I eventually headed for these to look for a site that was at least out of sight of the other campers.

As I was setting up camp, on a spot where I could only see the other tent if I stood up, two more backpackers came down Glen Tilt. When I went down to the river for water a grey dome tent was sitting next to the turquoise one. A desultory camp fire was burning in a ring of stones, giving off occasional puffs of blue smoke, and I could see a man scouring the hillside above for wood or, perhaps, heather roots. Another tent, a more unobtrusive dark green, was pitched a couple of hundred yards upstream.

The night was cold and very windy, gusts waking me several times. In the morning the sky was clear but the deep and narrow glen was still in shadow and a cold 5°. I lay in my sleeping bag while I had breakfast and watched the warm sunlight creeping slowly down the hillsides. Soon the far side of the glen was glowing brightly and the bridge and the trees round the falls were shining with the new light. The dog from the other camp barked. A loaded backpacker crossed the bridge, heading down the glen. I looked upstream. The green tent had gone. Suddenly the sun appeared over the hilltops and the world was a different place, colourful and bright. In the tent it was soon quite hot but outside the wind kept the temperature down and I set off for the day walk round the Ring of Tarf wearing my fleece top under the windshirt.

The Ring of Tarf is the name given to the four Munros that lie either side of the Water of Tarf, remote An Sgarsoch and Carn an Fhidhleir to the north and Beinn Dearg and Carn a'Chlamain to the south. The complete circuit is a long walk over rough, heathery ground with few paths. When I returned to the tent that evening I'd walked at least 25 miles (the farthest yet), climbed nearly 6,000 feet and been out ten minutes short of 12 hours. As most of the walking was off paths I had to adjust my route constantly so that where possible I could follow deer tracks and grassy stream gullies, even peat channels, rather than walk over boggy ground covered with ankle wrenching, spongy grass tussocks or thick tangled heather. It was very hard work and there was too much heather bashing, especially for just four summits. Overall this was one of the toughest days of the whole walk.

I went north first, to the hills that Irvine Butterfield characterises with the phrase 'dreary isolation and extreme remoteness'. Certainly the terrain isn't exciting, this being moorland rather than mountain walking, indeed a close counterpart to these hills would be some of the less well known tops in the northern Pennines. However the views, especially of the Cairngorms to the north, are extensive. On this occasion the light was dull however as the sky clouded over and the highest tops slowly faded away as I climbed An Sgarsoch. Out on the Great Moss across the Geldie Burn to the north Beinn Bhrotain was visible with the very distinctive little pointed peak of Sgor Gaoith beyond it.

From Carn an Fhidhleir it was a long haul south across the Water of Tarf to the lone granite peak of Beinn Dearg, a pointed, stony summit in a mass of moorland hills. Another tedious slog across yet more heather led finally to Carn a'Chlamain, whose pointed summit, although only small, is a distinctive landmark as there is nothing else like it in the surrounding terrain. The lonely piping of a golden plover rang out from the moorland near the summit. Throughout the day I'd heard the insistent thin calls of this bird, an appropriate sound for these desolate, deserted hills.

Thankfully a path runs up to Carn a'Chlamain from Glen Tilt. I followed this down steep slopes then headed back up the glen on a broad track. Noisy oyster-catchers and sandpipers kept me company. The wind had dropped and it was now quite calm, the darkening sky red from the setting sun and a half moon hanging in the fading light. I smelt cooking – frying – on the air long before I saw two tents pitched by the river a quarter mile below my camp. Three more tents were on the terrace immediately below the one I was camped on and another green tent had appeared up the glen where the one had been the previous night. I totted up the total. There'd been two tents nearby last night and one a little way away and tonight there were three nearby and three not far away. Nine in all. Yet until yesterday I'd only seen one other wild camp. It was beginning to feel overcrowded. Was this the start of the summer backpacking season?

At 5 a.m. I woke feeling slightly chilly. The temperature was 2°C. I pulled the hood of the sleeping bag shut and went back to sleep. Three hours later the temperature was 9°C, the sky was clear and the tent was soaked inside and out with condensation and dew. There was no wind. The only sounds were the gentle ripple of the river and the songs of birds.

Between Glen Tilt and Glen Shee to the east there lies a rather disparate scattering of hills, eight Munros and five Tops in total. As I was due to meet Denise in Glen Shee at noon the next day I had until then to climb these 13 summits. They are mostly typical Grampian hills, rounded with grassy slopes but also with steep sides and divided by deep glens and low passes. There is no easy way to link them, no high level ridge running between them, so I would have to do a great deal of out-and-back walking. Again it would be a long day, 11½ hours and another 25 miles though this time with over 7,000 feet of ascent, the extra climbing cancelling out the easier walking, on grass, mostly, rather than heather.

As I left on the path east to remote Fealar Lodge the other backpackers were heading up Glen Tilt. The sun was now warm and I walked in sandals and shorts with my sleeves rolled up. Beyond the lodge, one of the most isolated habitations in Britain, I followed the Allt Feith Lair up to a peaty col. Here I left the pack for the first out-and-back to the two summits of Carn Bhac. As I approached the south-west Top one of the four people by the summit cairn began to wave me to one side. I paused, puzzled, then, as she seemed quite agitated, moved sideways. 'There's a bird with young beside you,' she said when I was near enough for her to speak to me without shouting. I looked down and sure enough there was a dotterel with two chicks just a few feet away, so well camouflaged on the stony ground that I might never have seen them if they hadn't been pointed out.

After walking round to the eastern summit, which is the higher one though it's not named on the OS map nor given a height, I made a slanting descent back to the pack then climbed south to Beinn Iutharn Mhor, which I had to myself, then Mam nan Carn where another walker was sitting by the summit cairn. At the col to the south-west I stopped for a snack as two pairs of walkers came off Carn an Righ and another pair set off up. The hills were busy today.

Leaving the pack again I climbed Carn an Righ. There were good views across Glen Loch to Beinn A'Ghlo but high, thin clouds were dulling the light now and the wind was stronger and cooler too. The sharp point of Lochnagar was visible to the north–east, as it was from every summit. The other hills east of Glen Shee could be seen too but none of them stood out. Westwards, Ben Lawers and Schiehallion were clear whilst much nearer Carn a'Chlamain was surprisingly prominent.

Collecting the pack I took the footpath running east below Mam nan Carn, then crossed a broad watershed to Loch nan Eun. Seeking a camp-site I walked round the north-west shore. The banks were boggy and covered with peat and heather. The only flat dry ground was opposite the little island that lies at the northern end of the loch. A mass of pale birds whirled and wheeled in the air above, screeching loudly, some of the large colony of common gulls that nest on the islet. The din was far too loud for me to consider camping nearby. On the shore of the islet I could see many young gulls, grey and clumsy looking, opening and shutting their beaks as they squawked for food. Continuing round the loch I finally camped on the south shore not far from the outlet burn, a site I'd used before. This is a fine site with a wild atmosphere and a feeling of remoteness. At 2,600 feet it was the highest camp so far. Others had been here too however and recently. Stones lay on the turf, probably used to weigh down tent pegs. When I lifted them to toss them back in the loch the grass underneath was still bright green. Nearby bits of litter poked out from under rocks. I packed some of it to take down to the road the next day. This was the first despoiled site I'd used and it left me feeling annoyed and sad, as such sites always do.

To reach Glen Shee in time the next day without leaving any summits unclimbed in this group I needed to climb more hills that evening so at 8.45 p.m. I set off up Glas Tulaichean to the south. This is the highest and probably the finest hill of the whole group with a deep rugged corrie, Glas Choire Bheag, on its north-east flanks. I was up and down in 72 minutes. A longer excursion then took in the steep little peak of Beinn Iutharn Bheag which lay directly north of Loch nan Eun and the one-and-a-half mile long ridge of An Socach to the north-east. The latter peak has a summit at each end and, as with Carn Bhac, the height of the higher top, in this case the western one, isn't marked on the OS map while the name appears only at the eastern end of the hill. I've always found An Socach an awkward hill to fit in with other summits with much rough boggy terrain to cross to reach it. On the ridge it felt cold, especially as I was still wearing shorts and sandals, but the red sun sinking into pink clouds made up for the chill. A bright half moon gave a bit of light for the return to camp. Back at the tent at midnight I had the third course, or rather stage, of my dinner – dried apples and custard. The first bit had been soup before I went up Glas Tulaichean, then I'd had cottage pie (instant mash and a dried soya and onion mix) before the last three summits.

At 4.50 a.m. the gulls started to screech. I cursed them briefly then fell back to sleep. At 6.15 I was again woken, this time by the sun coming up. The gulls reacted to the sunrise with another raucous burst of noise. Every footstep seemed to start more hares darting through the heather as I set off straight up the hillside to the east to follow the broad ridge twisting towards Glen Shee. The distinctive knoll of Carn Bhinnein, a fine little peak, lies just to the south of the ridge so I did it without the pack. From the top there were good views of the deep curved green bowl of Glas Choire Mhor on Glas Tulaichean. Herds of deer watched me cautiously as I passed quickly over the lump of Carn a'Gheoidh and along a good path round the head of the steep walled corrie west of The Cairnwell. Then came desolation. The Cairnwell and Carn Aosda to the north are the most ugly, depressing summits in the Highlands. That's not because of the hills themselves but rather because of what has been done to them. They've been stripped bare, gouged raw and totally desecrated in the name of mass industrial tourism in the form of alpine skiing. This is often considered a mountain pursuit. It's not. It's a mountain-destroying pursuit. The Glen Shee ski area looks more like an abandoned quarry in which industrial junk has been tipped than a hill landscape. The scoured slopes are laced with lines of pylons carrying ski tows and fencing put up to trap snow while below bulldozed roads run all over the place.

On reaching the first fences I left the pack and went up the broad, eroded stony track past the ski tows to the mast and shed dotted summit of The Cairnwell. A few people who'd come up on the chairlift that almost reaches the top stood about looking at the view. I didn't bother but dashed back down and then up another wide track to Carn Aosda. I was in the car park 28 minutes after leaving that summit. These devastated hills were the only two I climbed purely so I could say I'd done them.

Denise arrived soon afterwards and we sat in the café talking at length then sorted out my food and gear in the car park. In four days she'd meet me in Braemar so I didn't have too much to pack though I did have a new pack, supplied by Lowe Alpine, which I hoped would prove more stable on steep ground than the one I'd had since Comrie.

Feeling tired after two long days and only four to five hours sleep the previous night I laboured up through the ski squalor east of Glen Shee to another ruined summit, Meall Odhar. I'd planned on camping at the head of the Allt Coire Fionn glen just east of this hill but it was sullied by ski tows that weren't shown on the map. That this development is in a National Nature Reserve makes a mockery of the designation.

As I desperately wanted to camp out of sight of the despoilation I continued on up all the way to the summit of Glas Maol then descended north-east to camp near the burn right at the head of Caenlochan Glen. At 3,100 feet it was my highest camp. There were views across the deep hollow of the Caenlochan Glen to the crags of Druim Mor but these weren't very clear as the light was dull and hazy under a covering of high cloud. I lay in the tent with the door open staring out at the sky and the space. I felt calm and content. All I could see was wild hill country. A cloud was brushing the top of Druim Mor and I realised that I could easily wake up in thick mist here. Just before I fell asleep the first tendrils of mist were creeping round the tent and dampening the flysheet. Suddenly there was no view.

Bright light, heat. What was going on? What was the time? Groggily I reached for my watch. 5.20! I looked out of the tent, straight into the newly risen sun. Below, Caenlochan Glen was a sea of white cloud. Suddenly awake and inspired I leapt out of the tent, grabbed the camera and tripod and started taking photographs. It was the first cloud inversion of the walk. As the sun strengthened the mist began to sink into the valley but the view was still spectacular with the hills all around rising above the cloud and shining gold and green in the low slanting light. Hares were everywhere and the dark shapes of deer could be seen moving across the hillsides.

The early wakening meant I'd climbed three summits by 9 a.m.! And the cloud inversion meant I'd taken over one-and-a-half rolls of film. It was a wonderful morning, the most marvellous of the walk so far. Leaving the dew-sodden tent to dry in the sun I headed south-east to Little Glas Maol, where a few flat planks were all that remained of a small wooden hut I'd stayed in 15 years earlier, then cut back west and south to the two summits of Creag Leacach, just dipping into the mist at the col below the peaks. The ridge to Creag Leacach is narrow and quite rocky with much scree and many boulders, very unusual for the Grampians and a welcome change from the miles of grass and heather walking.

Back at the tent I had a second breakfast before setting off across the hills lying between Glas Maol and Glen Doll. These form the southern half of the vast plateau known as The Mounth, an anglicisation of the Gaelic word *monadh*, meaning a mountain but in this instance more specifically a large area of hill country. The northern half of The Mounth stretches to Lochnagar. In total this plateau contains over 27 square miles of land above 2,500 feet, an area only equalled in size by the Moine Mhor in the Cairngorms, and seven square miles over 3,000 feet. On this great tableland there are 13 Munros and 16 Tops.

It took just over eight hours to do eight of these summits as I went first north, then east, then south between the bumps. From the first one, Druim Mor, there was a superb view down into the depths of Caenlochan Glen and across to the green vegetated crags of Glas Maol and Little Glas Maol. The westernmost pair of hills, Cairn of Claise and Carn an Tuirc, gave excellent views of the high Cairngorms to the north. All the cloud had now cleared from the glens. I met the only people of the day on these two tops, five in total. Tolmount, Crow Craigies and Tom Buidhe all came and went as I strode on over the rolling plateau. The walking was easy, mostly on dry turf with occasional bits of bog, peat or boulders. Finally there came a long walk south to the rather more distinctive though still rounded summits of Driesh and Mayar. Throughout the day the cloud slowly thickened from the north-west. At first it was just fuzzy, out of focus white cloud over the Cairngorms which contrasted with the deep blue sky and which I expected to look good on photographs. Soon darker, thicker, more solid clouds followed. The last sun was on Tom Buidhe, the first light rain on the ascent of Driesh, the last summit of the day. I donned a rain jacket here but stayed in shorts and sandals.

This is country for long, high-level walks rather than peak bagging as the summits aren't separate hills at all but just the high points on a vast plateau. Although I walked 28 miles over 11 summits (the most I'd climbed in a day), seven of them classified as Munros or separate mountains, the ascent was just 4,400 feet. Classifying these peaks in the same way as those in the west is an impossible task. But they're in the *Tables* and it's a daft game anyway so over them I went. I enjoyed it too. It was great to stay so high all day under the spacious sky, feeling the freedom of vast, open space. This is a good place for moorland birds too and during the day I saw dotterel, ptarmigan, grouse with chicks, golden plover, sandpipers and ravens.

I descended abruptly on the path that runs down the steep slopes of the spur of the Shank of Drumfollow into the plantations of Glen Doll, a deep, heavily forested and steep-sided glen at the head of long, straight Glen Clova. The path through the dark trees led to the Forestry Commission camp-site, a small field at the road-end. Half a dozen other tents were on the site. Rain was falling and I was soon zipped into the tent.

Going through my notes I realised that I'd passed 150 summits and the 550-mile mark during the day. Had I really come so far, climbed so many hills? I thought back. Mull, Ben Cruachan, Glencoe all seemed long ago. I had to look at my notes to remember the details. Yes, I thought, the journey was really under way. The beginning was over and I was now in the heart of the venture. An itchy ankle distracted me. A red spot marked the first midge bite of the walk. How it got through the layers of dirt, the result of three days of walking in sandals, I don't know.

I'd descended to Glen Doll because I wanted to climb the easternmost

Munro, Mount Keen, the following day. This solitary hill lies far to the east across difficult country ridden with deep peat hags. My plan was to use a bothy I knew of at the western end of this country as a base and go out and back to Mount Keen from there. I hoped I could do this in a day from Glen Doll.

The night was muggy and humid and by morning everything felt damp. A fair number of still sluggish midges were in the tent porch so I lit a mosquito coil and put on some repellent for the first time. I was trying a new type called Mosi-Guard Natural that was based on eucalyptus oils rather than frightening sounding chemicals that melted your watch strap. I hoped it worked but if it didn't it would be back to the more toxic stuff.

From Glen Doll I climbed up the Capel Mounth path. This is an ancient route marked as the Mounth Capell on a map dated around 1360 according to the Scottish Rights of Way Society's *Scottish Hill Tracks*. Leaving the path I went north-east for a few miles round the shoulder of the Black Hill of Mark to Water of Mark. A ring ousel, the white crescent on its black breast prominent, darted over the moorland. As I headed downstream a dipper zipped down the streamside ahead of me then a small duck scuttled across the water followed by five ducklings. Teal, I thought, noting the green flash on the wing.

Soon I came to the Shielin' of Mark, a little bothy near the head of Glen Mark. I'd discovered this unlocked shelter on the first Ultimate Challenge (now the *TGO* Challenge) crossing of Scotland in 1981. Then it was a private estate bothy, rarely used by walkers as it lay near no major summits. Now it is maintained by the Mountain Bothies Association (MBA). According to the bothy book, Shielin' of Mark bothy is still little used except during the middle of May when Challenge walkers cram into it for several nights. That night would be the 40th of the walk but my first in a bothy.

The MBA is a voluntary organisation which restores and repairs bothies throughout the Highlands and other hill areas of Britain. Everyone who uses bothies should be a member of the MBA. Whilst a supporter of the MBA I have mixed feelings about bothies. Remote ones that don't get too much use are fine but once they become popular then, unfortunately, problems arise with litter, vandalism and the disposal of human waste. There are certain bothies that I am no longer prepared to use and would like to see closed because these problems have become so severe. However when the weather is stormy, and particularly when the midges are biting, the space and shelter of a bothy can be welcome. One problem with bothies is that people use them as a substitute for self-sufficiency rather than as a supplement to it. This means they go to an area or undertake a walk because there are bothies available. Whilst I use bothies at times I always carry a tent or bivvy bag and am always prepared to sleep out if the bothy is full or I fail to reach it for some reason.

Before setting out for Mount Keen I had lunch in the bothy. It took two goes to make some soup. The first try ended abruptly when I nudged the rickety table and the pan tipped off the stove. A bit of paper wedged under one leg minimised the wobble and I tried again. Success! Cheese, biscuits and chocolate followed then it was time for Mount Keen.

The first time I'd come this way I'd followed the high ground round to Mount Keen. It looked easy on the map, mostly level with only gentle ascents and descents. However, these uplands are very boggy and covered with deep peat hags. Slithering in and out of these black, sticky runnels was arduous and slow. In between the peat bogs lay thick heather and dense tussocks. Learning, for once, from experience I avoided this nightmare walking by following Glen Mark downstream, preferring extra ascent to peat bogs. The glen is more attractive and interesting than the moorland above with the Water of Mark leaving little ox-bow lakes as it meanders through upland meadows before rushing down steeper, narrower, stony sections. I saw two more ducks with young. One of them left four ducklings paddling on the spot while she tried to lure me away with lots of splashing and fluttering, the other swam off with her young who then dived into various crevices in the bank while she tried to draw me away. I also saw deer, hares, sandpipers, meadow pipits, dippers, golden plover and red grouse with chicks. In the stream small trout – some 6-8 inches long – darted through the pools. The landscape may be less spectacular than further west but for wildlife it was the richest area I'd been through.

I finally left the Water of Mark to climb steeply beside the burn between two heathery lumps called Little Hill and the Hill of Doune. A stretch of peat and heather moor followed as I headed on a compass bearing towards the invisible Mount Keen. It had disappeared into cloud just as I'd arrived at the bothy and it had stayed hidden since. The last steep slopes to the top were all in dense mist. Reaching the summit meant I had climbed the southernmost and easternmost hills. Now everything left lay to the north and west.

On my return to the bothy I at first stayed higher, walking through the silent, misty, dry peat channels and bare flats of the Head of Black Burn, a mysterious, desolate and eerie country. Strands of stray mist drifted across the dusty ground and slithered round stones and over banks. The only sound was the gentle crunch of my boots and the thin piping of golden plovers. Occasionally a grouse would explode from the ground – 'Go back, go back, go back'. It felt more like the Dark Peak or even Dartmoor than the Highlands.

Soon the ground became rougher and wetter and covered with heather tussocks so I dropped down south back to Glen Mark and followed it back up to the bothy. The 11 mile round trip had taken seven-and-a-half hours.

Reading the bothy book that evening I found a note from the only other walker I'd seen all day, a man who'd been descending into Glen Mark from the north as I headed downstream for Mount Keen. Bill Scott from Dundee was doing a round trip from the road-end at Invermark, up Glen Lee and down Glen Mark. Apart from that there was only one other entry in the last month. Looking back through the pages I found that Mike Cudahy had stayed here on his record-breaking Munros run in 1994.

Before slipping into the sleeping bag I went outside. A bright three-quarter moon hung in the almost clear sky. To the east the final slopes of Mount Keen rose out of a pale, thick mist. It was wonderfully quiet and peaceful.

The only sound at dawn was the gurgling of the burn. Less than a mile from the bothy I joined the path that led down easily to the Spittal of Glenmuick. There was a phone here so I rang Denise and rearranged the meeting in Braemar for the next evening rather than the morning after as I was actually ahead of schedule for this section. The good weather had made a huge difference.

The easier walking on these gentle eastern hills also made for fast times and I surprised myself that day for, by the end, I'd done the remaining 16 summits in the Grampians, all of which lie on the plateau north-west of Loch Muick. Again the ascent, 5,900 feet, was low for the number of hills, especially as the distance was 21 miles.

After a pleasant wander through the mature Scots Pine in Glen Muick the ascents began with Lochnagar and its four Tops, Cac Carn Mor, Meall Coire na Saobhaidhe, Cuidhe Crom and Meikle Pap. The last gave excellent views of the great cliffs of the north-east face of Lochnagar, the mountain's finest feature. Unsurprisingly there were many other walkers on Lochnagar with eight on the actual summit, Cac Carn Beag. I saw none on any other peaks however and given the very few I'd seen during the last three days I decided I wouldn't have to adjust to seeing lots of people every day after all. From Lochnagar it was an easy stroll over the White Mounth hills – Carn a'Choire Boidheach, Creag a'Ghlas-uillt and the Top of Eagle's Rock – followed by Carn an t-Sagairt Beag and Carn an t-Sagairt Mor. Only Meall Coire na Saobhaidhe, which lies on a spur north of Cac Carn Beag, required any real effort and that was because I had to re-climb Lochnagar. The others are all just rounded bumps on the plateau even though two of them have Munro status.

Dropping down into the head of the Allt an Dubh-loch glen I found a good camp-site by the burn at 2,850 feet. To the south lay the remaining six summits on the plateau. I had time to climb them the next day but the sky was clouding over from the south-west so I decided to do them that evening while it was still clear and dry rather than risk having to do so in mist and rain. I was well aware that navigating over these featureless hills was difficult in poor visibility and that finding some of the less distinct summits could be almost impossible.

Fafernie, a rounded hummock, came first and then the rockier Munro of Cairn Bannoch and the two Tops of its south ridge, Cairn of Gowal and Craig of Gowal. The last was the lowest and least distinctive of the six summits but did give good views of Broad Cairn, the second Munro of the group which I climbed next. Across the deep glen holding the dark waters of the Dubh Loch, Eagle's Rock was an impressive face of big slabs with waterfalls cascading down a series of them. There had been no hint of this on the rounded lump above. From the last Top, Creag an Dubh-loch, I descended northwards to the Allt an Dubh-loch which I followed back to camp up a very rough glen full of bogs, peat channels, stream gullies, heather tussocks, pools and boulders of every size. It was the hardest walking of the day.

The expected rain began as I fell asleep and it was still raining when I woke. Only light rain but still rain. A dense wet mist hung outside. Everything was damp and I felt slightly chilly and very glad I'd no more summits to do before descending to Braemar. As it was I needed a compass bearing just to find the path that lay half a mile away on the slopes of Carn an t-Sagairt Mor. Then it was down out of the mist to gloomy Loch Callater and a walk under dull skies down the Glen Callater track to the A93 and a final few road miles into Braemar. I waited for Denise in The Old Bakery, which served excellent coffee and delicious cakes, of which I ate several. Outside it rained, on and off, and dripping tourists ambled about aimlessly, peering into shop windows and wondering what to do.

Denise turned up early and whisked me back to our house five miles

73

outside Grantown-on-Spey. I hadn't been totally happy about going home during the walk but I had some more much longer and detailed book proofs to check and this would be easiest done with the original on the computer screen in front of me. These proofs had been expected and we'd agreed some time ago that if they had arrived when I got to Braemar I'd go home for the day. 'They've come,' Denise had told me at Glen Shee. The work took ten hours the next day and a couple the morning after, an unreal interlude.

Chapter 5

THROUGH THE CAIRNGORMS

30 JUNE – 10 JULY BRAEMAR TO DALWHINNIE 159 MILES 59 SUMMITS

'The landscape at times seemed intent on personal destruction.'
Hamish Brown
Travels

The Cairngorms constitute the greatest wild area left in the British Isles, covering an area of over 385 square miles. Between the A9 in the west and the A939 in the east no paved road crosses the mountains whilst between Glen Feshie and the A939, a straight line distance of 28 miles, no roads of any sort cross the mountains. Here too is the largest area of high ground with 46 square miles above 3,000 feet and 23 square miles above 4,000 feet.

The Cairngorms are my local hills. From the windows of home I can see several summits including Beinn a'Bhuird, Bynack More and Cairn Gorm itself. They were also the first hills I ever visited in the Highlands, long before I moved here, and I probably know them better than any other mountains. Years of wandering the high plateaux on foot and on ski have shown me a few of their many secrets and also taught me to respect these mountains and to be wary of them in bad weather. Under clear skies the walking across the tops is easy and it can be hard to think of these hills as dangerous. However when storm winds sweep the tops and the mist clamps down the featureless plateaux can become hard to escape from as navigation can be very difficult and there are many cliffs and deep gullies below the gentle summits.

Knowing this was not encouraging as I left Braemar for the three mile cycle ride to Invercauld Bridge and Keiloch as I also knew that the weather forecast was dismal. A series of cold fronts was predicted, with gale-force winds due in two days' time and storm-force ones with sleet on the tops for two days after that. I decided to try and climb as many summits as I could over the next few days when it was only meant to be wet and windy, especially as this was the third day in a row on which I had not climbed any hills at all.

At Keiloch, at the end of the public road, Denise collected the bike. We were due to meet again in just three days time. I walked a few miles up Gleann an t-Slugain then camped by the burn. I felt tired and was soon asleep. A day and a half of desk-work at home had left me more exhausted than a long day on the hill.

Morning came with heavy rain and a barometer reading of 999 millibars, the first time it had dropped below 1,000 mb for a month. Clouds were pouring across the sky from the west. The weather had broken. A long, wet, windy, misty day ensued. My aim was to climb the nine summits on the easternmost of the three great plateaux that make up the Cairngorms. Two huge hills make up this tableland, Ben Avon, with one Munro and a wide scattering of four Tops, and Beinn a'Bhuird, also with one Munro plus three not quite so scattered Tops.

The day began badly. Worrying about the weather to come I headed north on the path beside Quoich Water. To the right lay the lower slopes of Creag an Dail Mhor, a distant outlier of Ben Avon that I planned to climb first. I walked right past it. Without realising I'd done so I turned east and began to climb the steep slopes above me. The altimeter gave the first hint I'd made a mistake. I couldn't believe the pressure had dropped that much so quickly. It hadn't. I was already higher than Creag an Dail Mhor and near the top of Carn Eas, the next summit to the north. I left the pack and went back to collect the lower peak. The mistake woke me up. I couldn't make careless errors like that and expect to cross the Cairngorms safely in bad weather.

So far the clouds had stayed above the tops and I'd had good views of the great cliffs of the eastern corries of Beinn a'Bhuird but as I approached Leabaidh an Daimh Bhuidhe, the highest point of Ben Avon, the summit rocks were black blocks against a dark threatening sky. The mist rolled in before I reached them. It cleared briefly while I scrambled up the granite tor that caps the peak but soon returned to remain for the rest of the day, turning it into a navigation exercise. The walking though was easy, over short grass and flat stones, as in much of the Cairngorms.

Ben Avon is a strange mountain, a vast undulating plateau dotted with weird granite tors rising abruptly from the flat grasslands, an unusual feature in the Highlands and reminiscent of the tors of Dartmoor and the hills of the Dark Peak in the southern Pennines. Ben Avon's Tops are situated at the far ends of the massif with many miles between them. I'd come over the south-western ones and now I headed for those far out to the east, West Meur Gorm Craig and East Meur Gorm Craig. The latter lies well over two miles from Leabaidh an Daimh Bhuidhe. I left my pack by the summit tor, reckoning that however bad my navigation I should be able to find the highest point again. At times the rain was very heavy and the wind strong and cold. All day I wore full rain gear plus my warm hat and windproof fleece gloves. I was glad I'd finally remembered to carry the latter and didn't have to use my spare dry socks as mitts. I'd need them for my feet in the evening. East Meur Gorm Craig is a rocky little knoll at the start of a spur running north from the main mountain. I could see little but steep slopes dropping away into boiling mists to either side and a jumble of rocks fading away in front of me so to be sure I had reached the summit I went along the ridge until it began to drop noticeably.

The pack safely regained, I headed west for Beinn a'Bhuird. Between the two massifs at a height of 3,200 feet is the Sneck, a narrow saddle separating the grassy slopes that lead south down to the Water of Quoich from the dramatic ring of cliffs rimming Garbh Choire to the north. There are good camp-sites just below the Sneck to the south, with water provided by little burns that run down from crags to the west, but I still had far to go. Above the Sneck lay the easily reached small bump of Cnap a'Chleirich. The next Top, Stob an t-Sluichd, is more awkwardly placed some two miles away at the end of the northernmost spur of Beinn a'Bhuird. However it was the most distinctive summit of the day, the cairn situated on a tor-dotted narrow rocky ridge whose serrated skyline I'd seen from the slopes of Ben Avon before the mist closed in. The North and South Tops of Beinn a'Bhuird were just cairns in the mist at either end of the almost flat, almost two mile long summit ridge. The first is the higher by some 65 feet and therefore the Munro. Magnificent corries cut deeply into the eastern side of the ridge but all I saw of these when the rims loomed up out of the mist were the big black holes of gullies disappearing downwards.

From the South Top I dropped south-west down steep slopes. Unstable rocks covered the ground at first and made the going slow and difficult. Lower down it became grassier and easier though still steep. I came out of the cloud at 2,700 feet. The sudden sight of the world spread out below was, as always, a shock. Brown moorland rolled way into the distance with the dark green of pine forest in the glen bottoms. Once down by the Alltan na Beinne I camped on the first flattish piece of ground I could find. I'd been out 11¼ hours, a long day, mainly due to the time spent navigating. I'd had the compass in my hand much of the day. For the first time in weeks my boots were totally sodden.

The rain had stopped and the cloud was slowly lifting and clearing to reveal patches of blue sky, encouraging me to get an early start the next morning in the hope that there might be a window of reasonable weather before the next storm blasted in. There was, just. The sky stayed mostly cloudy all day but the summits were clear and there was some good light at times with bits of sunshine here and there. There were showers but most of them were light and short. Only during a few heavier ones late in the afternoon did I need my rain jacket. By the end of the day my boots were almost dry.

Making the most of the clear conditions I linked 11 summits that lie either side of Glen Derry and the Lairig an Laoigh. First though came a walk through the magnificent old Caledonian Pines in the Dubh-Ghleann, a wonderfully inspiring and magical way to start the day. The great 200-year-old trees glistened with the rain of yesterday, their trunks glowing gold and red. Now that the National Trust for Scotland has taken over the Mar Lodge estate, which includes this area along with much of the Cairngorms, it is to be hoped that these forests will have a chance to regenerate. If not they will die, as it is 200 years or more since any seedlings survived browsing by deer.

Leaving the splendour of the trees I laboured up steep heather to the twin summits of Beinn Bhreac. To the west the central Cairngorms ran northwards in a line of stony slopes, rounded tops and rugged cliffs. I went north too on a boggy, arduous walk across the expanse of the Moine Bhealaidh to Beinn a'Chaorainn's two summits. This was the most tedious part of the day. Beinn a'Bhuird looked very dull too, just a long, featureless, flat-topped ridge.

To the west lay the Lairig an Laoigh, one of the two great passes of the Cairngorms that separate the three plateaux. I dropped steeply down to the head of Glen Derry just south of the pass then headed up the path into Coire Etchachan and the heart of the Cairngorms. It was familiar country but I still felt excited. I always do. When this landscape fails to stimulate me, I'll be dead. Outside the Hutchinson Memorial Hut, a small concrete shelter, five people stood talking. Wet gear was spread out everywhere, drying after yesterday's drenching. Three of the people were obviously staying in the hut, the other two, carrying large packs, went on up the path ahead of me.

At the head of the corrie lies the jewel of Loch Etchachan in a spectacular situation below the great cliff of Carn Etchachan. Leaving the pack near the loch I climbed south up the stony slopes to Creagan a'Choire Etchachan then went along the edge of Coire Etchachan to Stob Coire Lochan Uaine. To the north the pyramid-shaped black wedge of broken crags of Stob Coire Etchachan stood out on the hillside. A further climb took me up to the stony summit of Derry Cairngorm and a fine view of the Coire Sputan Dearg cliffs on the east side of Ben MacDui.

Back down at Loch Etchachan a tent had appeared, the first I'd seen on a wild site since the plethora at the Falls of Tarf. This is a fine camp-site and I was slightly envious, though this wasn't to last. A line of walkers was descending from Ben MacDui. I moved the pack a short distance northwards then left it again while I went up Beinn Mheadhoin which has one Munro and three Tops. It rained on Stob Coire Etchachan, making this the only summit of the day that wasn't dry. Then it was over the South-West Top to the main summit which, like Ben Avon, sports a granite tor the ascent of which involves a little easy scrambling.

Traversing the steep, loose slopes below the South-West Top to reach the last summit, Stacan Dubha, was a mistake. It's so close to the path to Loch Avon, which I would be taking next, that it would have been quicker and easier to climb it from there. As it was, I had to cut back south to collect the pack. Stacan Dubha is a fine rocky little peak perched high above Loch Avon with a superb view to the magnificent cliffs curving round the head of the loch. Far below I could see a large, bright yellow tent pitched on the green turf of the Avon delta below the tumble of huge boulders that hold the famous Shelter Stone. The artificial brilliance of the nylon tent was an intrusion in the scene, reminding me of why I prefer dull greens or browns for tents.

Not far beyond Loch Etchachan the path drops steeply to Loch Avon, twisting and turning through the boulder fields. On a flat boulder near the yellow tent three rock climbers were sorting out their ropes and ironmongery. Not wanting to camp too near them nor to crawl into the dark, viewless confines of the Shelter Stone or one of the other boulder refuges to be found in the vast pile of huge rocks, I followed the burn the few hundred yards down to the loch shore and pitched the tent by the lapping waters. Pausing, I looked round. The great square-topped block of the Sticil or Shelter Stone Crag, the more pyramid-like Carn Etchachan and the dark wedge of Hell's Lum Crag soared into the sky, forming a spectacular ring of cliffs round the head of the loch. Down the granite slabs that make up the back wall of the corrie the white waters of the Feith Buidhe and the Garbh Uisge Beag tumbled and crashed down from the plateau above, the first in an 800 foot waterslide, the second in a series of waterfalls for some 400 feet. This is a scene of wild grandeur, the finest place in the Cairngorms and one of the most impressive corries in the whole of the Highlands.

Three anglers carrying rods and creels passed my camp, rounded the head of the loch then headed up Coire Raibert towards Cairn Gorm. A breeze ruffled the water. I lay back in the tent and fell asleep.

I was shaken awake at 11.30. Literally. Huge gusts of wind were knocking the tent from side to side. The predicted storm had arrived right on time. I dozed until 1 a.m. but then decided that as the wind was worsening it was daft to stay put when there were several boulder shelters nearby. It took an hour to pack up and move in the pitch darkness. First I had to ensure nothing blew away or was left behind and then I had to pick a way back along the path in the tiny circle of light provided by my headlamp, looking for one of the shelters. I soon found a small one I'd passed earlier and crawled inside. The floor was covered with grubby plastic sheeting and there was a great deal of litter but although somewhat draughty it didn't shake in the wind and it was dry. It would do. I wondered how the other campers were getting on, especially those up at Loch Etchachan.

Overnight the pressure dropped 12 millibars. The only time such a rapid fall had happened before had been over a month earlier at the end of May on the day I'd retreated to Inveroran from Clach Leathad. Today I hoped to retreat over Cairn Gorm to Glen More where I was meeting Denise. If I couldn't do this it would be a long walk out via Strath Nethy.

Morning revealed my shelter to be under a huge sloping boulder, the upper edge of which rested on a smaller rock. Most of the gaps at the sides had been crudely walled, closed with rocks, leaving a narrow slot entrance that led upwards and admitted the only daylight. I was very glad it was here.

Rain started to fall as I walked up the path in Coire Raibert into the mist. The wind on Cairn Gorm was extremely strong, blowing me from side to side so that I staggered over the mountain as if drunk. Only because it was from the south and therefore at my back was I able to climb the hill at all. Fighting into it would have been impossible. The mist on the summit was dense and I needed compass bearings to find Cnap Coire na Spreidhe. In such a severe storm these two summits were enough so I abandoned plans for Bynack More and descended into Coire Cas through the ski resort that defiles the northern side of Cairn Gorm. At least the mist hid the worst of the devastation. I tried not to think about the diabolical scheme to build a funicular railway up Cairn Gorm to within half a mile of the summit. The purpose of this would be to take coach parties of tourists up the funicular to a 'wilderness centre', an unbelievable travesty and insult to the mountain. The plan is for 250,000 visitors each year. If the funicular is built the final destruction of the north side of Cairn Gorm will be achieved.

At the Coire Cas car park I phoned Denise to say I was early, then walked on down into the pine forests of Glen More, using the old road where possible, musing on the irony of building roads, railways and visitor centres in order to give people a 'mountain experience'. This is of course impossible. A mountain experience means dealing with the elements, with rough steep terrain, means feeling wind and rain and sun on your face, means sweat, aching limbs and sore feet. It also means the freedom to walk and climb as and where you will. Gazing through a window at a misty ski resort from a crowded visitor centre can never resemble a mountain experience. If there has to be a 'wilderness centre' let it be down in Glen More or in Aviemore, where people who truly love the mountains can ignore it and go to the real thing.

Denise and Hazel found me sitting over a cup of coffee in the Glenmore Café next to the campsite. There were yet more book proofs to check so off home I went. A rest day didn't seem a bad idea however as the forecast was for unsettled weather for several days with the low responsible described as 'unseasonably deep'.

I spent the rest of that day and the morning of the next proof-reading, writing another walk report for *TGO* and answering mail while the storm raged on. Chris Brasher phoned, Denise having told him I'd be home, and was keen to join me in the Cairngorms. We made a tentative arrangement to meet on the Great Moss in three days' time. A little after 24 hours after leaving I was back at Glenmore. It was still raining. On my feet was a new pair of boots. This mundane fact seemed significant. It marked a stage in the journey, showed the progress I was making. I had completely worn out a pair of boot soles.

The hills sheltered me from the wind as I walked through beautiful Ryvoan Pass, cheered by the many young trees visible amongst the grand old pines that line the steep hillsides of this narrow notch. As I rounded the end of the long spur that extends north from Cairn Gorm I caught the first gusts of wind, from the north-west now. In the distance clouds were brushing the tops of the pines of Abernethy Forest. I climbed into the storm and the mist. On the lower flanks of Bynack More the compass came out as visibility was reduced to a few yards. The bumps of Bynack Beg and A'Chailleach were found and left as the wind drove me on. From

81

the last top I descended to the foot of Loch Avon. The wind seemed less strong here so I started to pitch the tent. It was just about up when a gust that seemed to come from directly above smashed down and almost flattened it. Further, stronger gusts followed.

A night in a thrashing tent wasn't appealing so I repacked the tent and set off along the side of Loch Avon for the Shelter Stone, some two miles away. Owing to my late start it was now growing dark which made the rough path that rose and fell along the lochside hard to follow. I was in mist much of the time which gave an eerie and unreal feel to the surroundings. At times curling sheets of mist drifted above the loch and I found it hard to tell how far below me the water was. Everything looked insubstantial with hazy rocks and boulders fading in and out of view and dissolving into the night as I stumbled through the stream of water that ran down the path. If a kelpie or water horse (the Each Uisge) had emerged from the loch I wouldn't have been surprised. I lost the path at the head of the loch, so simply turned towards the black mass of crags visible to the south, knowing that the Shelter Stone lay somewhere at their foot. When I reached the river Avon I just plunged in, glad I had my poles for support.

The Shelter Stone or Clach Dhion is in the middle of the huge pile of boulders that lies below the Sticil. It's a cave-like howff under a house-sized boulder marked by a cairn on the top and resting on some smaller boulders. Over the years the gaps in the sides have been filled in with stones and earth and heather to make a reasonably water and windproof refuge.

In all my visits to the Cairngorms I'd never before stayed in the Shelter Stone, undoubtedly the most famous natural refuge in the Highlands and one that has been used by walkers and climbers for well over a century and by outlaws before that. In the *Scottish Mountaineering Club Guide to the Cairngorms* Adam Watson refers to an account from 1794 that says it was used by freebooters and could hold '18 armed men'. The first climbing club in Scotland, the Cairngorm Club, was founded here in 1887. It was about time I stayed in this historic shelter – 'an essential task for hill-men' according to Dave Brown and Ian Mitchell in their book *Mountain Days and Bothy Nights*. (Hill-women are exempt, presumably.) It somehow seemed appropriate to stay here during this walk though it wasn't planned. Appropriately too I was genuinely using it as shelter from a storm.

I found the Shelter Stone by following the well-worn polished route through the boulders. It was ten past midnight. I crawled into the cave-like interior, high enough for me to stand up at one end and big enough to house a half dozen or more comfortably. No one else was there however. The floor was lined with plastic survival bags, most of them fairly dry though rain was dripping in at one corner. I lit a candle and the warm yellow light instantly made the place seem more homely. A shelf of rock ran along the back wall. Over it I draped my wet waterproofs. Next I laid out my mat on the floor then slid my sleeping bag inside my bivvy bag to protect it from the damp air. Feeling shivery now I'd stopped, I pulled on my fleece sweater and crawled into the sleeping bag. Setting up the stove on the wooden box that held the bothy book I cooked and ate a very late supper of mushroom soup laced with fresh garlic and chunks of cheddar. The candlelight flickered on the wet, black walls. Outside I could hear the wind roaring and the rain hammering down. Inside there was just the occasional draught. I felt tired but strangely peaceful.

I was having breakfast, still in my sleeping bag as it was quite chilly, when a head popped through the narrow slot that does for a door. The owner was on a day trip from Coire Cas. 'More rain's forecast,' he said cheerfully. It had stopped for the moment though. Outside I was astonished at the sudden space in front of me. In the darkness of the previous night I hadn't realised how far up the glen side the Shelter Stone was. Below my feet the boulders ran down to the green grass of the corrie floor beyond which lay the deep black of the loch. Turning, I looked up at the huge cliffs towering above. An impressive spot indeed.

My original plan had been for a curving sweep round the 13 summits from Bynack More over Cairn Gorm to Ben Macdui and Carn a'Mhaim in one long day. The storm had ripped this scheme to pieces. In two days of walking I'd climbed just five of these tops. With the storm still blowing I didn't dare even think I could climb the remaining eight in one day so I just set off to see how far I could get.

It was another bundled up, hat, gloves and waterproofs day. The rain began as soon as I left the Shelter Stone, then kept up all day apart from a few short lulls. The wind stayed strong and cold too. Thankfully it was from the north-west so I had it at my back for much of the day. Firstly though I headed north up Coire Domhain to Stob Coire an t-Sneachda and Cairn Lochan, the peaks at the heads of the spectacular Northern Corries of Cairn Gorm, and then went out to Creag an Leth-choin (Lurcher's Crag), a rocky little peak that dominates the northern approaches to the great cleft of the Lairig Ghru which separates Cairn Gorm and Ben Macdui from the other two 4,000 feet plus summits, Braeriach and Cairn Toul. The views can be spectacular but this time all I had were occasional glimpses of mist-filled depths with dark slopes rising into the clouds on the far side. Turning back across the plateau I next had a three mile walk to Carn Etchachan, right above the Shelter Stone.

To the south-west lay Ben MacDui, the second highest mountain in Scotland and in Britain and one of the finest. A big, bulky hill, its glory lies in the deep corries that surround it and the cliffs that rim them. I reached the summit by way of the North Top, then sat by the massive cairn for a snack. A snow bunting joined me and I threw it a few crumbs of flapjack. There were no views.

Two spurs run south from Macdui. The shorter eastern one has a bump on it called Sron Riach that has Top status, the longer western one ends in a more distinct summit, Carn a'Mhaim, which is a Munro. Sron Riach was below the cloud and gave good views down steep cliffs to dark Lochan Uaine. It was the 200th summit of the walk, a figure that seemed highly significant. All long walks have important staging posts, usually places or distances. On this walk it was numbers of hills climbed. These stages affect how I view a walk. At different points I knew I would suddenly realise that there was more of the walk in the past than in the future. Two hundred summits had me firmly embedded in the heart of the walk. I couldn't see the finish or anywhere near it but the start was now far away too. Climbing hills was what I did. There was for the moment no other reality.

The rain stopped for the ascent of Carn a'Mhaim along a ridge that is surprisingly narrow for the Cairngorms and a nice change from the wide plateaux. This was the best part of the day, especially as it was below the cloud. Across the Lairig Ghru the black slabs of The Devil's Point looked impressive. The higher hills remained in cloud though Cairn Toul appeared briefly now and then.

The slopes immediately south of Carn a'Mhaim are stony and steep. Descending them doesn't look easy. I went down anyway and was delighted soon to discover a wide ribbon of grass running through the rocks. Down more quickly than expected, I reached the river Dee just as the rain began again. The ford was knee-deep. My boots were still sodden from crossing the Avon the night before so I kept them on. Camp was by the Allt Garbh which runs down to the Dee from the first summits I planned climbing the next day. The ground was wet and a bit bumpy but the wind wasn't too strong here. The tent was soaked from my attempt to pitch it the night before and it was only going to get wetter so I again used my bivvy bag to protect my sleeping bag. The stove warmed the tent a little and took the edge off the dampness for a while. Over supper I considered my options for the next day.

Chris Brasher was hoping to meet me at Loch nan Stuirteag sometime the following afternoon having travelled up on the sleeper train from London to Aviemore and then walked in. The fallback plan was to meet in Glen Feshie either that evening or the next day. Loch nan Stuirteag lies at 2,850 feet. I couldn't imagine camping there in this storm. Heading straight for Glen Feshie would mean missing out some of the summits on the Moine Mhor however. I was still musing on this when I fell asleep.

Luckily there is a difference between imagination and reality. The latter is always more surprising. By 2 p.m. the next day I was camped at Loch nan Stuirteag. This remote loch lies at the head of Glen Geusachan just below the col between Cairn Toul and Monadh Mor, a gloriously wild place. From the tent I could look across the loch, its surface rippling with waves, to the crags on the northern flanks of Beinn Bhrotain hanging above Glen Geusachan. The wind, still from the north-west, had eased a little and the rain could be described, just, as showery. I'd reached the loch via Carn Cloich-mhuilinn, Beinn Bhrotain and Monadh Mor. The first is a rounded bump that was demoted from separate mountain status to that of a Top in the controversial 1981 revision of the *Tables*. Sir Hugh Munro himself planned to climb it as his last Munro but had died without doing so. It was at least clear of mist unlike the next two summits, Beinn Bhrotain and Monadh Mor. The most interesting part of the walk over these was the bouldery descent from the first that led down to a narrow col, then the steep slope beyond the col leading to the long flat summit ridge of Monadh Mor.

To the east and north of my camp lay a chain of seven fine summits along the western edge of the Lairig Ghru, the main ones of which are Cairn Toul and Braeriach. The southernmost of these is The Devil's Point (Bod an Deamhain), an uprising of granite slabs formed when a glacier sliced the end off a spur running down from Cairn Toul. The anglicised name is a euphemism, created to avoid offending Victorian sensibilities, as the Gaelic means Devil's Penis. Cameron McNeish argues in his book *The Munros* that there should be a campaign to persuade the Ordnance Survey to revert to the original Gaelic name, which isn't even given on the 1:50,000 Landranger map. I agree and I'm pleased to see that on the Harveys 1:25,000 Cairn Gorm map the Gaelic name is given with the anglicisation in brackets. The walk from Bod an Deamhain to Braeriach is the finest high-level walk in the Cairngorms and one of the best in the Highlands. On this occasion though it didn't look as if I would see much.

I was below the mist at first as I contoured round the southern slopes of Cairn Toul to the col with Bod an Deamhain. A group of six walkers were heading for the summit of the latter. As I passed two of them they asked me if I knew anything about a helicopter they'd seen fly over earlier. Was it a rescue? I hadn't heard or seen it or anyone else. Their concern had been prompted by seeing some people in shorts scrambling beside the slabs on Bod an Deamhain who they didn't think seemed equipped for the conditions. The small summit felt crowded with seven of us so I soon left, passing two more people ascending. They'd come from Braeriach and this was the only view they'd had all day.

The mist stayed down as I went over Stob Coire an t-Saighde, Cairn Toul, Sgor an Lochain Uaine (sometimes called Angel's Peak) and then rounded the head of mighty An Garbh Choire to climb Braeriach. Occasional glimpses between walls of rock down dark gullies into hidden depths hinted at the grandeur of the landscape.

The stony slopes of Braeriach seemed endless. A brief spurt of hail greeted me on the summit. This is one of my favourite hills but today climbing it seemed a bit of a chore, as did going out and back to Sron na Lairige, the northernmost summit of the day. However the direct descent from Carn na Criche back to camp was very fast. There was no sign of Chris Brasher. Feeling very tired I was soon asleep despite the heavy rain and strong gusty wind.

When I woke the mist was very low, almost touching the tent. I shivered in the chilly dampness and pulled on my fleece sweater. After three very wet days and nights my gear needed drying out. There was no sign of a change in the weather however as I set off on what Irvine Butterfield calls 'perhaps the most psychologically intimidating walk in Britain', that is the crossing of the Moine Mhor (the Great Moss), that vast featureless upland plateau lying between the Braeriach – Cairn Toul Tops and Glen Feshie. Presumably this is because the navigation can be difficult as the walking is easy. I find exposed scrambles like the Aonach Eagach far more mentally unnerving than crossing open spaces however large.

Eight summits lie on this plateau, all of them on the western edges except for Tom Dubh which lies in the centre, not far from Loch nan Stuirteag. It's technically a subsidiary Top of Braeriach though it's almost four miles from the summit. Butterfield, who seems not to like this area, describes Tom Dubh as 'the most meaningless 3,000 foot "top" in all Britain'. Just what is a meaningful top, I wonder?

The summit of Tom Dubh lay just below the cloud. Brown moorland stretched out all around, merging into the grey cloud. Not far away I picked up a bulldozed track, a disgraceful scar on the landscape. It led almost the whole way to Mullach Clach a'Bhlair, a gentle swelling of a hill.

Mist washed the flat summit. I turned north, following the rounded edge of the plateau above hidden Glen Feshie. As I walked over the rolling terrain the cloud began to break and there were glimpses of sunshine in Strathspey to the north. The dull brown bumps of Meall Dubhag and Carn Ban Mor were just below the cloud but mist swirled around the top of the finest hill by far in this group, shapely, pointed Sgor Gaoith. The summit cairn lies right on the edge of the line of crags walling the west side of the deep trench of Gleann Einich. Through the thin haze I could see green gullies and long grey ribs of rock dropping steeply downwards as I walked along the edge of the cliffs to Sgoran Dubh Mor. In clear weather there's a superb view of Braeriach from here.

The last two tops lay below the cloud on a long spur jutting out north-west towards Strathspey. The first of these, another Meall Buidhe, isn't named on the OS 1:50,000 map though it is on the Harveys 1:25,000 sheet. On the last Top, Geal Charn, two walkers were sitting, the only others I saw on the hills all day. They were doing lower tops because of the bad weather. 'I've done enough hills in rain and mist,' said one. So have I, I thought, so have I.

Down below, the green forests of lower Glen Feshie were catching bursts of sunshine. The main forests in this part of the glen are planted but above these there is still a scattering of old pines and I was interested to note as I descended that long before I reached the first mature trees there were signs of regeneration with many small pines, birches and rowans springing up through the heather.

A quick descent led to the glen floor where I walked along the public road to its end at the farm of Achlean where I was due to meet Denise and Hazel. I sat on a hillock with a good view back down the road and read a book while I waited. Soon I could see the car approaching on the winding, single-track road. Then there was an hour-and-a-half of talking, sorting supplies, checking maps and eating the sandwiches and cake Denise had brought for me. Chris Brasher wasn't able to join me here, she told me, but he was now hoping to do so when I reached the Mamores in a few weeks.

As we were to meet again in just two days in Dalwhinnie I set off up Glen Feshie with a light pack. It was a beautiful evening with soft cloud-filtered sunlight slanting across the glen. The river Feshie roared and rumbled down the glen, the water brown with rain run-off. Flocks of noisy oyster-catchers circled over the meadows lining the banks.

The glen grew wilder and narrower and great Caledonian pines, last relics of the Great Wood of Caledon, started to appear along with aromatic clusters of juniper. I walked amongst the magnificent trees feeling, as always, a sense of awe. Glen Feshie has suffered years of neglect and abuse by absentee owners who've bulldozed tracks, planted blocks of non-native conifers and allowed deer numbers to remain high so that the pine forest cannot regenerate and the other vegetation is over-grazed. Still a magnificent glen, it is now owned by a rather secretive charitable organisation called the Wills Woodland Trust, which is meant to be committed to conservation but which seems to be more concerned with maintaining deer stalking. Instead of drastically culling the deer it appears that they intend erecting miles of deer fencing. As well as being an eyesore and destroying the wild feel of a place, deer fencing means the forest can only regenerate in blocks rather than throughout an area. Meanwhile the rest of the land is still over-grazed. Fencing is also unnecessary as has been shown by SNH and the RSPB at Creag Meagaidh and Abernethy where regeneration is well underway without need of fencing because deer numbers have been reduced by culling.

Not far into the old pine forest is Ruigh-aiteachain, a popular bothy. Nearby stands the remains of a chimney, all that is left of a house where the Victorian artist Edwin Landseer, famous for his romantic paintings of animals such as The Monarch of the Glen, once worked. In the 1930s frescoes by Landseer could still be seen on the walls of the ruined building according to Seton Gordon in his book *Highways and Byways in the Central Highlands*, first published in 1935.

As I approached the bothy I caught up with a party of five women backpackers just arriving. Several mountain bikes were leaning against the walls and a group of people were standing around a very smoky fire. I waved and kept walking. Sharing a bothy with one or two people I could enjoy, squeezing in with a crowd I could not. I didn't want to be confined in a building on such a fine night in such a fine place anyway. With the tent doors open I could still be in contact with the woods. Several hundred yards further down the glen I camped on smooth green flower-strewn turf under the tall pines. A gentle breeze drifted down the glen as I sat in the tent watching the trees and the river. A cuckoo called somewhere nearby. Otherwise all was quiet.

I woke to birdsong and bright sunshine. A buzzard was mewing high above. The world was green and rich with life. I felt quite content just to sit here and watch it but I had a long, complicated day ahead. To reach the four summits I planned climbing I had first to cross some lower hills to Glen Tromie. After splashing across the river Feshie, here a braided stream running between gravel bars, I followed a vehicle track that climbed westwards to some plantations and then a path that led down beside the Allt Bhran to the glen. This is spacious, rolling, heather moorland country full of wheatears, golden plovers, red grouse and hares. It is also home to large numbers of big deer flies. These would follow me, buzzing annoyingly round my head and trying to land on an arm or leg and then bite me, but when I stopped to swat them they, too, would stop only to reappear as soon as I started walking. Even so I must have flattened a dozen or more.

Walking down a steep section of the paved road in Glen Tromie I was nearly run down by two mountain bikers who sped silently up behind me. At the last moment one of them yelled a warning in an American accent. Startled, I jumped out of the way. The bikes vanished quickly into the distance.

Further down the glen I was disappointed to find a freshly bulldozed road running up beside the Allt na Fearna to a new weir, destroying the old and unobtrusive footpath. A sign at the bottom read 'Not A Right of Way' and advised walkers to go down the glen. I ignored it. From the end of the road I struck up to the broad north-eastern ridge of Meall Chuaich, a big round hill that is quite isolated and so has extensive views in all directions. Today though the sky was cloudy and the distant hills were just hazy smudges.

I now had a long three hour haul southwards over miles of featureless moorland to the next summit, Carn na Caim. Even though the visibility was good I needed to use the compass a couple of times as there were no landmarks at all in places. What gave interest to the walk were the deer. There were hundreds of them everywhere. I came over one rise to see around 50 stags just in front of me. Instantly they galloped away, making an impressive sight as they crossed the skyline, antlers silhouetted against the pale grey sky. Two hours more heather-tussock and peat-bog bashing led to A'Bhuidheanach Bheag and Glas Mheall Mor. Rain began to fall on these hills and mist rolled over the summit of the latter just after I'd left. As I descended into the long, straight, narrow and steep-sided valley of the Allt Coire Mhic-sith I felt very glad the cloud had held off until I'd completed these nondescript hills. Finding them in the mist would have required very precise navigation. As it was I'd been out for 12 hours. In bad weather it could have been much longer. Camp was on some bumpy tussocks by the stream, the flattest ground I could find. I was too tired for the lumps to keep me awake and I fell asleep straight after supper.

My camp was at least in a sheltered spot. After being woken by heavy rain, I sat and watched clouds racing overhead while I ate breakfast. Down here there was nothing more than a gentle breeze. Away to the south-west a small patch of blue sky caught my eye. Would it spread? It didn't but the rain soon stopped and I had an enjoyable walk over the four Munros west of the Pass of Drumochter.

Crossing the A9 again seemed significant. The Cairngorms and Grampians were now behind me. I went under rather than over the road, by way of a convenient stream culvert. Then it was up Sgairneach Mhor. On the summit a walker was sitting. He nodded brusquely at me then looked away, obviously wanting to be left alone. I continued on round to Beinn Udlamain, the highest of these hills and the only one whose summit was in mist. A different walker sat on the top. He barely acknowledged my presence. Another loner. The walk to A'Mharconaich gave good views down to Loch Ericht and across to the long ridge of The Fara, a Corbett. Ben Alder, further down the loch, was in cloud. Yet again a solitary male walker was on the summit. Yet again he showed no inclination to talk. I continued north to Geal Charn. For the fourth time a single walker sat by the summit. They were all different people, I was sure. This one certainly was as he not only greeted me cheerfully but followed this with questions as to where I'd been and was going and what the weather was like. Initially I was quite startled. I'd got used to the silent types. He was, he told me, just doing two summits on a day trip from the A9. If you're driving it on business it's easy to nip up here, he said. Perhaps that's why I'd met someone on every summit. He was using a global positioning satellite receiver (GPS) for navigation, the first time I'd met someone on the hills with one of these high tech instruments. Having tested a few models for *TGO* I'd briefly considered using one on the walk but had quickly rejected the idea. Too heavy, too complex, too battery dependent, too sensitive and too distracting I decided. A compass was perfectly adequate. There was to be one occasion though when a GPS might well have been useful.

I followed the long north-east ridge of Geal Charn down to Loch Ericht and Dalwhinnie. After a period of decline Dalwhinnie is coming to life again with a new village store plus The Tea Shop, an excellent café where I found Denise and Hazel waiting for me. After nine days without a break it was time for a rest day. I went home as it was so close and there seemed no point staying in Dalwhinnie. I spent most of the next day revising the route to take account of the need to be in Skye in 12 days' time. As Denise had suggested some time ago, I would cycle there from Fort William so I wanted to climb all the hills left south of the Great Glen, 86 in all, before doing so.

Chapter 6

LONG DAYS TO GLEN NEVIS

11 – 21 JULY DALWHINNIE TO GLEN NEVIS 177 MILES 86 SUMMITS

'Climb the mountains and get their good tidings.'

John Muir

I left Dalwhinnie by bike for Newtonmore and then Glen Banchor at the foot of the Monadh Liath. I wasn't looking forward to cycling along the busy A9 so was pleased to find that I didn't have to most of the way after I found the old road, much of which is hidden behind a screen of small trees and bushes. Some sections were very broken up and I had to lift the bike over a couple of fences but it was wonderfully quiet and peaceful.

In Glen Banchor we arranged a rendezvous for three days time at the bridge over the river Spean at Luiblea on the A86. As usual we checked the maps carefully to make sure we agreed on the exact spot. It would be all too easy to wait either side of a wood or loch, wondering where the other was. Then we loaded the bike back into the car and Denise and Hazel left and I set off into the Monadh Liath, the Grey Hills, originally named as a contrast to the Monadh Ruadh, or Red Hills, as the Cairngorms on the other side of Strathspey were formerly known.

The round of the seven nondescript summits of the Monadh Liath is a long moorland slog. Under snow in winter it makes a superb ski tour but as a walk it's not that interesting. The dull overcast weather didn't help either. Between the first two summits, A'Chailleach and Carn Sgulain, and the third one, Carn Ballach, lies nearly three dull miles. The only real diversion was the wildlife, the now familiar inhabitants of heather and peat moors: hares, golden plover, ptarmigan, red grouse and deer.

From Carn Ban I diverted south to the two tops of Carn Dearg. They lie above the steep slopes of Glen Ballach which gives them a bit of character. Next though comes a tedious six miles of undulating moor before the westernmost summit, Geal Charn. I read most of the way, a

Joanna Trollope novel that bore little relation to my surroundings, only stopping when I realised it was slowing me down. The east side of this hill sports a rugged corrie containing a little lochan but by the time I reached the top my main interest was in finding somewhere to camp. The south-west ridge led quickly down to the Feith Talagain, a sizeable burn. I camped beside it, a mile or so above Garva Bridge. As soon as I stopped the midges came out so I had to spend the evening shut up in the tent. Now it was mid-July I knew that this would occur often in the days ahead so I had to learn to accept it.

A long, fairly flat ridge runs slightly south west from Garva Bridge making up the eastern spur of Creag Meagaidh. On it lie four Tops and two Munros. The western end of this fine ridge lies above superb Coire Ardair, the lower slopes of which are now covered with regenerating woodland, the result of drastic reduction in deer and sheep numbers by SNH which owns the land and manage it as a National Nature Reserve. In upper Coire Ardair lies Lochan a'Choire under the magnificent Creag Meagaidh cliffs.

The journey along this ridge from Garva Bridge takes the walker into more and more mountainous terrain. After the initial steep climb the walking is easy and the summits come quickly, first Stob Coire Dubh then Carn Liath, Meall an t-Snaim and Sron Coire a'Chriochairein. There were several other walkers about and on the next summit, the East Top of Stob Poite Coire Ardair, a bearded man hailed me. 'You're Chris Townsend, aren't you?' This was the first time I'd been recognised and initially I felt a little awkward and not sure how to respond. A cautious affirmation was, I think, my reply. Gerry Parker wasn't so reticent however and we were soon talking about the hills and my walk, which he knew about from *TGO*. He shook his head at the idea of backpacking. Heavy packs, he said, didn't appeal.

After ten minutes he went off to Carn Liath and I continued west over Stob Poite Coire Ardair, then dropped down steep slopes to the narrow notch called The Window that separates this ridge from the main Creag Meagaidh massif. Two walkers passed me heading up. 'Will the weather hold?' one asked. All day it had been cloudy with hazy views and a gentle west wind but now thicker, lower clouds were approaching ominously from the south-west. 'I hope so,' I replied. However as I climbed up the steep, rocky slope onto the Creag Meagaidh plateau the mist swept across the highest summits.

Creag Megaidh is a large, complex mountain with many long spurs running out from the high central plateau. Fine craggy corries cut into the hill on every side. On the southern edge lie four tops. These are considerably lower than the main summit and I was pleased to see that they were below the cloud as they all have good views. I went for the furthest one first, An Cearcallach, at the end of the western spur above green and grassy Moy Corrie. The rim of this corrie leads to Meall Coire Choille-rais beyond which lies the broken, vegetated crags of Coire Choille-rais. Across this corrie the eastern pair of Puist Coire Ardair and Sron a'Choire are set right on the edge of Coire Ardair and you can look across the massive cliffs and down to the black lochan far below.

I'd left my pack high on Creag Meagaidh while I did the round of these tops. As I was returning to it a walker came striding down the hill dressed in blue jeans, checked shirt and sweatshirt rather than the more usual fleece and polyester though he did have a very shiny new pair of walking boots and a large, half-full rucksack. On seeing my trekking poles he gave a high, nervous laugh and asked if I was skiing. I gave a half-hearted grin. When I first started using a pair of poles I became resigned to comments about snow and skiing but this was the first time anyone had mentioned it on this walk. He told me, in between nervous laughs which I soon realised were a quirky mannerism rather than aimed at me as I'd first thought, that he often used a single walking pole. The idea of using two seemed astounding to him however.

'A nice day but a front's on the way,' were his parting words as he loped off down the hill. It's already here, I thought, as I entered the mist and got out the compass in order to find the summit of Creag Meagaidh and then the descent down the broad west flanks to the Bealach a'Bharnish. Here I dipped briefly out of the cloud but I was soon back up in it again as I finished the day with a walk along the mile long ridge, cliff-rimmed on its eastern edge, of Beinn a'Chaorainn. The highest point and Munro is the middle of the three summits on the ridge. Oddly, the height isn't given on the 1:50,000 OS sheet though it is for the northern bump, which doesn't even qualify as a Top, and for the South Top. From the latter I descended west to the Allt a'Chaorainn by which I camped on the first spot big enough for the tent. I had hoped to go on and climb Beinn Teallach which rose above me to the west but I was too tired. It would have to wait until the next day. The 14 summits had taken nearly 11 hours and I'd walked 23 miles and climbed 6,300 feet. I was soon asleep.

Drizzle and occasional bursts of rain greeted me in the morning, along with midges. The dampness made me feel chilly. On mornings like this a hot breakfast was nice. Most days I had cold muesli but I also had some packets of an oat based cereal called Hot Bran Start. On its own this was a little bland but this morning I added cinnamon, raisins, chopped dates and brown sugar to make a tasty warming meal. It seemed to give me some energy as I was up and down Beinn Teallach in an hour-and-a-half. The mist and rain helped too. There was no point lingering. As I set off up I was surprised to see a large dome tent pitched only a few hundred yards away but hidden from my camp by a bank of heather.

Camp packed away after a second breakfast, I descended through plantations to the A86, then slogged along the road for three miles to Luiblea. I was an hour late and Denise and Hazel were already there. Denise had brought the latest *TGO* with the first report on the walk in it. Reading it was a strange experience. Had the weather really been that bad? We listened to the lunchtime forecast on the car radio. A high was building and summer would start tomorrow, according to Peter Cockcroft. Deciding to believe him I put the sandals and sun hat I'd abandoned at Braemar back in the pack. Suddenly two hours had vanished and it was time to set off again, this time with a heavier pack. Our next rendezvous was at Fersit on Loch Treig in five days time.

To the south-east of Luiblea lies a group of three mountains all of which can be climbed from the high pass above Loch a'Bhealaich Leamhain that connects Loch Laggan with Loch Ericht. Just below the pass a good stalkers' path cuts north between Geal Charn and Creag Pitridh. Leaving the pack I followed this path to the col between the peaks then climbed the little rocky pimple of Creag Pitridh. Three people were sitting near the summit cairn, the only walkers I saw all day. They greeted me separately but appeared to be ignoring each other. The atmosphere felt tense and I felt as though I'd just intruded on an argument. I left them to it. There was no view anyway and the wind was strong and cold. Guessing the way off rather than using the compass – always a dangerous practice – I descended the western rather than the southern slopes and had to contour back round to the col. A steep climb up rough slopes into thick, wet mist and I was on Geal Charn. Again I started down the wrong way and had to contour back. I'd taken a compass bearing at the top but had then allowed the terrain to deflect me from the bearing. Although I'd corrected them quickly I was annoyed with myself for making these errors. Why was I being so careless?

I took greater care on Beinn a'Chlachair, whose long, gentle, featureless summit ridge seemed endless in the confining mist. The most enjoyable part of the day wasn't on the hills but on the start of the descent from the pass where the scenery was rugged and, more importantly, I could see it. A fine path led across the steep slopes above Loch a'Bhealaich Leamhain which lies in a narrow slot in the hills and down to the Allt Cam. I could have camped here but decided to go on to Loch Pattack. This was a mistake. If I'd thought about it I'd have realised that the loch shores would be very windy as it's set in a wide flat area. But this was not a day on which I seemed to be thinking clearly. Culra Bothy was only a few miles away but it was a Saturday and it's a popular bothy so I didn't head that way. Instead I ended up back at the Allt Cam pitched in the partial shelter of a high bank. There was a dark red sunset over The Fara. I hoped it meant the weather forecast was correct.

I woke to winds rattling the tent and clouds racing across the sky from the west but the rain had stopped and there were big patches of deep blue sky. The pressure had risen too, to the highest it had been for three weeks. After three long days during which I'd climbed 25 summits I decided I needed a rest day. It was only three days since the last one but I felt tired and was concerned at the misjudgements of yesterday. The moment I made the decision I knew it was right because I felt suddenly relieved. It felt good too to know that no car journeys would be involved and that I wouldn't have to check any proofs or deal with mail or phone calls. I would actually be able to relax.

I would, though, first walk round to Culra Bothy. It took 40 minutes. The slim tapering peak of Sgor Iutharn and the great bulk of Ben Alder lying between the rocky arms of the Short and Long Leachas rose impressively ahead as I approached the bothy. In the main room – there are three smaller ones – two sleeping bags were laid out on the wooden sleeping platform while three mountain bikes stood against the walls. Stoves and pans were set up on a table. I moved into a side room. It was bare but did have a wooden floor.

I'd just settled in when another walker arrived and sat outside brewing up over a noisy roaring petrol stove. 'I should have been here last night,' he said. Out for the weekend he'd walked in from Dalwhinnie two nights ago then gone along the Aonach Beag ridge the day before. This had taken him longer than expected and he'd ended up bivvying out just west of the Bealach Dubh. Now it was back out to Dalwhinnie and his car. 'I'll be in the bath by six.'

After he'd gone I pottered round the splendidly situated bothy looking at flowers, the hills and the clouds, just happy to be able to relax for a change. One of the mountain bike owners returned and left without my seeing them. Later the other two came back – one from Ben Alder, one from Aonach Beag. They were dressed in shorts, thin thermal vests and fell running shoes so I wasn't surprised to discover that both were fell runners and mountain bikers and believers in travelling as light and as fast as possible. One was a chemistry lecturer from Glasgow, the other an architect from Kendal. They hadn't met until the night before but had quickly developed a camaraderie based on how they travelled the hills which they clearly believed was superior to other ways from the casual manner in which they gently mocked people who carried what most walkers would regard as a normal load. 'I don't carry waterproofs, I travel fast enough to escape from bad weather,' said one. I gathered I was supposed to be impressed. I said nothing however, just thought of some of the storms I'd experienced and also what would happen if they twisted an ankle or got lost. Still, I thought more charitably, I was travelling much lighter than many people thought safe. It was in the end up to the individual.

Two heavyweight backpackers added to the numbers late in the afternoon, a young couple walking from Fort William to Dalwhinnie. The man was wearing big heavy mountain boots and said he had bruised feet. They pitched a tent outside.

Light rain fell and the west wind stayed strong but the pressure went on rising. I had a very early night and slept for ten hours. I really had been tired. The next day began with an edge of excitement. My plan was for the eight summits on the long Aonach Beag ridge that ran south-west from above the bothy. When I finished it I would have done 261 Tops, over half way.

On the advice – good as it turned out – of the fell runners I went up Sgor Iutharn by the Lancet Edge, a fine, slim arête ending in a narrow section of sloping 45° slabs, though it was nowhere as exposed or difficult as the spire-like profile suggested. Contouring below Geal Charn, over which I planned to return, to the col with Aonach Beag I climbed the latter peak then continued west to Beinn Eibhinn. I was descending from the last peak when I met a walker ascending, his freckled face red with the sun and the effort of the ascent. A talkative Geordie, he told me he'd hitch-hiked to Dalwhinnie from Newcastle and then walked over Ben Alder a few days ago. Later today he would descend north, pick up his camping gear and walk out to the road to hitch-hike to Fort William then home. He wasn't quite sure where he was on the ridge and admitted his navigation was a little shaky. I was to meet him again as I returned over Beinn Eibhinn.

At the west end of the ridge, Mullach Coire nan Nead and Meall Glas Choire, gave good views. The weather had been improving all day and now the sun was out. Heading back east I reached the halfway point of

On the summit of Ben More on Mull, the first peak of 517, 18 May

Stob Coire nam Beith from the climb to Sgorr nam Fiannaidh,
Aonach Eagach, 27 May

Ben Nevis from the Aonach Eagach, 27 May

Sunset over Rannoch Moor and the Blackmount hills from the Beinn Achaladair – Beinn a'Chreachain ridge, 2 June

Beinn a'Chuirn and Beinn Mhanach above Glen Lochay. Andy Hicks in foreground, 2 June

On the summit of Carn Mairg with Schiehallion on the skyline, 19 June

Inset: Andy Hicks crossing the rickety bridge over the Abhainn Shira en route for the Stob Coir'an Albannaich and Stob Ghabhar tops, 1 June

Studying the map in Shielin' of Mark bothy, 26 June

Ben Alder and Sgor Iutharn from near Culra Lodge, 14 July

Camp in Glen Tilt near the Falls of Tarf, 22 June

On the slopes of Stob Coire Easain with the Grey Corries
in the background, 18 July

Rainbow over Binnein Beag in the Mamores, 20 July

View across Coire Lagan to Sgurr Mhic Choinnich, Sgurr Thearlaich, Sgurr Alasdair and Sgurr Sgumain, 24 July

The hardest summit. Chris Ainsworth below the Inaccessible Pinnacle, 24 July

the walk (it's 258½ summits of course!) between Geal Charn and Diollaid a'Chairn. Many of the hills of the last 58 days were in view during the day from the serrated crest of the Aonach Eagach over Bidean nam Bian to the Blackmount, Ben Starav, Ben Lui, the Bridge of Orchy and Glen Lochay hills I'd climbed with Andy, Ben More and Stob Binnein, Ben Lawers and the fine cone of Schiehallion. It was hard to grasp I'd climbed all of these.

From Diollaid a'Chairn I continued on to Carn Dearg from where I descended directly to the bothy where I found two new mountain bikes outside and two packs inside. All the people from the night before had gone. I moved my cooking gear outside and sat in the sun. A steady trickle of people passed heading east. One eventually stopped, a German walker with a very large pack. 'Too heavy,' he said, dumping it on the ground. He'd walked in from Kinloch Rannoch with a camp in a forest the previous night. 'Too many little flies,' he said with a shudder, 'I couldn't eat breakfast until 11 o'clock.' He'd never heard of bothies before but now he was here he would stay and head out the next day. Another walker arrived, the owner of one of the bikes and one of the packs in the bothy, having been up Ben Alder after cycling in from Dalwhinnie. Not a lightweight fanatic, he had a pack which was full of tinned food and cans of beer. He was a little concerned about the owner of the other pack whom he'd met on the walk in and had gone up Ben Alder with and who he described as an 'older' man. He'd descended from the Bealach Breabag as he had a sore leg and should have been back first, as the man talking to me had continued on over Beinn Bheoil. An hour later the other man walked in. He'd been going to walk out to Dalwhinnie that evening but decided he couldn't catch the last train and so would stay here and get up at 4 a.m. and go for the first train in the morning. He had no sleeping bag or mat but did find an abandoned air mattress in the bothy which he draped over himself as a blanket and was soon asleep, lying fully clothed on a bench with his boots still on. The air mattress rustled noisily every time he moved and I was glad I was sleeping in another room. I didn't want waking at 4 a.m. anyway.

Then John Thompson from Manchester, a walker I'd met that morning, returned from Ben Alder. He'd arrived from Dalwhinnie late the night before and was intending to go to Fort William via Loch Ossian youth hostel where he knew the warden. I'd noticed that Culra had been renovated extensively since I was last here some dozen years before. John told me the old wall panels had been made of asbestos and the bothy had been redone when they'd been taken out.

The final arrivals were a father and two sons, who set themselves up in another room. For the second night there were seven of us in the bothy. I hadn't spoken to so many people on the walk before and whilst it was interesting I was looking forward to solitary camps again.

That night I dreamt of a weather forecast predicting hurricane force winds and snow! However, hot sun and a clear sky greeted me when I woke and I left Culra and set off for Ben Alder wearing sandals, shorts and sunhat. The path to Loch a'Bhealaich Bheithe had been recently rebuilt, making for an easy walk to the Bealach Breabag. Here I left the pack and climbed the initially steep slopes of Ben Alder for only my second ascent of this big impressive mountain. The summit lies on a huge flat plateau, which belies the steep, craggy slopes that fall away on every side. The air was sharp and clear and the views were excellent, especially to the west where Ben Nevis towered over the rippling line of the Aonachs and the Grey Corries, the shape, a steep curve one side and a vertical slash the other, suddenly reminding me of Half Dome in Yosemite valley in the Sierra Nevada mountains in far off California.

Across Loch a'Bhealaich Bheithe from Ben Alder lies the long ridge of Beinn Bheoil. Back at the bealach I shifted the pack to the base of this hill, then made the short climb to the Top at the southern end, Sron Coire na h-Iolaire, from where there is a good view down the length of Loch Ericht. A couple on the summit were waiting for some others whom I could see heading up Bheoil itself. The couple had cycled in to Culra then climbed Bheoil from the far end, meeting their four friends, who'd walked in from Loch Ossian, en route. Next they were going up Ben Alder where one of the group would celebrate completing his round of the Munros. The rest of the party were descending Beinn Bheoil as I ascended and told me that it had been a long, hot, sweaty walk in from Ossian as it was very warm and humid lower down.

Collecting the pack I dropped down to Benalder Cottage, an old and famous bothy on the shores of Loch Ericht. As I descended I admired the stands of conifers – larches, mostly – scattered amongst green meadows beside the loch. For some reason the wildernesses of North America were in my mind today as the scene reminded me of ones I'd seen in the Rocky Mountains. Sitting outside the bothy were the father and sons who'd been in Culra the night before. They were heading for Fort William on a passes and glens route. I was heading there by a rather more up and down route.

The next stage of this involved crossing the three summits that lie between Loch Ericht and Loch Ossian. These are pleasant hills but the approach from the east is not the best one. It's tediously long and very boggy and this time I was also walking straight into the sun, now blindingly low in the sky. It was with great relief that, hot and sweaty, I dumped the pack at the Bealach nan Sgor and turned away from the sunlight to climb the peaks on either side, Sgor Choinnich and Sgor Gaibhre. The distant views were quite good with many peaks visible but the immediate surroundings were a bit dreary, just wide shallow glens full of peat bogs. Over Creag Meagaidh to the north some towering white clouds looked as though they could develop into thunderheads. Back at the bealach I contoured beneath Sgor Gaibhre to the Mam Ban then climbed the sixth and last hill of the day, Carn Dearg.

Descending west from this peak I met John Thompson again. He was going to bivvy out high on the hill having found a spring – 'brackish but it'll do'. No midges he said, not here, above 2,500 feet. I was tempted to join him but I had a rendezvous with Denise at Loch Treig at 3 p.m. the next day and between here and there lay five more tops so I went on down to the Allt a'Choire Odhair Bhig. I stopped here as I knew that camping wasn't allowed near Loch Ossian which lay not far below while the walkers I'd met on Beinn Bheoil had told me the Ossian youth hostel there was full. I was still at over 2,000 feet here so I hadn't descended far. Loch Ossian is at 1,300 feet. As I cooked dinner a pink sunset faded away to leave a darkening and totally clear sky.

A cool 5° night gave way quickly to hot sunshine. From the tent door I could see the slightly hazy hills of the Blackmount and Buchaille Etive Mor, nearer now than they'd been for many weeks. Ben Nevis, the Grey Corries and the Mamores were slightly sharper. High on the hillside I could see John descending. I was soon doing the same, down to Loch Ossian where several people and two obviously tame stags were standing outside the hostel. The loch shone in the sun and the trees fringing it glowed green.

Beyond the loch there was a long, boggy haul up the featureless whaleback of Beinn na Lap. This is generally agreed to be one of the easiest Munros yet I failed to climb it on my first attempt. This had been in a December storm during my first winter visit to the Highlands. My friend Steve and I had battled up it against the wind from a camp near the railway at its foot but were reduced to crawling over the snow as we neared the top. Some few hundred yards from the summit cairn we gave up and let the wind blow us back down. Our other companion, Fran, had sensibly stayed in camp.

On this easy, if tedious, ascent the monotony was broken by the flowers, yellow tormentil and pink and white orchids plus the first purple heather. A heat haze shimmered over the hills all around. A steep boggy descent led down to the Allt Feith Thuill from where it was straight up again to Meall Garbh. Two women were sitting on the summit. I dashed past, concerned I'd be late for the rendezvous. From the col below it took 15 minutes to go up and down Chno Dearg. I did have time, just, to admire the soft light playing over the craggy slopes of Stob Coire Sgriodain, whose two summits were my next destination. On their ascent I met another walker, Don from Falkirk, who recognised me from *TGO*. We had a short chat, then I hurried on. The rugged slopes of Stob a'Choire Mheadhoin and Stob Coire Easain looked impressive across the deep trench containing the reservoir of Loch Treig, whose waters are piped 15 miles under the mountains to come out on the far side of Ben Nevis to provide electricity for the aluminium smelter in Fort William.

Once over the summits I tried to race down the 2,300 foot descent. I couldn't do it. The north ridge of the hill was all steep rocks, bogs and tussocks, difficult terrain over which I couldn't easily run. Hot and thirsty and sticky with sweat and dust I reached Fersit 50 minutes late. On a blanket on a knoll above the car park I could see two figures sitting. One was Denise, the other, I was delighted to see, was her elder daughter, 17-year-old Rowena who was visiting from England where she now lived. Wearing high heels, a long flowing skirt and a broad-brimmed, stylish hat, she stepped delicately down through the heather, looking as though she should be at a garden party in the English countryside rather than on a rough Highland hillside.

Denise had as usual brought plenty of tasty food for me and I settled down to a late lunch. The fresh fruit – oranges, plums and bananas – was particularly welcome. Unfortunately she hadn't brought much to drink and I'd stupidly not stopped for water since the Allt Feith Thuill, a great deal of time and effort earlier. I was very thirsty and felt quite tired and irritable as I tried to sort out food and gear. This involved changing packs as Aarn Tate had sent another version of his pack for me to try. After I'd got quite hot and bothered Denise went to one of the nearby houses where the occupant kindly filled a water bottle for her. While I tried to sort out the gear Don returned from his round of the tops. I'm afraid I was a bit brusque as I had rather too much to think about. As well as suffering from the lack of water I was also feeling a growing sense of confusion, something that seemed to be increasing each time I came down to a resupply point. It always seemed such a hectic rush with no real time to talk with Denise. Information on a range of subjects came at me, far too much for me to absorb properly or understand. I was in a different world and couldn't leave it quickly. The walk had developed a simple rhythm to which I was now attuned. Each day fell into the same pattern. The camping was just about automatic while the walking was very immediate, my concentration focused on the next few minutes or at most on which route to take to the next rise or dip. The intrusion of the outside world into this life was becoming harder to deal with.

After two hours Denise and Rowena departed. I felt a bit lost, as I did every time Denise left. For a short time my world had abruptly changed. Now it was just me and the mountains again. I knew, though, that once I started walking I would very quickly slip back into the walk.

The next summits, the Easains, lay above, a long way above. I set off up the steep slopes. Once before, at the start of a 500-mile walk from Corrour to Ullapool (see *The Great Backpacking Adventure* for a full account), I'd climbed the peaks on either side of Loch Treig in one day. It had been hot and humid then too and I'd fallen asleep on the slopes of Stob a'Choire Mheadhoin. That didn't happen this time. It was late in the evening and there wasn't time to stop and rest.

As I reached Stob a'Choire Mheadhoin the sun dropped behind some thin clouds and a spectacular sunset began. Streaks of bright white cloud radiated across the blue sky from a splash of red just above the ragged silhouette of the peaks out to the west. By the time I was on Stob Coire Easain the colour was fading and I descended west into a grey, colourless world. Not far below the summit, at 2,700 feet, a broad shelf ran across the face of the mountain. There was water here, the start of the Allt Ruigh na Braoileig, which runs down into the Lairig Leacach, so I camped on the lip with a fine view to the Grey Corries, pale in the dying light. I'd climbed nearly 8,000 feet and been out 12½ hours. It was time for sleep.

The only sound in the morning was the gentle trickle of water. There wasn't a breath of breeze. The sun was shining on the Grey Corries, turning their quartzite screes silver, but I was still in the shade. Way out to the west a dirty purple-red heat haze hung above the horizon. Don had told me the forecast was for the high to continue with temperatures rising each day. After all the days of cold wind and rain this was welcome. I didn't mind how hot it became.

The Grey Corries is the name given to the splendid rocky ridge, containing four Munros and eight Tops, that lies south of Glen Spean. The name comes from the light coloured quartzite scree that covers much of their slopes. Many of the Tops are *Stobs*, literally a short stick or upright post, but here meaning a peak, and usually a pointed one. I was looking forward to walking the ridge as I'd only done it once before, on the same walk on which I'd fallen asleep on the Easains, a long 17 years earlier.

While I waited for the sun to appear and dry the condensation-soaked tent, I stuck some Kamillosan cream and a dressing on a crack in the skin under my big toe. I'd walked in sandals for the last two days and the skin on my feet was drying out. I smeared them with sunscreen to try to keep them at least slightly moist. The sun hit the tent and the temperature was 20° within seconds. Far below I could see people and tents outside the tiny Lairig Leacach bothy. By the time I reached the pass the people had gone though there was gear laid out in the bothy and some socks drying outside.

My first summit of the day was Stob Ban, a fine outlier of the Grey Corries. To reach it I took the intermittent path that runs beside the Allt a'Chuil Choirean. There were excellent views of the pointed peak up the tree-lined stream gorge, a Himalayan scene in miniature. The path continues to the col north of the summit from where steep scree leads to the top. Lying well south of the main Grey Corries ridge Stob Ban is a good viewpoint for the rest of the range. Four people and a dog were descending from the summit as I reached it.

Next came the highest peak, Stob Choire Claurigh, another pull up steep and very unstable scree. This Munro has two inconveniently placed Tops out to the north, Stob Coire na Ceannain and Stob Coire na Gaibhre. They are fine peaks however, the first with a narrow ridge running out to it and the second with excellent views of its parent peak. These were the last sharp views of the day however as thin, high clouds were gradually covering the sky. This overcast layer, through which the weak sun was just visible, stayed the rest of the day. Distant views were lost in the haze while nearer peaks became pale silhouettes.

Back on Stob Choire Claurigh I began the traverse of the main ridge, a marvellous walk, much of it on rock or stones, along narrow ridges and over neat little summits. Ravens floated over the ridge and perched on summit cairns and I saw one dotterel. All the last eight peaks of the day, bar one, Beinn na Socaich, lay on the ridge. Stob a'Choire Leith, Stob Coire Cath na Sine, Caistell and Stob Coire an Laoigh came and went. From the next summit, Stob Coire Easain, I went out to Beinn na Socaich, then it was a long peakless walk out to the last two summits, Sgurr Choinnichs Mor and Beag. The first of these was perhaps the most impressive summit of the day with a steep climb onto it up a narrow buttress. These last two peaks are a little different from those to the east, more green and with more dark rock and less quartzite.

My plan had been to drop south to the Water of Nevis to camp and then traverse the Mamores ridge the next day. Now though it seemed a waste of the height I'd gained to do that when without descending far I could link the Grey Corries with Aonachs Mor and Beag, whose vast east wall had been facing me all day. Tiny lochans dotted the unnamed bealach between Sgurr Choinnich Beag and Stob Coire Bhealaich and I camped by one of these. The first peak of the next day, Sgurr a'Bhuic, was only 750 feet above my camp. The tent faced south and from the door I could see across the Water of Nevis to Binnein Beag and Binnein Mor in the Mamores. A touch of late sun caught the latter and it glowed gold. The big mountains to the west soon hid the setting sun however, leaving me in the shade.

Voices passed by as two walkers descended to Glen Nevis. I watched them fade into the distance. Then I looked at the mountains. There was nothing else to see. I realised as I did so that these camps alone with nothing but wild country were a very important part of the walk, the part that separated it from a series of day walks, from returning to car, hostel, B&B or roadside camp site surrounded by other campers each night. Wild camps like this, with no sign of human presence or activity, were relaxing, invigorating, inspiring. They allowed a deeper contact with the mountains. Here I felt at home and at peace. The world seemed perfect. That's why camps with views of power lines, dams, bulldozed roads, the unnatural straight edges of plantations, ski lifts and other man-made intrusions were so depressing. It was like looking at a magnificent painting that someone had scratched and marred with graffiti. Low-level camps in glens with farms and fields aren't quite the same as these human features are part of people's lives, part of the way people live in the country. The stark, ugly, high-level constructions are soulless; functional but graceless they speak of a lack of contact, understanding, rapport or appreciation; they represent the dull, colourless, unimaginative aspects of human nature. They disturb me because I cannot understand how anyone cannot respond to the wild beauty of the hills.

High, thin clouds still lay in sheets across the sky when I woke. Occasionally spots of rain spattered individually on the tent. A westerly breeze blew. Out to the east pale yellow and pink tinged bands of cloud marked the rising sun. The summits were all clear but looked dull and flat in the soft light. However it was still a wonderful, an incredible, place to be.

Surmounting the precipitous rocky slopes rising above my camp to the west looked as though it could be difficult. A steep groove slanting up under overhanging rocks offered a potential way through the crags. I scrabbled up the loose earth and scree below the dark, wet rocks. There

103

was a steep step near the top over which I had to push the pack before I could haul myself up but once over that the angle eased. On the ridge above five walkers were heading for Aonach Beag, the only people I would see until I reached the summit of Ben Nevis many hours later. I went the other way at first, out to the little Top of Sgurr a'Bhuic, the southernmost point on the Aonachs ridge. From the summit I turned northwards to climb Stob Coire Bhealaich and then Aonach Beag. Although the name of the latter means the little ridged mountain it's actually higher than Aonach Mor – the big ridged mountain. The reason is the overall size of the mountain rather than the height of the highest point, as the names were given long before summit heights were accurately measured and refer to how the mountains look from the glens. Together they form a superb, long, high ridge lying east of Ben Nevis. Wild remote corries and long, rocky ridges lie below the Aonachs, country I wanted to return to explore thoroughly, the first time I'd felt this on the walk.

I had to do some exploring straightaway as Aonach Mor has two outliers, Stob an Cul Choire and Tom na Sroine, on its north-east ridge. As the map showed unbroken crags below the summit of Aonach Mor I was concerned as to how easy it would be getting down to this ridge so I was relieved to find a fairly narrow but not too steep spur running down to a col at the start of the ridge. Although rough this was easy to descend. It took an hour-and-a-half to do the round trip to the two Tops which gave good views of the vast east face of Aonach Mor.

The steep descent to the col with Carn Mor Dearg was much harder than I remembered from my last visit, over a dozen years before, as the path, mostly on scree, was eroded and slippery. A cool wind blew over the col where I had lunch in the shelter of a stone wall. The path up to Carn Mor Dearg was also steep and loose but going up is always easier. This delicate, pointed peak is a total contrast to the great bulk of Ben Nevis just across Coire Leis. It's a great viewpoint for the magnificent northern cliffs of the latter, the biggest in the Highlands, but on this visit it was dark and hazy and I could see little detail. After going out and back to Carn Dearg Meadhonach, just to the north of the main summit, I set off along the granite blocks of the Carn Mor Dearg arête which curves round the head of Coire Leis to the south-east slopes of Ben Nevis. The scrambling isn't very exposed or difficult but the situation is spectacular and thrilling. It's without doubt the best way for walkers to climb Ben Nevis. The final steep climb of Britain's highest mountain is over a mass of huge rocks and boulders. I reached the summit at 4.45 p.m. There were still around 20 people there and more could be seen toiling up the tourist path from Glen Nevis. Earlier I expect there were hundreds.

The Ben has two Tops, Carn Dearg NW and Carn Dearg SW. I went to the latter first, picking a way over the rough stones that cover the summit plateau then following the edge of the great cliffs. Some rock climbers were coiling their ropes while below I could see more perched on narrow ledges and spread-eagled on sheer faces. From Carn Dearg NW the summit of Ben Nevis was a mass of people moving seemingly at random around the large cairn.

I crossed the plateau in the other direction to a stony descent that led to the col with Carn Dearg SW. From there it was grass to the top. From this, the last and 11th summit of the day, I had to find a way down into Glen Nevis. I started with a steep and rough descent of scree, tussock and rock into Coire Eoghainn. There were tempting camp-sites here but stopping now would probably make doing the Mamores ridge the next day impossible. A path leads down from the corrie but it's such a loose, eroded mess that I cut well away from it frequently for more stable ground. The descent as a whole, nearly 4,000 feet in less than two miles from the summit of the Ben, hammered my feet and made my knees ache for the first time in the walk. As consolation there were good views of the tree-lined deep Nevis gorge with beyond it the Steall waterfall and the Mamores. There were masses of flowers too, especially orchids.

Once down in the glen I walked up through the gorge into the upper glen and camped on the flat, smooth, turf below the ruins at Steall. In a straight line I was only a mile or so from where I'd been the night before though much lower of course. I'd camped here 17 years earlier on the Corrour to Ullapool walk. It had been a beautiful site then and it still was. To the north I could see and hear the waterfalls on the Allt Coire Guibhsachan. Across the Water of Nevis to the south little crags covered with birch trees dotted the hillside. I was tired but content. It had been a long, hard but wonderful day.

Bird song and waterfalls were the only sounds when I woke. There was still lots of high cloud but also sunshine breaking through in places. It was hot too, 19°C before 7 a.m. Another day for shorts and sandals. The soles of the latter, well used before the walk, were starting to disintegrate. A chunk had fallen out of one heel and the cushioning layer seemed to be collapsing. That was probably the reason my feet had felt pounded yesterday. Today's walk, although longer and with more ascent, was on the softer terrain of the Mamores, a magnificent high-level ridge running some ten miles between Loch Leven and Glen Nevis and containing 11

Munros and six Tops (at the time of the walk – ten Munros and seven Tops following the 1997 revision of the *Tables*). The ridge twists and turns and is quite narrow in places. Big corries cut into it both north and south and there are long rocky spurs running out into these. I'd done the whole ridge in one day a few years earlier, though from a high-level camp, and knew that it would take a good 12 hours, probably longer. I also knew that it was a superb walk, one of the best in the Highlands.

Fourteen-and-a-half hours after setting off I'd done 17 Tops, walked 18 miles and climbed 11,000 feet. It was to remain the most ascent and the most Tops in a single day of the entire walk. The visibility had improved and there'd been sharp, clear views of nearby hills all day though distant views were mostly hazy and Ben Nevis vanished into drifting cloud a couple of times during the afternoon.

After fording the Water of Nevis I climbed the northern outlier Binnein Beag then took the excellent traversing path round to Coire an Lochain from where I climbed the easternmost peak, also an outlier, Sgurr Eilde Mor. On the descent I passed a woman ascending who'd arrived on Binnein Beag just after me. We were to meet several times in the hours ahead before she descended from Sgurr a'Mhaim. There were several other people about too, some of whom I also saw several times, but I still had ten of the summits to myself. Sgorr Eilde Beag, which gave the best views of the day across to Sgurr Eilde Mor shining in the sunlight above the dark waters of the lochan in Coire an Lochain, marked the start of the ridge proper. The summits now just rolled by. Two on Binnein Mor, two on Na Gruigaichean, Stob Coire A'Chairn where I left the pack while I scrambled out on the narrow rocky ridge to An Garbhanach and An Gearanach, Am Bodach, Sgor an Iubhair where I dumped the pack again while I went out along the Devil's Ridge over Stob Choire a'Mhail to the highest peak in the Mamores, Sgurr a'Mhaim. The only water on the ridge, apart from the lochan in Coire an Lochain at the start, is the small Lochan Coire nam Miseach which lies between Sgor an Iubhair and the next peak, Stob Ban. Very thirsty, I drank deeply here and was tempted to camp. I resisted the urge and pushed on. From Stob Ban the haze that had hung over distant peaks all day began to sink into the valleys and mountains began to appear, especially to the south where the Aonach Eagach and Bidean nam Bian could be seen sharp and clear having been silhouettes all day. To the west and north dark lines of indistinct peaks appeared as the sky turned pink from the sinking sun.

The last hill, Mullach nan Coirean, has two Tops. On the higher one a map and route sheet encased in plastic lay near the cairn. It was labelled

Grantown-on-Spey RAF OTC. Reading the dates I saw it could only have been left a few hours earlier so I put it under a rock on the cairn in case the group who'd lost it returned. I knew one of the RAF instructors in Grantown and wondered if it was one of his parties. The climbing finally over, I descended the north-east ridge on a path that led to the plantations in Glen Nevis. A metal disc on the ladder stile over the deer fence read 'Walkers Welcome'. However the path in the trees was an eroded slippery mess and hard to follow as it went steeply down to emerge on a road in a clear cut area. On the edge of this a big sign said 'Closed to the Public due to Felling Operations'. The mass of boot prints I'd followed down the path showed that many people were still using this route though. Presumably the Forestry Commission had assumed the route would be used only from the bottom.

The logging road eventually brought me to Glen Nevis and the public road. I walked down the glen in search of a camp-site but there were many 'No Camping' signs, a new addition since I was last here. Very tired now, I eventually forded the river Nevis in the dark and pitched the tent on a small sloping meadow on the far side, hidden from the road by the fringe of trees on the riverbank. As soon as I stopped clouds of midges appeared. The Mosiguard Natural repellent stopped them biting me but didn't prevent them crawling over my face and head, a maddening feeling. I threw the tent up quickly, not exactly where I'd intended, chucked in the pack, dashed down to the river to fill my water containers, then dived into the tent to sort everything out. A burning midge coil made my eyes water but kept the midges outside. Too weary to concentrate properly I then burnt my dinner so badly I couldn't eat it. Minestrone soup, a large lump of cheese and some trail mix had to do instead. I didn't mind. It had been another wonderful day in the mountains. In the last three days I'd climbed 40 peaks and they'd been three of the best days of the walk. I'd also now done 313 summits in total, all those south of the Great Glen.

The night was moist and misty and condensation was dripping from the roof of the tent the next morning. My matches, which I'd left lying on the groundsheet, were too damp to light. Luckily I also had a lighter as I needed some coffee after a fitful night's sleep on the sideways slope. In the daylight my camp looked very makeshift indeed and I was ashamed of the way the tent was pitched. The Glen Nevis Caravan and Camping Park lay only a mile and a half away. If I'd been down earlier or been less tired I'd have made it there the previous evening. Forty-five minutes along the road and I was there, paying £5.20 to camp in a corner. It seemed a bad deal after all the free sites high in the hills but today was to be a rest day and I wanted access to showers, shops, cafés and other bits of decadence I'd been away from for ten days. I rang Denise and arranged to meet her in a café the next morning. She would bring the bike with her so I could cycle to Skye.

I spent the rest of the day in Fort William, browsing in the outdoor shops and almost buying lots of interesting books in Nevisport. I restricted myself to one. Dinner was a pizza in The Grog and Gruel which had a very American atmosphere, reminding me of a pizza place in Yosemite Village. It did serve excellent real ale however. The pizza was an American sized one too and I could only eat about a third of it despite feeling very hungry. I took the rest away to nibble in camp. After half a day I'd had enough of Fort William. It's not the most interesting town. What did the visitors who thronged its streets see in it? Above the town clouds hung round Ben Nevis. The weather had broken and showers started during the afternoon. By evening this had become a steady downpour.

Chapter 7

A CUILLIN DIVERSION

'Graceful and beautiful as dream mountains.'

Seton Gordon
Highways and Byways in the West Highlands

Eggs, beans, tomatoes, mushrooms, vegeburger and toast made for a different and excellent breakfast in the Café Beag just along from the camp-site. Outside the rain poured down. Denise and Hazel joined me in the café during the morning and we repaired to Fort William to collect my now unneeded food parcel which had been sent before my plans changed. I hadn't picked it up the day before because it had been a Sunday.

With the rain still hammering down I left on the bike for Mallaig and the ferry to Skye. No bridges for me! The real reason was that Denise had worked out that this was a shorter route than going by Kyle of Lochalsh. It was also less hilly. The rain lasted until Lochailort, about two hours into the ride. The clouds remained low but I was at sea level or thereabouts so still had views. The silver sand beaches of Arisaig and Morar looked lovely and for a while I could see the attractions of cycle touring. Every so often though a lorry would come too close and nearly force me off the road and I changed my mind. The distinctive serrated crest of the Cuillins appeared in the distance. Wonderful!

Ten minutes short of four hours and I was in Mallaig. 'This is the way to go to Skye,' I thought as I leant over the side of the ferry to Armadale watching Mallaig slowly fade away and the far shore grow nearer. Onshore again a hilly hour-long ride took me over Skye's bleak southern moorlands to Broadford on the north coast. I have strange memories of Broadford. For a few summers in the early 1980s I led backpacking parties for Outward Bound Loch Eil on a venture called Skye Trek which involved walking through Knoydart then across Skye to the Cuillin and Glen Brittle. On one trek one of the students had a stomach upset and we were forced to wait out a day while he recovered. It was a Sunday and we were camped just outside Broadford. Nothing was open, not one shop, not one café. It was like a ghost town. We did find someone surreptitiously selling newspapers from the back of his car down a side street. I'd never expected to feel guilty buying *The Observer* but I felt it should have come wrapped in a plain brown envelope. Back at the camp the midges were out and so was the sun. The tents were just too hot so we had to sit outside fully clothed. I have one surreal photograph showing a student dressed in full waterproofs with gloves on and a balaclava pulled down over his face sitting in bright sunshine reading a newspaper.

Today Broadford seemed boringly normal and much more tourist orientated than I remembered. I met Denise and Hazel in a café. They'd driven round by the bridge and been impressed by Glen Shiel where the mist had been swirling round the crags. I cycled on, around the coast and then up a very long, slow hill before descending to Sligachan with a somewhat sore backside. Seventy-eight miles was the most I'd ever cycled in a day.

A small boggy, bumpy field just beyond the Sligachan Hotel was packed with tents. This is the Sligachan camp-site. When I first came here camping wasn't restricted. You just camped on the river bank. Too many people and too much litter and damage ended this and resulted in the camp-site. Denise and Hazel were in the café/restaurant/bar – a long new building extending out from the old hotel, a historic place where the first mountaineers to explore the Cuillin stayed in the late 1800s.

Leaving me at the camp-site, Denise and Hazel drove off to their accommodation some ten miles away. They would return in the morning before going home. Denise had left me three cardboard boxes of food, fuel and various bits and pieces. I could hardly move in the tent but I had to squeeze both them and myself inside as there were showers during the evening and, much worse, lots of midges.

The tent somewhat sorted out, I retreated back to the bar where I phoned Chris Ainsworth. He and Paul Riley were driving up the next day. As the weather forecast was for good weather the day after, but then bad the day after that, Chris was keen to get a very early start and try to do as much of the ridge as possible. I nervously agreed. The Cuillin summits were the most difficult part of the walk, the crux to put it in rock climbing terms, which is appropriate as walking and climbing on the

Cuillin are hard to separate at times. The thought of moving fast for hours on high, exposed, rocky terrain was exciting but also a little scary.

There are 23 Tops in the Cuillin, 21 on the main ridge or its radiating spurs. The odd two out are the summits of Bla Bheinn, a fine mountain away to the south down Glen Sligachan. After Denise and Hazel had come to say goodbye I walked down this wide, boggy glen on a very damp and misty morning. The clouds were hanging along the hillsides just a few hundred feet up. Two mountain bikers accompanied me down the glen. The path was rough and rocky with many muddy sections and they were no faster than me. Every so often the path would be smooth for a few hundred yards and they'd speed off but then it would become bouldery again so I'd catch up and, in places, pass them. Overall, cycling looked much harder work than walking.

It was a pleasure to know that Bla Bheinn and the lands either side, the Strathaird and Torrin estates, are now owned by the John Muir Trust, a conservation organisation dedicated to buying land in the Highlands in order to restore and preserve it. The Trust is named for the Scot John Muir, known as the father of national parks in the USA. After emigrating there as a child with his family, he was the main force in the establishment of Yosemite National Park and also founded the Sierra Club, a major environmental organisation.

Once past Loch na Creitheach I began to ascend the hidden rocky slopes of Bla Bheinn. This had been Denise's first Munro many years earlier when we'd climbed it from Camasunary to the south. The weather had been stormy then too. This time at a height of about 2,000 feet I entered the mist which was very dense with visibility of no more than a few yards. It was very dark and strange, with pale rocks quivering insubstantially in the shifting light. Other walkers were about and figures would loom suddenly out of the mist or else I'd hear voices, seemingly close by, yet see no one. Once I heard a shepherd far below shouting at barking dogs. The ground was wet and slippery and required care. Where possible I stuck to the rock, the rough volcanic gabbro that makes up most of the Cuillin and which gives very good grip. Although wet it wasn't cold and I walked most of the day in shorts and rain jacket. There's a short steep dip between the two summits but it's not difficult. Both summits done without seeing a thing, I made a rapid descent, then slogged back up the glen where the path was now running with water.

Chris and Paul arrived that evening and camped in Chris's big orange Vango ridge tent which towered over my little backpacking shelter. The early start for the next day was on as the forecast was still good. They'd done the whole ridge in 13 hours several years before and Chris was confident we could get a long way. I wasn't planning on the whole ridge as some of the summits, notably those of Bidein Druim nan Ramh, are below 3,000 feet while some of the Munros and Tops didn't lie on the main ridge. Could I do them all in one day? I doubted it. This wasn't the Mamores. The 14 *Sgurrs* give an idea of what the ridge is like. The name generally denotes a steep rocky peak. The Inaccessible Pinnacle and Bhasteir Tooth are also suggestive. The Cuillin is unique. The main ridge is only seven miles long but those seven miles are a roller-coaster of extremely narrow arêtes, rock towers and cliffs, the most impressive rock scenery in Scotland and unlike anything on the mainland. It's a paradise for rock climbers and confident scramblers but can be quite overwhelming for walkers. I'd done all 11 Munros and most of the ten Tops before and knew that on some of them I'd be at my limit psychologically. The record for the ridge is an astonishing, no, an unbelievable, 3 hours, 32 minutes and 15 seconds, achieved by hill runner and rock climber Andy Hyslop in 1994.

We left at 6 a.m. on a cool morning, loaded with harnesses, slings, helmets, carabiners and other bits of climbing gear plus of course a rope. Cloud hung over the peaks as we climbed the rough slopes of Coire a'Bhasteir. At times the sharp spires of the Pinnacle Ridge of Sgurr nan Gillean appeared dramatically through the mist. A cold breeze blew through the Bealach a'Bhasteir where we left the packs while we went up the West Ridge of Sgurr nan Gillean, the northernmost Munro on the ridge. The crux of this is Nicholson's Chimney, a dark, dank, steep 80 foot cleft graded Moderate by rock climbers (which means very easy in their jargon) where we used the rope both for the ascent and descent. This was for my benefit as Chris and Paul were quite happy soloing. The climbing was easier than it looked but I still wouldn't have wanted to do it without the rope, especially in descent. The summit gave a bit of a view but it was still very misty. I thought back to the day in 1981 when this had been my last Munro the first time round. I'd been impressed then and I was impressed now.

Back at the col we paused for a bite to eat and to sit and stare down the rugged slopes to the south to Loch Coruisk, the spectacular loch that lies in the heart of the Cuillin with the main ridge curling round it. The Coruisk basin is arguably the most magnificent mountain landscape in Britain. Beyond the loch rose the great prow of Bla Bheinn. Replenished we headed, still packless, west for Am Basteir, a sharp wedge of rock. The south-east ridge is mostly easy, though exposed, except for one steep step of ten feet or so. This seemed harder than any of us remembered it and we used a sling as an extended handhold on both the descent and the ascent on the return.

Reclaiming the packs, we descended east down steep scree and a series of ledges into Lota Corrie. Once lower than the cliffs of Am Basteir we contoured across the slopes to the base of the Bhasteir Tooth, a great black fang of rock jutting out of the ridge next to Am Basteir and the summit I was most worried about – no let's be honest, frightened of – on the whole walk. This was due to its appearance and the advice in the guidebooks rather than previous experience as I'd never dared attempt it before. 'No possibilities for the scrambler' said Bull in his *Black Cuillin Ridge Scrambler's Guide*. Another guide, Wilson Parker's *Scrambles in Skye*, was worse: 'the tooth cannot be entertained by non-rock climbers' and 'the most difficult 3,000 feet Top in Britain'.

'Nonsense,' said Chris and Paul, 'it's easy. You won't need the rope.' I insisted on taking it anyway. They were right. And I was amazed. And relieved. The Ordinary Route, first climbed by the great mountaineer and Cuillin explorer Norman Collie along with the guide John Mackenzie in 1889, went some 400 feet up sloping ledges and little chimneys to the Nick between Am Basteir and the Tooth. The scrambling was simple and not very exposed. From the Nick a walk up easy, angled slabs led to the top. The hardest 3,000 Top in Britain it most definitely isn't. Spectacular it is though, an airy perch high above the corries on either side with the intimidating west face of Am Basteir rising into the mist above.

We returned to the packs then contoured round to the Bealach nan Lice and two easy summits, Sgurr a'Fionn Choire and Bruach na Frithe. The mist was clearing now and Loch Coruisk was a deep blue in the sunshine. A decision had to be made. Ahead lay the peaks of Bidein Druim nan Ramh, technically difficult, for a non-climber, followed by the equally challenging north Tops of Sgurr a'Mhadaidh, none of them reaching 3,000 feet. Not wanting to make the day harder than necessary we decided to traverse below Bidein and descended into Coir'a Tairneilear. Here Paul announced he would keep on down and return to Sligachan for the car then meet us in Glen Brittle at the south end of the ridge. Chris didn't fancy taking me over the Mhadaidh Tops on his own so we went down too, then round the end of Sgurr Thuilm and all the way back up to An Dorus, the notch in the ridge between Mhaidadh and Sgurr a'Ghreadaidh. This diversion took three-and-a-half hours and an awful lot of effort.

The summit of Sgurr a'Mhadaidh was now an easy scramble and was soon done. Next came the incredibly thin knife-edge of Sgurr a'Ghreadaidh. Having so far coped with the exposure well I suddenly felt very shaky and insecure on this breathtaking ridge. Chris belayed me between the two summits at either end of the ridge, then we had a short break. Sitting there staring at the unbelievably fantastic view calmed me down and from then on I felt fine. Why did this occur? I don't know but it wasn't unexpected and was one reason I'd wanted experienced companions here. I hadn't expected problems on Ghreadaidh specifically though as I had traversed the peak on my own twice before, once in a storm.

The views were now superb, the sky almost clear with a fine golden evening light over the jagged, spectacular peaks ahead. Romping over the rocks now with a sudden burst of confidence we quickly climbed Sgurr Thormaid and Sgurr na Banachdich and arrived on Sgurr Dearg. To the north the ragged black silhouette of Sgurr nan Gillean looked far away. Immediately above us the Inaccessible Pinnacle looked sensational. This massive monolith emerges from the scree just below the summit of Sgurr Dearg and rises some 25 feet above it. This makes it a Munro, the only one requiring rock climbing ability to reach the top as there's no gentle side to the Pinnacle. The 'easiest' way up is by the 120 foot long East Ridge, a steep, extremely exposed narrow arête graded Moderate by climbers and the route used by the first ascensionists, the Pilkington brothers, in 1881. The Victorian description of it as having an 'overhanging and infinite drop on one side and a drop longer and steeper on the other' only seems a slight exaggeration during the ascent.

Chris led the way up and I followed on the end of the rope, the only way I will ever climb the Inaccessible Pinnacle. I find the exposure overwhelming and hard to deal with even when tied on securely. The ascent is thrilling and exciting. It's not actually difficult though there is one high step that is a little awkward. It's the situation that makes it remarkable. The route is obvious and the rock, slippery basalt rather than gabbro, is extremely polished as this is, unsurprisingly, a very popular climb. Even late in the evening others were about. We passed, by climbing over them, a couple sitting on the ridge half way up who made it clear they wanted us to go on, and then were passed ourselves by a solo climber with a rope over his shoulder. Above us high, thin streaks of cloud raced over from the north, dissipating as they passed over the summit, and creating a surreal and dizzying effect. The summit is a small platform. The view was astonishing and spectacular, with all the peaks of the Cuillin spread out around us and turning gold in the rays of the now low-in-the-sky sun. Descent was by an abseil down the vertical 60 feet of the west face. I'd enjoyed the climb but was glad to be back on what felt like solid ground. The Inaccessible Pinnacle is without doubt the hardest 3,000 foot summit in Britain.

To reach the next peak we skirted below the Pinnacle and the disintegrating pile of rubble called An Stac to rejoin the crest of the ridge at the Bealach Lagan. From here we climbed the north-west ridge of Sgurr Mhic Choinnich, yet another superb peak. I was feeling tired now though and there was also a sense of anti-climax after the Inaccessible Pinnacle, the high point of the day in every sense.

We descended Mhic Choinnich by Collie's Ledge, a narrow shelf that slants across the steep west face of the mountain to the Bealach Mhic Choinnich. From Glen Brittle and Coire Lagan scramblers on the ledge look sensationally exposed as they appear to be crossing vertical walls but in fact the exposure isn't that great and the scrambling is easy. The sky was clouding over now, the marvellous light just a memory. Light rain began to fall as we reached the bealach. Sgurr Thearlaich lay above. Chris looked at me. I could see what he was thinking and agreed. We'd done enough. One-and-three-quarter hours later we were down in Glen Brittle, arriving just as darkness fell. We'd been out 16½ hours and had done 14 summits and climbed 9,900 feet, almost all of it on rock. It had been a brilliant day – exciting, frightening and inspiring. I would never forget it.

Paul was waiting in the glen. The tents however were in Sligachan. He'd brought my bike but I couldn't imagine cycling to Sligachan now. The link would have to be made another day. Paul drove us back to camp. I had a quick meal then fell asleep as the rain and wind began in earnest.

A stormy night ensued. Or so I gathered from the battered look of the camp-site in the morning. Several tents were flapping in the wind, pegs ripped out and flysheets torn, and one had blown down. The wind, rain and low cloud persisted all day. The site fee collector woke me at 7.30 a.m. but I went straight back to sleep, reawakening at 9. After the efforts of the previous day and given the weather a rest day seemed inevitable. We went to the hotel for breakfast and didn't leave for six hours. Outside the rain streamed down. The climber who'd passed us on the Inaccessible Pinnacle arrived in the afternoon having bivvied between two of the Tops on Sgurr a'Mhadaidh then given up the complete traverse on Bidein Druim nan Ramh.

Dragging ourselves outside in the late afternoon we packed up the camp and moved to the busy camp-site at the end of Glen Brittle so as to be well placed for the remaining peaks, which all lay at the southern end of the ridge. Chris and Paul had to leave by the next evening at the latest and there were still a couple of summits I thought I might need assistance on so we planned for another early start though the forecast was worrying. Forty to fifty m.p.h. winds were predicted along with a 1,500 foot cloud base.

I had been going to start the cycle ride back to the mainland the next day but after a few phone calls with Denise I decided it would be too late to set off when we returned from the hills so I would stay here and leave the next day. Given what was to happen this decision was a good one.

Chris woke me at 5 a.m. saying there was no wind and we should go at once. He'd slept badly, waking frequently thinking about the route and the weather. By 6 a.m. we were on our way into Coire Lagan. The mist was down to the corrie floor. We found the bottom of the Sgumain Stone Shoot and scrambled up this wide bouldery ravine and walked along the ridge above to Sgurr Sgumain. A descent to the Bealach Sgumain led to Sgurr Alasdair, the highest peak in the Cuillin, which we climbed by its south-west ridge, turning the awkward, exposed Mauvais Pas by a loose, greasy chimney to the right. Another scrambler followed us up then disappeared into the mist. We saw no one else all day. There were no views on Alasdair so we quickly descended to the Head of the Great Stone Shoot, a very long scree slope that is the least exposed though most arduous way up Alasdair. We were now on the other side of Sgurr Thealaich from where we'd stopped two days before. This peak, which I hadn't been up before, was my main remaining concern as the initial climb was up a very steep wall. The rope was used here and left in place for the descent. The mist was damp and cool and the rock was slippery in places but there was no wind or rain yet.

Back at the Great Stone Shoot Paul left to go back to Glen Brittle and dismantle the camp. Rather than tackle the notorious Thearlaich-Dubh Gap, Chris and I went back over Alasdair, down the chimney and then further down on the Coir'a Ghrundda side to the east, where we contoured round the upper slopes of the corrie intending to regain the ridge somewhere near Caisteal a'Garbh-choire. In fact we hit it on the slopes of Sgurr nan Eag further south as we saw when the clouds lifted a little to reveal the Caisteal to the north. Unfortunately given what was to happen we didn't climb Sgurr nan Eag at this point. A burst of heavy rain immediately followed by powerful gusts of wind nearly persuaded us to retreat but we found that below the crest of the ridge the wind was much less strong so we continued, turning the Caisteal on the east side, where we had views under the clag into boulder-strewn An Garbh-choire and down to Loch Coruisk, then climbing easily up the rubble of Sgurr Dubh na Da Bheinn. In thick mist we descended eastwards to a narrow col then followed worn and scratched rocks up a sometimes exposed scramble to Sgurr Dubh Mor, the highest point on the great Dubhs ridge which descends east from the main ridge to Loch Coruisk. Worried about the weather worsening and with no views we turned back immediately and retraced our steps to Sgurr Dubh na Da Bheinn.

We now went drastically wrong. I still don't know exactly what happened or why. The main reason I think is that we relaxed as we thought all the difficulties were over, a classic mountaineering mistake. All that remained was the easy summit of Sgurr nan Eag followed by the descent back to Glen Brittle. As we found, there are no easy summits in the Cuillin, especially in minimal visibility, and relaxing is very unwise. We were also probably still tired from the long day two days before. But there's no real excuse. We were very careless. What we did, as we worked out later, was to descend north and west instead of south from Dubh na Da Bheinn, contour the upper slopes of Coir'a Ghrunnda and end up back on Sgurr Sgumain which we not only didn't recognise but which we tried to convince ourselves was Sgurr nan Eag. We must have been really tired. Wherever we were, Chris had to get down soon so we descended north-west on bits of path and down steep slabs and gullies, a slow process as we kept zigzagging across the slope looking for safe ways down. We were in fact on the edge of the Sgumain Stone Shoot. At one point I saw a drinks can on the scree that looked remarkably similar to one I'd seen on the ascent. My mind clearly wasn't functioning properly as I assumed it was a different one. It wasn't.

The edge of a lochan appeared in the mist. Loch Coir' a' Ghrunnda we assumed. The mist was so thick we could only see a tiny bit of it and we descended the path from the lochan still not aware of where we really were. It is surprising how easy it is to make the land fit your idea of where you are. Even when we started to drop out of the cloud at Loch an Fhir-bhallaich we didn't realise what it was and took the path to the Eas Mor (Great Waterfall) rather than the camp-site. Only when we were approaching the Eas Mor did I begin to suspect what we'd done. A look at the map confirmed it. We had made an embarrassing mistake! And the penalty for me was that I had to go all the way back up to Sgurr nan Eag after what had already been an eight-and-a-half hour day with 5,500 feet of ascent.

First I went down to the camp-site with Chris. Paul was waiting impatiently, ready to go. I said farewell and they drove off. Without them

I couldn't have done the Cuillin and I felt very grateful for their support.

I retired to the tent for a short rest before setting off for Sgurr nan Eag. An uneventful boggy walk across moorland rich with yellow bog asphodel and pink and purple orchids, and with views south to the islands of Soay and Eigg, led to the base of the mountain. The ascent up loose, broad slopes of grass, bog, scree and boulders was easy. The fleshy leaves and pink flowers of roseroot grew in many places. The mist had risen a little but was still down to 2,000 feet so there were no views from the cold, windy summit. I didn't mind. I had now completed the Skye peaks.

I was back at the camp after four hours. Supper was a tin of vegetable soup with some oatcakes followed by a tin of pineapple slices. There was no need to eat dehydrated food when there was a shop nearby. Since arriving in Glen Nevis it had been a week of roadside camp-sites, cycle rides and day walks. I could understand why Rick Ansell had only done the mainland Munros on a continuous round in 1984, omitting the islands because 'the ferries would have spoiled the purity of the walk'. I was looking forward to going back to backpacking. But first I had to cycle back to the Great Glen.

Chapter 8

THE ROUGH BOUNDS

'The scenery of the Highlands and Islands is that of solid rock.'
F. Fraser Darling and J. Morton Boyd
The Highlands and Islands

I was waiting at the camp-site entrance, my gear all packed, when Denise drove up with Hazel. I'd been reading an informative notice which gave details of the work of the Skye and Lochalsh Footpath Trust. I'd seen evidence of their restoration work on the path into Coire Lagan, once a wide eroded scar, now much improved.

The cycle ride up Glen Brittle, with nearly 600 feet of ascent, was tough enough for me to be glad I hadn't tried it after the long day on the Cuillin ridge. My backside still felt sore from the ride to Skye and I stood up in the saddle whenever possible. The day was broken by stops for refreshments, Sligachan for lunch, Breakish where the Seagull Restaurant served an excellent Greek salad, Balmacara for soft drinks and fudge from the shop. As arranged I met Denise and Hazel at the first two. Cycling over the massive out-of-place new bridge I didn't feel as though I was leaving an island. I could barely see the sea. The tolls are an outrage. Petitions against them were everywhere on Skye and around Kyle of Lochalsh. At Shiel Bridge I had a final reunion with Denise and Hazel. As it was 7 p.m. and Invergarry, my cycling destination, was at least three hours ride away, I decided to stay on the camp-site there. I'd only come 28 miles but I was tired.

As it was a Saturday night the site, a small, somewhat boggy field tucked away behind the Glen Shiel general store and restaurant, was crowded and quite noisy. The weather had been dull and cloudy all day. Now occasional short showers kept me in the tent while I ate the delicious home-cooked chickpea stew Denise had brought for me. The sharp, fresh taste was a joy after all the tinned and dried food.

The night was warm and humid. I fell asleep around midnight to the sound of recorded accordion music booming out. The same music woke me at 6.30 a.m. I suspected it had been playing all night. Still, I thought, tonight should be my first wild camp in a week.

All packed up, I sat in the café reading. Denise arrived mid-morning and we loaded my full pack into the car. A box of supplies was left at the shop as I would be back here in 12 days. I cycled up Glen Shiel and past Loch Cluanie, joining Denise for lunch on a grassy bank near the Cluanie Inn. The toughest part of the day was the long 1,000 foot plus climb above a very low Loch Loyne reservoir. Compensation for that was a very fast descent down to Glen Garry. The cycling finished in the Great Glen at the southern end of Loch Oich and I left the bike with Denise, glad I would not be seeing it for a while and that there weren't any long cycling sections left. My backside was very painful!

My route now lay west to Knoydart then back north to Shiel Bridge. This is all wild, rugged country with steep, rocky hills. There are few long ridges and I didn't expect to be able to climb more than a few summits a day. Great sea lochs, reminiscent of Norwegian fjords, push inland either side of the stubby peninsula of Knoydart, cutting it off from the lands to either side. The only village is Inverie on the coast near the mouth of Loch Nevis. There is no road to it, the only village of which this is true in mainland Britain. Access is either over the mountains or by ferry from Mallaig. Denise had sent a food box there as it was the only resupply place for the next 12 days.

Knoydart was still some way off however as I started along the forestry track beside Loch Lochy, my pack heavy with six days supply of food. My immediate aim was a high-level camp between the two Munros west of the loch, Sron a'Choire Ghairbh and Meall na Teanga. A good path led up beside the Allt Glas Dhoire to the Cam Bhealach. I camped right on the summit of the pass at 2,000 feet. A wild site again! The only sounds were the right ones, the wind and the trickle of a burn. A breeze kept the midges away and I sat in the tent doorway looking out on a pink sunset fading over the hills to the west. Deer barked sharply on the nearby hillsides.

The silence of the mountains had a soothing effect and I slept for nine hours, the most for over a week. In the morning a thin, dry mist covered the pass though I could see the line of the hill above. The deep, twisting, guttural call of a ptarmigan broke the quiet. The two hills either side of the pass were climbed quickly. Sron a'Choire Ghairbh was swirling with cloud but by the time I reached Meall na Teanga the mist had lifted though distant hills were still covered.

With a full pack now I walked west to Gleann Cia-aig and then down through forest to the Eas Chia-aig, an impressive double waterfall. Here the glen reaches the road through the Mile Dorcha, the Dark Mile, a steep-sided wooded glen linking Lochs Arkaig and Lochy. Turning west I followed the track along the south side of Loch Arkaig to the start of Glen Mallie. The scenery was pleasant but somewhat undramatic after the Cuillin. I read much of the way on the track down through the forest to the Dark Mile and then again along Loch Arkaig. The book, a thriller I'd bought in the Glen Shiel shop, was not very good.

Inver Mallie bothy stands at the foot of Glen Mallie. I had been going to walk further but the bothy was empty and a strong, gusty wind made camping less attractive than a night between solid walls. Also I'd felt listless, uninspired and a little weary all day. An anti-climax after the exhausting excitement of the Cuillin I guessed. Inver Mallie is a fairly large building with four rooms downstairs, two of them quite big, and three attics. Inside it was fairly clean and tidy though there was a large collection of beer cans and whisky bottles. It's a fairly accessible bothy, only a few miles from the nearest road, and the bothy book showed that some visitors came here mainly to have a party. In the last nine days only three individuals had stayed here however.

Rain fell most of the night – at least I heard it on the roof both times I woke up, once disturbed by the scratching of a mouse, once by deer calling outside. Morning brought short, sharp showers and a strong south-west wind. The shorts and sandals of yesterday were swapped for long pants and boots.

The day started with an uneventful five-and-a-half mile walk up Glen Mallie to the foot of Gulvain. As I began the climb to the col north-east of the summit ridge of this hill the rain began, light at first, but soon becoming heavier. I donned my rain jacket and pushed on into the cloud to the col. Here I was greeted by a very strong, gusty, south-west wind and lashing rain. I hastily pulled my rain pants on and climbed to the north and highest Top. The ridge along to the South Top, which although lower, has a triangulation point on it, was narrower and more interesting than I remembered from previous visits. The weather was now dominating the day however and I quickly left the ridge, descending north down steep, slippery, moss and rock covered slopes, thoughts of attempting any further summits abandoned. Instead my aim – and great desire – was to reach the bothy in Glen Pean. The shallow bowl of Fraoch

Mor above Gleann Camgharaidh was dotted with hoary old birch trees, purple orchids and masses of new burns swirling with brown water. Once across the glen I climbed the ridge to the north then descended more rough, tussocky slopes to the bridge over the river Pean just west of Strathan. Vehicles were parked outside the houses there and a party of walkers was coming down the track from the forest.

I went the other way, west through the plantations to Pean bothy. Foxgloves gave an occasional bright touch to the dull green dripping trees. One other walker was in the bothy, his wet gear strewn everywhere. He had spent the last two days walking from Inverie and was heading for Glen Finnan where he'd left his car. Richard's main interest was in competitive rowing, a subject about which I know little and in which I'm not really very interested, and he talked at great length about coaching teams and international competitions. I half-listened, nodding at what seemed appropriate moments, while I cooked dinner and scanned the pages of the bothy book. Pean was a bothy I'd used often a decade and more ago but it was now some years since I'd been there. In the interval it had been much improved. The single barn-like downstairs room had now been divided, the smaller section having wooden sleeping platforms, a table and chairs.

In the evening many deer came down to the meadows by the river to graze. A notice in the bothy spoke of the need for stalking, how it gave local employment, kept families in the glens and reduced the deer numbers so the forest could regenerate. It sounded like a social service. Outside there were no young trees however, no trees at all apart from the fenced-in plantations. Nor were there any families. A rejoinder had been added to the bottom of the notice that started reasonably but ended up totally intemperate. I agreed with the general sentiments however. The main point was that the glens supported more people before the sporting estates were created. Here on the edge of Knoydart stating that stalking kept people in the glens was an audacious not to say insulting claim given the numbers who were cleared from the area, initially to make way for sheep and then for deer.

Bothies are not, as is often believed, the homes of those cleared from the land. In fact they were built after the Clearances and are mostly either old shooting lodges or cottages built for keepers or shepherds. According to notes made in the 1980s by a Canadian descendant of the family who lived here, and copied into the current bothy book by Sandy Cousins, Pean was built in 1880 to house the shepherd Ewen Campbell and his family of seven. They'd previously lived in a house across the river, the ruins of which are still visible, but had been flooded out twice. Potatoes were grown here, other supplies coming in twice a year by boat up Loch Arkaig. The family left in the 1920s. It was hard to imagine them living here. It feels isolated now, despite the road along Loch Arkaig. Back then, with no modern communications, it would have been extremely remote and cut-off.

The storm continued into the morning. Richard staggered off under a massive load. I dawdled over a prolonged breakfast, hoping the weather would improve. For once this ploy didn't work. The rain grew heavier and the cloud dropped lower down the hillsides. The pressure was the lowest since the big storm in the Cairngorms a month ago. On the long, rough ridge to the south across Glen Pean lay two Munros. I finally set off for them in mid-morning. It was an even wetter day than the previous one with lashing rain all day. The hillsides were covered with white, foaming burns. Water was just covering the stepping stones in the river but I could still cross them without the water running into my boots. I climbed south-west into Coire Dhuibh and then Coire nan Gall, aiming for the west end of the ridge. Walking the ridge west to east would put the wind and rain at least partly at my back. The cloud rose a little and I could see Loch Morar far below and, in the other direction, Glenfinnan, as I reached the ridge just east of the first peak, Sgurr nan Coireachan. At the summit I sat in the shelter of the cairn and gulped down a chocolate bar before venturing onto the traverse to Sgurr Thuilm. Walking the stony, bumpy ridge was quite interesting as hail blasted in on gusts of wind that blew me about, nearly knocking me over at times. The grey shapes of nearby peaks appeared and disappeared in the clouds, sometimes quite solid and sharp, at others vague and insubstantial. From Sgurr Thuilm I descended directly north to the bothy. The ground was completely sodden with pools everywhere and a myriad tiny but powerful burns spurted down the hillside.

I was back in the glen in less than five hours. The stepping stones were now well underwater with rapids pouring over them. I waded across a little further downstream where the river was wider and a spit of gravel jutted at an angle across it. Even here the flow was strong and the water knee-deep. I had considered packing up and moving to A'Chuil bothy in Glen Dessary to be nearer the hills I planned on climbing the next day but decided to stay in Pean and try to dry out some of my wet gear. To this end I went out to search for some wood but could only find a bit of kindling in the plantation. I filled my water bottles at the river then returned to the bothy. With no need to go out again and feeling clammy and chilly I changed into dry clothing. I'd worn my rain pants over bare legs so my trousers were dry. I had some dry socks too and my fleece sweater. Everything else was damp or soaked. I wore my warm hat as well as the temperature had dropped and was now 13°C, which felt quite cool in the damp air. Outside white sheets of wind-driven rain were sweeping down the glen.

The streams on the hillside opposite had vanished or dwindled to trickles when I looked out in the morning. The rain had stopped but the wind still blew. Bursts of sunshine suddenly illuminated patches of mountainside. It was the first of August and the 76th day of the walk.

I walked on forest tracks round into Glen Dessarry and up to A'Chuil bothy. To the north lay another Sgurr nan Coireachan. Steep slopes led to the summit. I reached it just as the cloud lifted. To the west lay the extremely rough and rocky, winding, twisted Garbh Chioch ridge, a favourite from several previous traverses. Cloud swirled over the mountainsides, giving sudden, startling views of sheer drops and big cliffs on either side. A wall runs along the crest, in places set right on the edge of the crags and climbing at absurd angles in others. The cloud was thick on Garbh Chioch Beag but abruptly vanished on higher Garbh Chioch Mor to reveal the soaring pyramid of Sgurr na Ciche straight ahead and the silver, sun-reflecting flash of Loch Nevis far below. Mist coming and going at all levels and the very strong wind made for a disorientating descent to the col below Sgurr na Ciche. For a brief moment the enveloping clouds split apart to reveal a more distant cone of bright, white cloud tapering down to the shining surface of Loch Nevis between banks of grey mist.

Sgurr na Ciche, a splendid rocky peak, is steep on all sides. From the col I scrambled up rough scree and boulders to the tiny summit. I could barely stand up in the wind so set off down straightaway. The long south-west ridge runs all the way down to sea level. It's steep at first and I had some fun scrambling down rocks in the high winds. It then becomes easier and broader for the main part before ending in steep craggy slopes above Loch Nevis. I didn't choose a good line here and it took quite a while to pick a way round small crags and smooth slabs and then stumble through tall bracken that hid knee-high boulders to the shore. Loch Nevis was as beautiful as ever, shining calmly between steep hillsides. The smell of the sea greeted me and the shore was covered with strands of seaweed and broken shells. There is a small bothy here, Sourlies, but in maybe ten visits I'd never found it empty. This time it was. Inside the single room there are sleeping platforms and cooking benches plus old fishing nets and floats and other flotsam gathered from the loch shore hanging from the walls and the low ceiling giving it a quaint fisherman's cottage look. I moved in for my fourth night in a row in a bothy. Outside a pale rosy sunset coloured the western sky. I'd run out of books to read but the bothy sported a copy of *The Hobbit*, sans the first 50 pages, and a thriller I'd never heard of and quickly abandoned as it was all super-tough macho-violent nonsense. Tolkien would do for now. By the next evening I should be in Inverie collecting my supply box.

Gentle, misty drizzle greeted me the next morning. It was high tide so I had to climb through the bracken and crags above the loch to cross the headland north of the bothy then descend to the marshes bordering the river Carnach. I crossed the bridge to the ruins of Carnoch. A large notice said 'No Camping except around Sourlies' and informed me that the Camusrory estate was now managed as a nature reserve and there was no commercial stalking, though 80 hinds and 30 stags were shot each year.

An old stalkers' path runs from the ruins up to the Mam Meadail and then down Gleann Meadail to Inverie. Although it was running with water it made for fast progress. Fine, drenching showers kept sweeping in and mist was down on the pass. I was now entering Knoydart and directly north of the pass lay one of the three Knoydart Munros, Meall Buidhe. Like the others it's a steep, rugged, stony mountain. Indeed, the area used to be known as the Rough Bounds of Knoydart. Dumping the pack I climbed some steep, wet, greasy gullies filled with moss, tussocks and stones to easier ground which I then followed to the two summits which lie either end of a broad curving ridge. As I returned the same way the clouds suddenly parted and I could see down to Inverie Bay. Nearer to hand I could see a much easier way back to the pass than the one I'd ascended. The sun shone for a few minutes before the cloud closed off the view. Back at the pack after 1½ hours, I swung down the path in Gleann Meadail and was soon in Inverie, most of which consists of a line of white-washed houses looking out on the bay and the jetty. One of these was the Pier House Guest House where my supplies were and where I'd planned on staying. Until, that is, I discovered that the annual Inverie Games were being held the next day and that all accommodation was full and the camp-site packed. I repaired to The Old Forge, which claims to be the remotest pub in Britain, for coffee and toasted sandwiches while I thought about what to do. The only option seemed to be to move on a few miles then camp. The bar was crowded and cheerful. Several people had brought musical instruments – fiddles, guitars and whistles – and lively tunes rang out. The celebrations for the Games were beginning. I was strongly tempted to stay but in the end allowed the pressures of the schedule to overrule my immediate wishes.

Leaving the bar I visited Inverie's small store where I bought a few chocolate bars and gas cartridges. Denise had checked for me that the latter were sold here as I didn't want to emulate Hamish Brown who'd arrived here on his Munros walk to find no gas cartridges so had had to cook over fire-lighters for a few nights.

I was back outside packing my supplies, having just decided to move on for a few miles, when the lady from the guest house hailed me with a piece of mail from Denise that had just arrived on the afternoon boat. With her was a man who said he could provide some accommodation. Roger Trussel ran Torrie Shieling, a self-catering place a mile outside the village. Three expected guests hadn't been on the ferry so he had some space. I slung my pack in the back of his Land-Rover and climbed in. The Shieling was a converted byre and was well-appointed with showers, drying room, kitchen and comfortable living area. I shared a four bunk room with one other person. I went back to The Old Forge for dinner, happy to forego cooking for myself for once.

In the morning I went back to Inverie to phone Denise and have breakfast in the Pier Café. My plan for the day was to camp somewhere up Gleann an Dubh-Lochain and climb Ladhar Bheinn to the north from there. I read my way along the track to Loch an Dubh-Lochain. Climbing the path beyond the loch I looked for places to camp but everywhere seemed windswept, waterlogged and sloping. As I reached mist-shrouded Mam Barrisdale, the pass that separates Inverie from Barrisdale on Loch Hourn and also Ladhar Bheinn from Luinne Bheinn, heavy rain started to fall and the wind came in leg-shaking gusts. Camping up here in this seemed crazy so I didn't bother looking for a site but sloshed on down the path, hoping to find one somewhere lower down. I prospected a few possibilities but they were all sodden and exposed to the storm. Eventually I accepted that I was going to end up at Barrisdale, a small estate cottage beside Loch Hourn where you can camp on the turf outside for a token fee of 50 pence or even, for slightly more (£2), stay in the estate bothy which has electricity. When I arrived four tents were already pitched on the grass and six sleeping bags were laid out in the bothy. Strong gusts of wind swept the site but the ground was dry and firm. Most people were cooking inside the bothy but it was a bit crowded and the air was thick with cigarette smoke so I set up my kitchen in the tent porch.

Two loaded backpackers walked past the site in the early evening. A man, who I was told was the estate manager, rushed after them. I could hear nothing but the body language told me an argument was in progress. Another camper went over and joined in. Then the group broke up, the backpackers continuing up the track. The other camper told me the estate manager had told the walkers that no wild camping was allowed anywhere on the Barrisdale estate and they had to camp by the bothy. The walkers had rejected this and apparently said they came here to camp wild and weren't going to camp outside a house. Anyway, they'd said, if they headed west they'd be on John Muir Trust land and could camp where they liked. I wondered if the manager really meant anywhere on the estate or just down here near Barrisdale. It's a big estate, covering some 14,000 acres and stretching over to Loch Quoich. I'd be camping wild on it the next night.

Now that I'd had an unplanned day with no summits I would have to have some long days if I was to reach Glen Shiel before my food ran out, or without leaving too many hills unclimbed. More people arrived during the night, waking me with talking and the clashing of tent poles as they pitched camp. In the morning five more tents sat close by. The sky was clearing and I was optimistic about the weather. Ladhar Bheinn is a magnificent mountain, one of the finest in the Highlands, but my previous two ascents had been in misty weather so I hadn't really seen it. Its glory is in the great corries and ridges on its northern flanks, especially Coire Dhorrcail, and in the situation on the shores of beautiful Loch Hourn. All this is the property of the John Muir Trust. The JMT is trying to regenerate the Caledonian forest and new growth can be seen on the lower slopes of the hill.

The circuit of the two long arms that enclose Coire Dhorrcail is a superb walk. The clouds began to clear as I rounded the end of the easternmost of these arms for a view up Coire Dhorrcail to the broken cliffs at its head. After climbing up to Creag Bheithe I followed the ridge up to the foot of the final very steep slopes of soaring Stob a'Chearcaill, which doesn't reach 3,000 feet and so isn't a Munro or a Top. It's still a fine peak though. A traversing path bypassed the most precipitous section for what was still a very steep scramble up mud, grass and rock. From the top there was a wonderful walk along the narrow lip of the corrie down to the Bealach Coire Dhorrcail and then up to Ladhar Bheinn. The sky was now clear and the light sharp, probably because of the strong south wind which prevented any haze forming. There were fine views into the corrie and across Loch Hourn to lonely Beinn Sgritheall. A few other walkers were about, clearly exhilarated and

127

inspired by the views and the place. A narrow ridge led out from the summit to Stob a' Choire Odhair then down Druim a' Choire Ardair and into Coire Dhorrcail with excellent views back to the ridge.

I was glad now I hadn't climbed Ladhar Bheinn in yesterday's storm. Today the conditions had been perfect. I still had far to go however, so back at Barrisdale I had lunch before packing up and starting south on the path into Gleann Unndalain, a narrow, closed-in valley with steep sides, typical of Knoydart. There were good views ahead to bulky Luinne Bheinn and back over Barrisdale to Loch Hourn. At the unnamed pass at the head of the glen I left the pack while I climbed Luinne Bheinn, skirting round crags and following up shallow, green gullies. The sun was low in the sky now and the light dramatic. The mountain has two summits, the main one being just six feet higher than the subsidiary one. The view from both was excellent. Sgurr na Ciche and the adjacent Corbett Ben Aden, which I hadn't seen when close to because of the weather, looked impressively steep and rugged. Mealle Buidhe, not far to the west, was black and hazy (the walk between the two summits is incredibly rough and tortuous but well worth doing), while Ladhar Bheinn was darkening as the sun dropped, its shadowed peaks and ridges different shades of grey. To the north the light was less good but The Saddle above Glen Shiel stood out as two rugged ridges meeting at a tiny point. Further north faint peaks were visible while further west the Cuillin were a hazy mass of jagged outlines, the individual summits just identifiable.

Tearing myself away from the view I trotted back down to the pass, collected the pack, and continued on, still on a good path, to long, narrow Lochan nam Breac, which had stood out from Luinne Bheinn, with beyond it Loch Quoich and the cone of Sgurr Mor looking very smooth and symmetrical after the seemingly random complex ruggedness of the Knoydart peaks. Lochan nam Breac fits neatly into a narrow defile between Ben Aden and Druim Chosaidh, an impressive location.

The path stays above the crag-lined shore then descends to the east end where there is a sandy beach backed by a flat area of grass and reeds. This was where I intended camping. As I approached I saw someone else had had the same idea. A grey tent was pitched by an inlet stream. To camp away from it I had to ford this stream. It looked more than boot deep so I crossed in just my socks – they needed a wash! After a bit of searching amongst the tussocks and bogs I found a dry, grassy spot, close to the lochan, on which I could just squeeze the tent. It was a lovely spot.

Chris Ainsworth and Paul Riley in Coire a'Bhasteir on the way to Sgurr nan Gillean and Am Basteir, 24 July

Chris Ainsworth on the Bealach a'Bhasteir looking to Bla Bheinn and Loch Coruisk, 24 July

Sgurr Eilde Mor in the Mamores, 20 July

Sgurr a'Mhaim and Stob Ban in the Mamores, 20 July

Chris Ainsworth on Sgurr na Banachdich with Sgurr Dearg behind, 24 July

Ladhar Bheinn and Coire Dhorrcail, 4 August

Beinn Sgritheall and Loch Hourn from Coire Dhorrcail, 4 August

Luinne Bheinn and Lochan nam Breac, 4 August

Rainbows and storm at dusk, Glen Torridon, 26 August

John Manning, Katarina Tomcanyova and Jan Dulla on Liathach, 26 August

The finish! Celebrating with Chris
Brasher on the summit of Ben Hope,
12 September

With Denise and Hazel after the
ascent of Ben Hope, 12 September

Meall Buidhe rose up beyond the far end of the loch as a shapely pointed peak. Behind it a splendid sunset spread across the sky. The steep slopes round the lochan supported little tree-covered crags. The weather wasn't so good however. Powerful gusts of wind roared down the loch and shook the tent. In the total calm between the gusts midges appeared. It had been a magnificent but hard day and I'd been out 12 hours and had climbed 8,600 feet of rough terrain. I felt tired and hoped the wind wouldn't keep me awake. Unfortunately it did. The night was possibly the windiest of the whole trip. Strong gusts shook the tent, waking me frequently. In the morning the summits were clear, the sky hazy with a weak sun appearing at times though thicker clouds were streaming across from the south. When the wind paused I could hear bird song and running water.

The weather ended my original plans for the day. I followed the path on down east to the ugly, artificial shoreline of the Loch Quoich reservoir. A rough mile and a half mostly on the whitened stones of the shore led to an old path up into Coire Reidh, the northern end of which now simply disappears into the waters of Loch Quoich. As I climbed into the corrie I began to wonder what to do. It was starting to rain and I felt tired after two nights of broken sleep and a long, hard day the day before. The wind was still very strong and I didn't fancy another night in a shaking tent. My plan had been to traverse the long ridge between Loch Quoich and Glen Kingie over Sgurr Mor and then Gairich, which would be a long, high-level day. This didn't now seem a good idea. Instead I decided to head for Kinbreack bothy in Glen Kingie to the south and climb Sgurr Mor without the pack from the col.

This proved to be the right decision as the storm worsened. I went up Sgurr Mor in wild weather, with lashing rain, dense mist and a wind it was hard to walk into. Staying high all the way to Gairich with the pack would have been exhausting and unpleasant even if actually possible. Just before the summit I met two walkers descending. 'I thought we were the only ones mad enough to be out in this,' said one of them as they passed me.

Back at the pack I continued on the path into boggy Glen Kingie. The bothy lies on the far slopes of the wide glen so once I could see it I forded the river and struck up to it. As on other visits I was struck by the wide, open feel of the glen after the narrow, hemmed-in Knoydart ones. In the Kinbreack bothy book a writer said how much she wished she could have seen the glen when it was still forested. I agreed. It's now a desolate place. Other writers praised it however, though one said he didn't find Knoydart that scenic (Glen Kingie isn't in Knoydart of course) but reading on it appeared that what he was really missing was a pub.

Kinbreack is unusual in that the main shelter is upstairs. Downstairs is a rough stable-like room with a cobbled floor. When I first came here, again in stormy weather, I can remember feeling disappointed on seeing torn plastic sheeting in the downstairs windows and an open doorway as I approached. After going in, it was a little while before I noticed the door in the ceiling at the top of a short set of stairs. The bothy is like this because the downstairs floods periodically. The wet was the main factor in most people's comments in the bothy book with lots of descriptions of fording the river and of finding the lower room under water. One woman wrote that her boots felt no wetter after wading across the river than before. Mine had been like that on this occasion. The long upstairs room used to be very dark as there were no windows. Now there are plastic skylights so candles aren't needed at midday as they were before.

Once I'd unpacked my gear and settled into the bothy the rain stopped, the Tops cleared and the wind dropped. It was much the same in the morning though I'd been woken during the night by a very heavy shower pounding on the roof. Mist was clearing from the glen floor as I set off for Gairich. It took four hours to climb this isolated peak and descend to the dam at the east end of Loch Quoich. There was a good path most of the way including one down the steep and craggy east ridge of the mountain. The best views of the peak were looking back to it over Loch Quoich. There were no views from the top as it was very hazy.

There were cars and tents by the dam but no sign of any people. A steep, relentless, hot and sweaty climb led straight up Spidean Mialach to the north. This peak lies at the eastern end of a fine ridge that separates Loch Quoich from Easter Glen Quoich. The south side of the ridge is fairly featureless, the north is more dramatic with rocky spurs and craggy corries. Beyond Easter Glen Quoich rises the huge southern wall of the South Glen Shiel Ridge, massive and unbroken.

From the small rocky summit of Spidean Mialach I walked west along the ridge to Craig Coire na Fiar Bhealaich and Gleouraich. On the descent of the former I paused to take a photograph of silvery Loch Quoich and the grey hazy peaks rising beyond it. After I'd put the camera back in its pouch I realised it was absolutely silent. No wind, no distant running water, no engines of planes or cars, no insects, no birds. Total quiet. Total stillness. It felt as though the world had stopped and was waiting for something to happen. A pause in time. After some moments during which I almost held my breath I broke the spell and moved on, pack

130

harness creaking. Soon a breeze whispered in the grass and I could hear the trickle of a distant burn far below. But it had been a rare moment of magic. How often can you hear the silence?

From Gleouraich, another neat little peak, I turned north on a sketchy path that led down the narrow ridge of Sron na Breun Leitir. Beyond this faint trail I located an old stalkers' path that zigzagged down to the northwest. This path is marked on the map but much of it is grassed over and appeared little used even by deer. Down in the glen it joined the track to the lodge at Alltbeithe where cars were parked and windows were open. Preparing for the stalking season I guessed. I'd hoped to go on to Sgurr a'Mhaoraich but as I'd been out over nine hours on what was a humid, enervating day I decided instead to look for a camp-site in Glen Quoich. Like other deforested western glens it's mostly bog and not ideal for camping. After half an hour searching I ended up on a small island in the river Quoich. It wasn't flat but it was dry and grassy. I'd camped here once before, in 1981, on my 500-mile walk from Ben Lomond to Ben Hope. I'd been joined here by a friend, Alain Kahan. By luck we'd timed our meeting at Alltbeithe perfectly, he walking down Easter Glen Quoich as I walked in from Loch Quoich.

For the first time on the walk my feet ached and it was with relief that I took my boots off. Both they and my feet steamed profusely. The heat was the problem. I should have worn sandals. There was much fresh cattle dung on the island and in the river so I was careful with water, either boiling it or else treating it with Micropur tablets, the only time I used these on the whole walk. The day ended with the midges coming out and a subdued reddish sunset. Bands of mist floated down the valley.

Midges covered the inside of the flysheet the next morning so for the first time I put my start-of-day anti-midge procedure into action. This consists of lighting a midge coil in the inner tent, unzipping a short section of the inner door, slipping the smoking coil into the porch then zipping the inner shut. While the smoke drives the midges out, or kills them, I get dressed. Then I open the inner door and use a piece of tissue to wipe the dead midges off the porch walls.

Outside the sky was overcast and cloud covered the Tops. The six mile round trip up and down Sgurr a'Mhaoraich and Sgurr a'Mhaoraich Beag took three-and-a-half hours. This hill lies at the head of Loch Hourn and has good views down the loch. I was not to see these however as dense mist lay above 2,500 feet. A hazy sun was just visible through it which made me think it might lift or dissipate. It didn't and compass bearings were needed to find both summits.

131

Having struck camp I followed the cow-churned muddy path up Glen Quoich, passing through a herd of 50 of the beasts at one point. Higher up the glen the path disappeared and then reappeared again faintly on the climb to the Bealach Duibh Leac. On the misty pass I met the first walker I'd seen for two days. A cairned path led down to the A87 in Glen Shiel along which I then slogged to the camp-site. Overall it had been a dull, uneventful day. I read *The Brothers Karamazov* up the track in Glen Quoich – a gloomy book in keeping with the weather. There had been few birds or animals around, just one buzzard near the A87, then a heron in the reed beds by Loch Shiel. Overall I was seeing much less wildlife in the rugged west than I had on the moorland mountains in the east.

The camp-site was quite full. One of the campers I recognised. It was Richard from Pean bothy who'd driven from Glenfinnan and was now sticking to day walks. The shop produced a newspaper and some tinned food plus my supply box. I had dinner in the restaurant and thought about my plans for the next few days.

I would start, I decided, with a rest day. Skye didn't seem that long ago but it was two weeks since the day off at Sligachan. The Rough Bounds of Knoydart had lived up to their name and it had taken ten days to climb 23 Tops. Due mainly to the bad weather I had reached Glen Shiel without climbing The Saddle or Beinn Sgritheall. The first could be done as a day walk but the second would probably take two days. Then I would walk the two long ridges either side of the glen. This meant I was probably going to be based in Glen Shiel for at least four nights.

Chapter 9

KINTAIL DAYS

8 – 13 AUGUST SHIEL BRIDGE 65 MILES 28 SUMMITS

'The mountains are the ultimate realm of wild nature.'

Jim Crumley
Among Mountains

A lazy day ensued. During the afternoon I wandered down the glen to look at placid Loch Duich but most of the time was spent sitting in the café at the camp-site as the weather was dull with rain in the afternoon. My journal was brought up to date, another report for *TGO* written, some postcards scrawled and sent. Much of the time though I spent poring over the map working out my plans for the next few days, having been told when I rang Denise that Chris Brasher would arrive the next day and had offered to put me up in luxury in the Kinloch Lodge Hotel. With him would be Bill Wallace, whom I knew from his work in various SMC guidebooks, especially *Ski Mountaineering in Scotland* of which he was one of the editors, and who I was to find out was a past President of the SMC and a trustee of the JMT.

After playing with various possibilities I came up with a plan that seemed to make sense. I would find out if the weather let me. The forecast was promising: clear weather for the next three days. The idea was to climb The Saddle, which I'd originally planned on doing on the way over from Glen Quoich, the next day and be back in time to move to the hotel in the early evening. With Chris and Bill I would do the South Glen Shiel Ridge, camping at Cluanie and then returning to Shiel Bridge along the North Glen Shiel Ridge. Beinn Sgritheall, another hill I'd planned on having done by now, would come next. It looked as though Shiel Bridge would be my base for the next five days. Luckily the café was a relaxed, not to say laid-back, place in which I could spread out my maps and sit over cups of coffee for hours while the shop provided extra

133

groceries, newspapers and odds and ends of camping gear. The staff were very friendly though communications could be difficult. When I asked the young assistant, whose accent suggested she came from Spain, if she had any tent pegs she produced a box of Tampax. By the end of my stay the owner had become curious about me and I was chatting to him about the walk. Although obviously fond of the area he was not a hill-walker and clearly regarded my walk as madness.

A breeze sprang up during the night so there were no midges at dawn. The cloud had risen too and bits of mackerel sky – that pattern of small fish-scale-like clouds that often presages good weather – gave hope for a fine day. My goal was The Saddle (An Diollaid in Gaelic), one of the great mountains of the Highlands. Long, narrow ridges meet at the summit above deep rocky corries and it's steep on every side. The size of the mountain is shown by the six Tops that lie on the ridges either side of the Munro.

The finest ascent route is the classic scramble up the knife-edge Forcan Ridge. However four of the Tops lie west of the main summit, the opposite side to the Forcan Ridge, and as I wanted to go on to another hill, Sgurr na Sgine, from The Saddle it made sense to climb those summits first. Passing through the gate at the back of the camp-site I took the path that runs up beside the Allt Undalain and then into Coire nan Crogachan. Eventually this path crosses the north end of a long ridge that leads to The Saddle and descends into Glen More to the west. I intended walking up this path to the ridge then following the latter to the Tops, a long approach but seemingly the most practical one. However at a height of about 1,000 feet I found the faint line of an old, little-used stalkers' path that traversed south across the upper slopes of Coire Uaine, a fine corrie backed by steep slopes and green vegetated crags, and then climbed to the ridge at a little lochan. Following this forgotten path was interesting. Every so often it would disappear and I would have to guess the line. I amused myself at how satisfied I felt when I got it right and the path reappeared.

Although the sky stayed dark and overcast the summits were clear and the walk on the fairly narrow rocky ridge round the head of Coire Uaine over Sgurr Leac nan Each and Spidean Dhomhuill Bhric to the cluster of four summits that make up The Saddle was enjoyable. There wasn't much in the way of distant views as the sky was hazy but the immediate scene was very impressive. The West Top and East Top are really no more than little bumps on the ridge but the distinction between the Trig Point and the actual summit, which lies some 100 yards away on a level stretch of grassy ground, is minimal. In *Munro's Tables* both points are given the same height. A note says 'observation on the ground gives the impression that the main summit of The Saddle is slightly higher than the Trig Point.' Perhaps. But whether there's a height difference or not this is clearly only one summit not two. (In the 1997 revision of the *Tables* the East and West Tops and the Trig Point were all deleted.)

A scramble, mostly easy but with one awkward steep bit, leads along a narrow rock ridge from The Saddle to Sgurr na Forcan at the top of the Forcan Ridge. This airy little peak is a true separate summit. The view back to The Saddle is dramatic, the connecting ridge looking far harder than it actually is. Steep slopes fall away on either side but as everywhere on The Saddle the crags are small and broken and there is a surprising amount of green. I was able to make a direct descent west from Sgurr na Forcan down green gullies between splintered rock slabs to the Bealach Coire Mhalagain. Immediately above lay the twin summits of Sgurr na Sgine. Again I'm not sure that the North-West Top merits its classification as a Top as it's just a brief stroll from the main summit.

From Sgurr na Sgine I returned to the bealach and then traversed below the Forcan Ridge to the col at the head of Choire Chaoil down which I descended back to Glen Shiel. A few people were on the path near the camp-site but otherwise the hills were empty, which surprised me as most people on the crowded camp-site seemed to be walkers.

After moving down the road to the Kinloch Lodge Hotel, which lies on the shores of Loch Duich, I had time for a much-needed bath before Chris and Bill arrived. After a good dinner we went to Morvich to visit the head ranger on the NTS Kintail and Affric estates, whom Chris knew as he was on the management committee for the latter. Willie was preparing for the stalking season, during which he was to test a new high-topped Brasher boot. So far he seemed to feel that they were too smart for the hills but fine for the bar.

An overcast sky greeted us the following morning. The walking began on the path up to the Bealach Duibh Leac. Undulating east from this high col is the South Glen Shiel Ridge. There are seven Munros on the seven mile long ridge and only once does it drop below 2,600 feet. The traverse of the whole ridge is a wonderful walk with, when it's clear, good views. We however were not to have these. The rain began on the first summit, Creag nan Damh. The forecast was for showers but as Bill remarked this looked the sort of rain that sets in for the day. And it did – all the way along the ridge. There was no wind, just a steady downpour and thick mist.

On the second summit, Sgurr an Lochain, we stopped for lunch. Chris produced a tiny ultralightweight titanium gas stove and a small pan from his rucksack and made up a packet of onion soup, which was welcome. These first two Munros were new ones for Bill. He'd previously skied the rest of the ridge.

With no views, Sgurr an Doire Leathain and Maol Chinn-dearg came and went in the mist. On the highest peak on the ridge, Aonach air-Chrith, a party of walkers was sitting by the cairn. Bill and I chatted to them and discovered they were a Ramblers' Association group from Peebles walking the ridge the other way to us. Meanwhile Chris walked about trying to get good reception on his mobile phone. One of his horses, The Maid, was racing that day and he wanted the results. Someone in the group we were talking to recognised him. 'Isn't that Chris Brasher?' We said it was. There was a pause. 'Er, what's he doing?' 'Listening to a horse race,' we said, as though it was obvious. Chris came over. The Maid hadn't won but had done well and he was pleased.

Chris and Bill left me on the penultimate summit, Druim Shionnach, for a direct descent to the Cluanie Inn so I did the last Munro, Creag a'Mhaim, alone. I was still down at the road before them, mainly because they had a mostly pathless boggy descent while I found a path just beyond Creag a'Mhaim that led north down to the bridge over the Allt Giubhais a couple of miles from Cluanie. Although not on the map it was a well-used path. In the lower section a large forestry plantation appeared with a high deer fence around it. There was no gate or stile but the path clearly continued inside the enclosure so I climbed the fence. On the other side I had to do the same again.

As I descended the sky began to clear. At first blue sky and sunshine were visible far to the east under a blanket of grey. Then the cloud began to break above me and the rain faded away. By the time I reached Loch Cluanie it was a beautiful, clear evening. The ridge we'd just walked looked tremendous, the summits gold in the evening sun. After my last traverse of the ridge, many years earlier, I'd camped by Loch Cluanie and I was planning on doing the same this time. A large sign however stated that camping was strictly forbidden. As the road and the Inn were visible from here ignoring the notice seemed unwise. I hadn't been thrown off anywhere yet and I'd rather it stayed that way.

All the camping gear was in Bill's car in Shiel Bridge as the idea had been that he would hitch-hike back to collect it. This way we'd been able to carry light loads. We still needed the car so Bill looked round for a lift. He approached a man in the car park. 'I can't take the risk,' was the alarmed response. The driver was clearly not a hill-walker (seeking a ride after a walk of one of the Glen Shiel ridges is quite common) and also somewhat paranoid as Bill looks quite inoffensive and had obviously been out walking. The next person he asked was a walker who gladly whisked him down the glen.

Meanwhile Chris was in the bar ordering some pints of ginger beer shandy. He was also trying to find rooms for us plus dinner. 'The Maid's done well,' he said, 'she can stand us a room.' The Cluanie Inn was full however, as was everywhere he rang. A Saturday evening in August was not a good time to find accommodation. The Inn had also just stopped serving food although it was only 8 p.m., much to the disgust of two walkers who'd arrived just before us and whom we'd met on and off all day. They'd left bikes here and were soon pedalling off down the glen in search of food.

Once Bill returned we followed the cyclists down the glen, seeking accommodation as well as food. Between Cluanie and Dornie we must have knocked on the door of every B&B and stopped at every restaurant. The first were all full, the second all closed. 'Try the pub in Dornie,' we were told, 'they do bar food.' We did and they did. Fish and chips. The bar was packed but the accents were mostly American, along with a few German and Spanish ones. It turned out a pipe band from the USA was staying here.

Having failed to find a room we returned to the Glen Shiel camp-site. Bill had brought a giant bright yellow geodesic dome that dwarfed my tent and had plenty of room for the three us to sit inside having a night-cap of the Lagavulin whisky Chris had brought. I used my steel mug but Chris and Bill had plastic mugs and complained that they could still taste the onion soup we'd had for lunch.

A beautiful starry sky made for a cool night, just 8°C in the morning. We breakfasted in Bill's tent, making camp coffee by tipping hot water on ground coffee in a pan. A tap on the side with a spoon settled the grounds. 'I can still taste onion soup,' said Chris, 'and whisky.' He and Bill were now going to Loch Mullardoch where Bill had access to a private estate cabin as he knew the owner. They dropped me at Cluanie.

The North Glen Shiel Ridge parallels the ridge to the south then turns northwards and continues as the Five Sisters of Kintail. Together the two are sometimes called the Brothers and Sisters Ridge. It's an even more splendid ridge than that of South Glen Shiel with more rugged scenery and steep, more distinctive peaks, six of which are Munros and four Tops (at that time of the walk, seven Munros and three Tops after the 1997

137

revision). It's only a slightly longer walk but even starting from the higher Cluanie end there's 1,725 more feet of ascent (8,100 feet as opposed to 6,375 feet) so it's a more arduous undertaking.

Instead of rain and mist I had sunshine and good visibility however. There was no haze either. Ben Nevis was in and out of cloud all day but all the other hills were clear. The Cuillin were a jagged silhouette while to the north Liathach in Torridon looked surprisingly close. I could see details of ribs and gullies on its flanks. It would still be two weeks before I was there. To the south-west a tangle of peaks and ridges rolled into the distance with Sgurr na Ciche and Ladhar Bheinn, the first a sharp pyramid, the second a flat-topped wedge, dominating the view.

The most awkward hill on the North Glen Shiel Ridge is Ciste Dhubh which lies out on its own to the north. After walking up An Caorann Beag I joined the ridge at the Bealach a'Choinich and went out and back to Ciste Dhubh. It's a fine, pointed little peak that gave good views of the main ridge. Sgurr an Fhuarail and Aonach Meadhoin are the first Tops, lying either end of a dipping, narrow crest. The peaks then came thick and fast. On a ridge like this it's the continuous high-level walking that is the joy rather than reaching individual summits. I met a few people but was surprised there were not more about on a fine Sunday in August.

Beyond Aonach Meadhoin a long, gentle descent is followed by a short, steep uphill climb to Sgurr a'Bhealaich Dheirg. The top lies at the end of a little rocky arête just off the main ridge. A large well-built cairn stands on the tiny summit, completely blocking the ridge. As I clambered round this cairn another walker arrived and started out along the arête. He moved awkwardly and was clearly unhappy on the rocks, stopping before he reached the summit. I'd found the walk simple but I was well aware that it was all relative. The way he looked to me was probably how I'd looked to Chris and Paul in the Cuillin.

Next came Saileag, at the head of a northward-running spur separating rugged Fhraoch-choire from huge Choire Dhomdain, and then Sgurr nan Spainteach, the Peak of the Spaniards beyond which the Five Sisters begin. Someone had left a large white flag on a pole with 'Spainteach' emblazoned on it on a subsidiary top. The name comes from the Battle of Glen Shiel, a minor skirmish in 1719 which involved a Spanish contingent. The ridge becomes steeper and rougher as it traverses Sgurr na Ciste Duibhe and Sgurr na Carnach to the highest and finest peak on the ridge Sgurr Fhuaran. These peaks encircle Coire Dhomhain, a fine sight with its craggy walls falling into steep, grassy depths. The view across the corrie from Sgurr na Ciste Duibhe to Sgurr Fhuaran is particularly spectacular though the views throughout the walk over these peaks are superb.

As I left Sgurr Fhuaran small white clouds began to cover distant hills while other clouds were creeping slowly up some of the glens. This didn't seem significant yet within minutes of leaving the next and final summit of the day, Sgurr nan Saighead, dense mist swept up from Glen Shiel and enveloped me, a rapid and unexpected change. I followed a path north-west towards little Sgurr an-t Searraich, its dark pyramid summit fading in and out of the swirling clouds and glowing gold in the sun, whose pale disc, silver in the mist, appeared now and then. It was an unreal, magical sight.

I came out of the mist but lost the path on the final descent down very steep craggy slopes and then through head-high bracken to the river just south of Shiel Bridge. Darkness was falling as I reached the tent after an 11-hour day.

Denise and Hazel arrived the next morning, the first time I'd seen them for a fortnight. Apart from a short stroll beside Loch Duich we spent most of the day in various cafés talking and snacking. After climbing 26 Tops in the last three days I was quite happy to have an easier day though I was intending moving on later. We collected a box of my stuff from the Kinloch Lodge Hotel, then left another box at the Glen Shiel shop. Denise and Hazel set off for home in the late afternoon and I walked over the pass at the head of Coire Crogachan, the one I'd almost reached the day I'd climbed The Saddle, and descended to Glen More and Suardalan bothy. A Dutch couple were inside and a fire was smouldering in the grate. 'Skye next,' they said. Their great desire was to see some red deer though so far they'd had no luck.

Dense mist hung just above the bothy as I set out for Beinn Sgritheall the next morning. I went up by the north-east ridge, a fine route finishing with a narrow, rocky section with steep drops into Coire Min. It was calm, windless and very humid and I was soaked with sweat when I reached the top. There were no views however, a shame as this mountain is in a superb situation overlooking Loch Hourn. Two people and two dogs were sitting by the summit cairn. 'I'd been wondering when I'd meet you,' said one, a young man with an earring and ponytail. Ben was a hill-walking guide based in Glenelg just to the north. He knew about my walk and as he was out most days in the western and northern Highlands had expected to bump into me somewhere. Today he had one client, Ken from Devon, who'd never climbed a Scottish mountain before. After talking for a while they went off down to Arnisdale and I navigated on compass bearings to the NW Top before returning to Suardalan. In Gleann Beag I met three walkers by Loch Iain Mhic Aonghais, a tiny lochan at the head of the glen. They seemed very disappointed at how small it was. Maybe the name made it sound large.

The skies started to clear as I walked back to Glen Shiel. Loch Duich was sparkling in sunlight as I descended for my sixth night on the Glen Shiel camp-site. I felt glad I was moving on. Although my total of summits was still rising I felt as though the journey had stalled.

Chapter 10

THE EMPTY HEART OF THE NORTH

14 – 24 AUGUST SHIEL BRIDGE TO TORRIDON 178 MILES 67 SUMMITS

'The attraction of beauty and unexpected strangeness which may lie round any corner on a mountain . . . '.

Alastair Borthwick
Always a Little Further

I began the day with a shower. It would be the last one for a while. Ahead lay a great tract of wild country, uncrossed by roads between Glen Shiel and Glen Carron, the land of the great east-west-running glens of Glen Affric, Glen Cannich and Glen Strathfarrar. Denise would drive out twice to resupply me in this remote area. Otherwise I'd have had a very heavy pack indeed. My previous walk through the region over all the Munros had been the only time I'd run out of food in the British hills. Back then I'd carried some compressed emergency rations called Turblokken which had kept me going for two days. Now I relied on walking out. More than a few extra snacks was too much to carry.

Returning to backpacking and wild camping was appealing after the last seven nights, six of which had been spent in Glen Shiel, five on the camp-site and one in a hotel, and only one in the hills, in Suardalan bothy. The walk seemed to be going in jerks and starts. Progress of course was in numbers of summits climbed not in distance covered or in moving from one place to another which made it rather an unusual journey.

As it was mid-August (already, I thought, where has the summer gone?) it was now the deer stalking season and many estates would be trying to limit where walkers could go or even exclude them completely. I did not intend asking permission to walk on the hills as to do so was to acknowledge the right of estates to control access, which I don't accept. However, I was interested to see how the estates were now reacting to walkers given the Concordat on Access, agreed between landowing and

141

outdoor recreation bodies earlier in the year. It would also be useful to know which estates might not want me there so I could keep out of the way of stalking parties or lodges. Denise offered to phone the estates to find out what they said. I would try to comply with reasonable requests, I decided, but not orders or blanket restrictions. I wasn't bothered about possibly interfering with the 'sport' of stalking. Killing animals for fun has always seemed a disturbing activity to me. As I have already made clear I think that deer numbers need reducing drastically, both for the sake of the forests and the deer, but this should be done by professionals not by paying tourists. Of course a professional hunter should take pride in being efficient and effective but I think this is totally different from killing for pleasure. Stag stalking also has little effect on deer populations as one stag can fertilise many hinds. I think it's significant that many estates don't bother about keeping walkers off when they are culling hinds, usually from mid-October to February but do during stag hunting, mid-August to mid-October. The real reason for wanting walkers to stay away is to avoid disturbing rich clients who've only got a short time in which they 'must' shoot a stag.

I could forget about stalking for the next few days however as in Kintail and Glen Affric I would be on NTS land where walkers are welcome year round and commercial deer stalking doesn't take place, though there is an annual cull by estate staff.

Finally leaving Glen Shiel I rounded the head of Loch Duich and walked up Strath Croe and Gleann Choinneachain. A good stalkers' path ran up to the Bealach an Sgairne through rugged scenery. As I climbed the cloud lifted and the sun shone. Dumping the pack – I hadn't done that in a while I realised – I climbed north up the rocky and initially steep south east ridge of A'Ghlas-bheinn to the broad slopes leading to the summit. The extensive views were dominated by the seven mile long unbroken ridge of Beinn Fhada (the name means long mountain) directly to the south.

Above the col steep, craggy slopes rose to the stubby nose of Meall a'Bhealaich. I skirted round the steepest crags then climbed steeply to a broad spur that led onto the big grassy summit plateau of Beinn Fhada, the Plaide Mhor. I hadn't been on a high-level tableland like this since Ben Alder. To the west were impressive cliffs and corries and rocky knolls. I went towards these first, to the westernmost Top, Meall an Fhuarain Mhoir.

Walking back along the length of the mountain I had superb views in the sharp late afternoon light. The finest sight was the North Glen Shiel

Ridge glowing gold in the slanting sunlight. Ladhar Bheinn, The Saddle and Sgurr na Ciche were all easily identifiable silhouettes while to the north Beinn Bhan in Applecross, a magnificent Corbett, was very distinctive. Far below on Loch a'Bhealaich in Gleann Gaorsaic a thickly wooded island stood out, contrasting with the bare shores and showing what the glens could be like if overgrazing was ended.

West of the main summit the mountain narrows, curving round Coire an t-Siosalaich to the final Top, Sgurr a'Dubh Doire, from where I descended to green-roofed Camban bothy in Fionngleann. The light on the peaks to the south was beautiful with the large cairn on craggy Sgurr a'Bhealaich Dheirg sharp and clear and below it a huge jumble of rock and boulders in Ghlas-choire. Two figures were standing outside the bothy, the Dutch couple I'd met in Suardalan the evening before last. They'd put off going to Skye for a day or two, they said, while they walked down Glen Affric in the hope of seeing the deer which still eluded them.

Camban is fairly basic even by bothy standards, with a stone flagged floor, large rocks for seats and a piece of corrugated iron laid on top of a column of rocks as a table. There is an attic upstairs. The situation however is tremendous, right underneath soaring Ciste Dhubh.

The Dutch couple were asleep and I was just about to climb up to the attic and into my sleeping bag when the door was flung open. A weary-looking large bearded man in a check shirt and shorts and heavy walking boots, and with a huge pack, came in followed by two boys, aged around nine or ten. They were from Germany, a father taking his sons walking in the places he'd visited years before. They'd not left Morvich until mid-afternoon and had walked in up Gleann Lichd intending to camp long before now. The midges were too bad though, he said, so they kept walking. The man remembered the bothy from his previous visit but couldn't remember the scenery. He was obviously relieved to be here, having found the walking tiring and the midges almost unbearable.

Dumping gear out on the floor as he rummaged through his rucksack the man produced a stove and some pans and began to prepare a meal of spaghetti, tinned luncheon meat and cup-a-soups, all mixed together. He couldn't find his torch so I moved the candle I'd been using next to his stove. I then produced my can opener after one of the boys tried to open the tin of meat by stabbing the top with a large sheath knife. The man was so exhausted that doing anything was clearly difficult.

Sunshine, dew and midges greeted me when I stuck my head out of the door early next morning. The man and his two sons went down to

143

the river to bathe. A foolish idea. They were back very quickly. 'The midges are destroying Scotland!' he said animatedly, several times. I explained that they were only a big problem in July and August. 'But that's when I'm here!' he replied.

Before climbing the huge ring of 11 peaks that lay to the south-east, a circuit sometimes called the Cluanie Horseshoe as it lies north of Loch Cluanie, I walked down upper Glen Affric and into Gleann na Ciche, in the heart of the horseshoe, to camp. Indeed, the Gleann na Ciche Horseshoe would be a better name. Outside Alltbeithe youth hostel stood a new shining windmill, bringing electricity to one of the most remote hostels in Britain. In forested lower Gleann na Ciche much work was going on. Large areas had been fenced to keep out the deer and allow regeneration of the natural woodland while many of the plantations had been cleared. The fallen trees had been left where they fell, the Forestry Commission having decided that taking them out would cause too much damage to an area they want to restore. Whilst this is to be welcomed it is very ironic that some 30 of 40 years after this land was cleared, ploughed and planted yet more money, time and effort is now being spent undoing that work and trying to return the area to what it was. Not wanting to be too conspicuous I climbed into the mouth of Coire Allt Donaich and pitched the tent above the deer fence on a dry though slightly sloping site near some fine old gnarled and twisted birch trees. There was an excellent view down to Loch Affric.

Above my camp an old stalkers' path led up the corrie. This soon disappeared and I climbed directly up a rough, steep ridge to Mullach Fraoch-choire, a bulky peak lying at the end of a south-north ridge, the western arm of the horseshoe. There's a Munro at each end of the ridge and a Top in the middle. Immediately south of Mullach Fraoch-choire is an entertaining row of rock pinnacles followed by a climb to Stob Coire na Cralaig and then on to massive A'Chralaig. The views had been hazy all day but now all the surrounding peaks were dark silhouettes and beginning to vanish in the thickening cloud. From A'Chralaig the circuit turns east and descends to the Bealach Choire a'Chait. Before this pass is reached however a grassy spur juts out north-east to the Top of A'Chioch. Leaving pack, camera and trekking poles leaning against a rock I ran out to the summit and back, trying to beat the deteriorating weather, or at least to be out in it as short a time as possible.

Collecting the gear I pushed on quickly over Drochaid an Tuill Easaich to Sgurr nan Conbhairean. Here another and longer spur runs south-east to Creag a'Chaorainn and Carn Ghluasaid. I jogged most of the way to and from these summits. Back on Conbhairean mist and wind-blown drizzle blotted out the few remaining views. Heading north on the last leg now I hurried over Sail Chaorainn, Carn na Coire Mheadhoin (my 400th summit) and Tigh Mor na Seilge.

A steep descent into the glen and a walk through the felled plantations finished the day. Coming down I saw several deer in their red summer coats. From above the black stripes down their backs were very prominent. It was dark when I reached the tent. Nearly two months had passed since the longest day and the nights were lengthening noticeably. So was my list of summits climbed, 401 now. With only 116 left, for the first time I had a brief thought that the end was almost in sight. 'Brief' and 'almost' were the key words though. There was still far to go.

Masses of condensation and thousands of midges filled the porch in the morning. Light rain was falling but there were hints that the sun was trying to break through. It did, within minutes of me starting walking. Towering cauliflower-like cumulus clouds and sunny periods replaced the rain and low cloud which were blown away on the breeze. It took two-and-a-half hours to walk down to the car park in Glen Affric some six or so miles away where I had a rendezvous with Denise. I stopped to take many photographs as there was a wonderful sharp post-storm light. A rainbow curved over the buildings at Athnamulloch. Walking along the track south of Loch Affric it was a joy to see so much natural woodland – pine, birch, rowan and alder – and many signs of regeneration. The combination of forest, loch and mountain was beautiful and complete. This is what a glen should look like. The Forestry Commission have long preserved much of the remaining natural pine forest on their land around Loch Affric and are now removing the plantations from elsewhere in the upper glen so the forest can regenerate.

Denise and Hazel had already arrived and were sitting on a bench overlooking the river and feeding crumbs to the local chaffinches. Three hours were spent talking, having lunch, wandering along the rocks by the river and paddling in the cold water. I had another new pack, a final model from Aarn Tate. It would see me to the end. As requested it was a sombre green and blue. The others had been bright red, not the right colour for the stalking season. (In fact, I prefer dull colours in the wilds at all times but having agreed to test items I couldn't complain at the colour.)

In the early afternoon Denise and Hazel left and, later than intended, I walked up into Gleann nam Fiadh to the north of Glen Affric past a large fenced area where there was much regeneration, especially of rowan.

Notices said that this work was being done by the group Trees for Life. Beyond the fences there were no young trees at all. I'd rather see deer numbers reduced than fencing but the latter is preferable to simply leaving land simply to deteriorate further due to over-grazing. However it seems daft to fence in the forests and then have to feed the deer, whose natural habitat is the forest, in the winter because there isn't enough natural food. This in itself signals a badly unbalanced environment.

Well above the trees I found a good flat camp-site beside the burn. A breeze kept the midges away. A nearby path ran up beside the Allt Toll Easa to the col between Toll Creagach and Tom a'Choinich, the easternmost summits on the long ridge that separates Glen Affric from Loch Mullardoch. From the col a short, steep pull led to the West Top of Toll Creagach after which a long walk over easy ground took me to the rounded lump of the main summit. Tom a'Choinich was much better, a rocky peak with green corries topped by gently angled small ribs of rock on its eastern flanks. There was a good zigzag stalkers' path up the narrow ridge to the summit. Beyond it I went out to two Tops, the bump of Tom a'Choinich Beag and neat little rocky An Leath-creag. Further west a pinnacled ridge ran towards Carn Eighe, one of the two highest peaks in this group. Five summits were enough for that evening however so I turned back and descended to the now midge-ridden camp, the breeze having died away. I dived into the tent, shut the doors tight and was soon asleep.

The mist was very low, drifting round the hills only a few hundred feet above the tent, when I woke. Rain was falling but there was no wind so there were still myriads of midges. For the first time I wore the head net I'd been carrying for months, pulling it over my wide-brimmed sun hat while I took down the tent and packed up. Once I was walking the midges faded away. They are not strong fliers. Thankfully.

I began the day with an ascent of Sgurr na Lapaich, the fine pointed peak that dominates upper Glen Affric. It used to be classified as a Munro but is now just a Top. This demotion can't be blamed on the modern revisions however. It was Sir Hugh himself who made the change. The peak lies well over two miles from its 'parent', Mam Sodhail, with another Top in between and is certainly more of a separate mountain than some Munros. But the important thing is that it's an impressive hill not what position it has in a set of Tables.

Passing over the small swelling of Mullach Cadha Rainich I soon reached the massive cairn on Mam Sodhail, the second highest mountain north of the Great Glen at 3,862 feet. The highest, Carn Eighe, is just 18 feet taller and lies just to the north. Both of them are big bulky hills, a pair of huge domes that can be seen from many distant summits. It was a Saturday and others were about. A runner passed me just below the summit of Mam Sodhail then three pairs of walkers appeared in quick succession.

Before I climbed Carn Eighe I went out to two Tops south of Mam Sodhail, each lying on a different spur. Sgurr na Lapaich had been clear but I was in mist soon afterwards and needed the compass to locate these Tops, An Tudair and Creag Coire nan Each. Not far from Mam Sodhail on the ridge out to the latter there are some curious rock formations below a prominent cairn. Nearby in a narrow ravine are several pits which I estimated at ten to 12 feet deep and 15 to 20 feet across. They didn't seem natural but rather the results of quarrying. Not far away are the remains of a small building just south of the summit of Mam Sodhail. From the foundations it looks as though it was once a well-built stone hut. The giant summit cairn on Mam Sodhail is well constructed too, a hollow structure with no entrance so the walls have to be scaled to get inside. I guess the stone for this and for the hut came out of the pits. The cairn was built in the 1840s during the Ordnance Survey's primary triangulation of Scotland when this hill along with Sgurr na Lapaich – above Loch Millardoch – to the north were important stations.

A drop of some 400 feet lies between Mam Sodhail and Carn Eighe. As I was ascending the latter a figure ran down towards me out of the mist. He wasn't in so much of a hurry that he couldn't stop for a chat. He and his companion had walked from the Loch Mullardoch dam away to the east and were going to descend to the west end of Mullardoch to camp. He wanted Mam Sodhail, his friend wanted a rest so he'd left his pack with him on Carn Eighe. Carrying heavy packs over the Tops is hard, he said, 'and ours are full of tins of beans!'. His brother was meant to be with them but hadn't turned up. 'I hope he's walking along Mullardoch to meet us as he's got half my tent.' They were descending via Beinn Fhionnlaidh. So was I but first I had to go east from Carn Eighe to the two Tops on the ridge to Tom a'Choinich I hadn't climbed the previous day, Stob a'Choire Dhomhain and Sron Garbh. On the former peak the ridge is quite narrow and there's a series of pinnacles. Back on Carn Eighe I had a strange sensation in my mouth as I was eating some flapjack and felt something hard. I took it out and looked at it. A cracked crown. Until the end of the walk I would have a stubby post in the front of my lower jaw instead of a tooth.

A long ridge runs north from Carn Eighe over a Top, Stob Coire

Lochan, to Beinn Fhionnlaidh. It's 1,000 feet down to the lowest point of this ridge. The first time I climbed these hills, from Alltbeithe youth hostel in Glen Affric, I walked the whole ridge from Toll Creagach to Carn Eighe and then went out and back to Beinn Fhionnlaidh. I remember the climb back up to Carn Eighe as exhausting and endless and was happy not to repeat it. One advantage of backpacking is that you don't have to return to your start point so instead of toiling back up Carn Eighe I descended the very steep slopes of Beinn Fhionnlaidh to Gleann a'Choilich to the west. On the grassy hillside I found the first blaeberries of the year, big dusty pale ones that didn't have much of a taste. Down in the glen I camped on a large sward of bright green, smooth turf not far from where the burn ran into Loch Mullardoch. It was a pleasant, comfortable site where I would stay for two nights. From the tent I could hear water running and the sound of a waterfall upstream, relaxing sounds that I love to listen to. A gusty breeze held off the midges. Later in the evening it brought rain from the south-west.

To the south lay a complex group of hills, a massif centred on Sgurr nan Ceathreamhnan, a singularly unpronounceable mountain. Cameron McNeish suggests 'keroanan' in *The Munro Almanac*, Peter Drummond 'kayravan' in *Scottish Hill and Mountain Names*, Hamish Brown 'kerranan' in *Hamish's Mountain Walk* – you get the idea. It means 'hill of the quarters', which apparently refers to land shares. A long central ridge runs up to Sgurr nan Ceathreamhnan between Gleann Sithidh and Gleann a'Choilich. From Ceathreamhnan other ridges run north and east, the latter eventually continuing to Mam Sodhail. There are three Munros and six Tops on these three ridges.

The air felt fresher and less humid than it had for days the next morning. The rain had stopped but the gusty wind was still blowing. Although the sky was overcast the cloud was high and from the tent door I could see hazy, pale hills rising to the north-east, the Lapaich group on the far side of Loch Mullardoch.

I started the day by climbing steeply up a rocky spur above the camp to Mullach Sithidh and Mullach na Dheiragain. The first of these was summit number 417. There were just 100 left. The ridge now curved over Carn na Con to the last steep slopes of Sgurr nan Ceathreamhnan. As I approached the latter a walker descended towards me, the only other person I met all day even though it was a Sunday. 'What a coincidence. I was reading one of your articles in *TGO* yesterday.' From Inverness he'd cycled out that morning for a round of Ceathreamhnan and Mullach na Dheirahain, two of the few Munros – 'just teens' – left on his second round.

From the neat, pointed, stony summit it was just a step to the West Top then a slightly longer walk north along a rocky ridge to Stuc Bheag and Stuc Mor. The views were very hazy with the near hills pallid silhouettes and distant ones invisible. The immediate scenery was dramatic however with narrow ridges and deep corries. Back over Ceathreamhnan there was a long walk east over Stob Coire nan Dearcag to An Socach. To the south the hills of the Cluanie Horseshoe stood out with Ciste Dhubh to their west looking very isolated.

A short way beyond An Socach lies the Bealach Coire Ghaidheil where a path crosses the ridge from Glen Affric to Loch Mullardoch. On the north side it's little used and hard to follow in places but still a relatively quick way down. Back at camp I had a few midgeless hours with the tent doors open before the breeze dropped and I had to zip myself in. A small bird was mobbing a larger one in the birch trees upstream. A meadow pipit and a kestrel, I guessed. Just outside the tent big bumblebees were buzzing heavily between blue flowers with tight wire wool heads. 'Teasel?' I wrote in my journal. I'd got the family right as later, on consulting a clutch of field guides, I decided it was probably Devilsbit Scabious. I'd like to have carried some natural history guides with me but the weight was just too much.

Rain fell for much of the night. I was woken twice by bites from midges that had slipped into the inner tent before I closed it, despite the smoking coil in the porch. Due to the heat, a humid 20°C, I was sleeping half out of the sleeping bag. The zipped tight tent was unpleasantly stuffy but I couldn't let in any air without admitting midges too.

The morning was humid and still. By the time I set off the sky was slightly brighter but the weather still looked like it was going to be similar to the previous two days; dull and nondescript with bits of rain, sun, mist and wind. I just wished it wasn't so muggy in the glens. It was fairly typical for mid-August though.

Heading north I crossed the mudflats at the west end of Loch Mullardoch. The water in the reservoir was very low. A wide, ugly, pale grey bathtub ring ran round the edge, an obviously unnatural feature. In places the mud was very soft and I started to sink a little too deeply. Many deer had crossed the flats and I quickly learnt to gauge the softness by the depth of their hoofprints.

Glen Cannich, in which Loch Mullardoch lies, and Glen Strathfarrar to the north, where I would finish the day, are both wild, remote glens surrounded by big mountains. They were once regarded as being two of the most beautiful glens, as glorious as Glen Affric just to the south, but sadly they have both been wrecked by hydro-electric schemes, the felling of most of the natural woodland and the planting of commercial blocks of conifers.

Between Loch Mullardoch and Glen Strathfarrar is a remote group of hills, known as the Lapaichs from the highest peak, Sgurr na Lapaich, with four Munros and five Tops. Long, steep and fairly tedious grassy slopes led up to the first summit, another An Socach. Like the one I'd finished on the previous day it's not named on the Ordnance Survey map. The name means a snout. There were plenty of flowers on the hillside and a couple of large herds of deer, 50 plus in each one, in Coire Lungard.

The walking was easy as I traversed the long ridge of An Riabhachan which has three Tops (West, South West and North-East) as well as the Munro. The views were hazy and minimal, just vague outlines of nearby hills with below the dark slashes of lochans and the large Mullardoch and Monar reservoirs. The terrain became slightly rockier as I approached Sgurr na Lapaich. On the way out and back to Sgurr nan Clachan Geala to the south I found a well-constructed stone shelter and nearby another carefully built edifice that looked like a mine entrance or perhaps just a fancy seat.

The east side of Sgurr na Lapaich is complex and rocky, the finest feature of the range. An excellent path runs down the east ridge, most of the way cutting across the steep slopes below the crest. The last time I had been here was one October after an early snowfall when we'd ascended this path. Descending it now I could see why we'd regretted not having ice axes.

The short burst of excitement over, easy walking led to the last two summits Carn nan Gobhar and Creag Dubh after which I descended northwards down boggy slopes to Gleann Innis an Loichel, picking up a track lower down and then passing through a fenced area in which there were some impressive, if small, stands of old pines. I camped by the burn, the Uisge Misgeach, in some large flowery meadows, a beautiful site. But there was no wind so, as I expected, hordes of midges appeared the instant I stopped. I had an action plan. Repellent on face and hands first, then trousers tucked into socks, windshirt cuffs tightened and headnet pulled over hat and the neck drawcord pulled in. Up with the tent, throw the gear inside, place lit mosquito coil inside the door, then down to the stream, just a few yards away, to fill water containers. Into the tent, zip door shut and kill midges inside with repellent spray, hands and bandanna. The whole process took less than ten minutes. Later there was a pink and orange sunset but I could only briefly glance at it through a few inches of open door due to the midges. I spent most of the evening rereading Mike Tomkies' *A Last Wild Place*, about the time he spent living in a remote house in the western Highlands studying wildlife. His midge horror stories made the problems of camping with them seem insignificant. One that made me shudder tells how he spent a hot humid summer night in a cramped hide photographing a buzzard's nest. There were masses of midges and he'd forgotten his repellent. He describes smearing orange juice and onion juice on his skin to no avail and ending up tying a scarf round his face and neck and wearing gloves.

'Desperate midges! At least I'm desperate!' I wrote in my journal the next morning. A thin, high-pitched whine filled the porch, the sound of thousands of the tiny horrors. A few had managed to get into the inner tent and I was bitten a few times before I could get repellent on all exposed flesh. Even with a coil burning midges were coming into the porch so I ate breakfast in the inner tent with the doors shut. The coils were a different brand from ones I'd used before and they didn't seem to be as effective. It appeared to be dull outside, as far as I could tell from the light coming into the tent. I didn't dare open the flysheet door as I could see midges crawling all over the outside. The only sound was the bubbling of the burn over pebbles. A roaring wind would have been welcome.

I had a rendezvous for 11 a.m. arranged with Denise in Glen Strathfarrar near the Loch Monar dam just a mile or so away, which was just as well as my supplies were reduced to a little coffee, a little dried milk, a few cloves of garlic, some herbs and spices and a few sachets of drink powder.

We met on the road and I dived into the car to get away from the midges. As well as four days' food Denise had brought various bits and bobs including more midge coils, a new notebook, a waterproof pen, waterproof matches, a candle and Darling and Boyds' classic natural history study, *The Highlands and Islands*. She'd rung the four estates I'd be crossing over the next three days and been given four different replies. The Braulen estate, where I was now, just said 'walkers not encouraged in August and September' which wasn't very useful. East Monar said they might be stalking on Maoile Lunndaidh the next day, when I'd be climbing it, and would certainly be stalking somewhere as the owner was there. They said nothing about access though. West Monar was more helpful. Walking was okay everywhere except on Beinn Dearg, a Corbett. Achnashellach said there was no stalking until 20 September. They also thanked Denise for calling, the only estate to do so.

As we sat and talked some vehicles came and parked at the foot of Toll a'Mhuic. Some little off-road vehicles were unloaded and set off up the track up the glen. As this was presumably a stalking party I decided to climb the Strathfarrar hills, four Munros and two Tops, from the other end and descend this track. After Denise had left I took my supplies back to the tent then started out, at three o'clock, to walk down the glen. I'd not gone far when a doubt entered my mind. Had I brought my spare headlamp batteries? I checked. I hadn't. As it seemed likely I'd be out in the dark I went back for them, though I knew by doing so I was making that a certainty. In Glen Strathfarrar there were lots of nice bits of woodland, mainly alders along the river but also birch, rowan, oak and hazel, on which the first soft white-shelled nuts were appearing, plus one stand of old pines and a line of sweet-smelling limes. A heron floated over the snaking course of the river. In Loch a'Mhuillidh a large island was overflowing with a dense forest. The glen must once have been like that.

Some five miles down the glen a path led into Coire Mhuillidh. Here I saw the first signs of autumn. Clumps of leaves on some of the rowans by the burn had turned red, brilliant flashes of colour in the general gloom. Where the path ended I turned up the steep, smooth slopes of Sgurr na Ruaidhe, the easternmost top of the range. It was 7.30 p.m. when I reached the summit and I realised I would have to move fast to avoid being caught high up in the dark, now only two hours away. I was on the sixth summit, a good five miles and much ascent away, an hour-and-a-quarter later. The weather helped, driving wind and rain from the north-east and therefore at my back. Even so, I was surprised at my fitness. Thick mist meant no views so, after pausing to put my rain jacket on and to swallow an energy bar on Sgurr na Ruaidhe, I didn't stop at all.

The route was obvious over Carn nan Gobhar and Sgurr a'Choire Ghlais, the highest summit, but I made a mistake coming off the next peak, Creag Ghorm a'Bhealaich. Thinking I knew which way the route must be, and not bothering with a compass bearing as I was in a hurry, I descended the north side instead of the west ridge. I quickly realised my mistake as I was on a broad slope not a narrowing ridge and contoured round to the correct route. On Sgurr Fhuar-thuill I tried to guess the right way off before taking a bearing, and was 30° out.

As I trotted along the tops I saw more wildlife than I had in several days including some hares, a dotterel and a few ptarmigan. There were many fresh deer tracks. There were also more signs of autumn. Rusty red tips were appearing on the rough grasses. I had a few anxious moments coming off the last peak, Sgurr na Fearstaig, when I couldn't find the path into Toll a'Mhuic that is marked on the map. The slopes here were very steep and it was growing dark. There was no real problem. I was just expecting the path too soon as I found when I checked the altimeter. When I reached the right height, there it was. Where the ground levelled out at Loch Toll a'Mhuic the path became a narrow vehicle track. Fresh gouges showed this was where the little off-road machines I'd seen earlier had been heading. It was dark now but the white rocks in the track stood out so I didn't need the headlamp. Above me the edges of hills appeared black against the dark sky in the swirling mists.

Back down in Glen Strathfarrar I went down to the bridge at Inchvuilt rather than risk a ford in the dark. I then took a wrong turning and went up the track beside the Allt Innis a'Mhuill. I soon knew I'd gone wrong as the path climbed which it shouldn't have done. As I turned back I suddenly had a strong feeling of a presence nearby, of something or someone waiting and watching. I paused but could hear nothing in the heavy rain nor see anything in the black night. The sense of another being was overwhelming and I was certain that whatever it was knew I was there. There was a hint of hostility but overall I felt the presence was waiting for me to depart. For a second or two I felt frightened. I switched on the headlamp. The tiny pool of warm yellow light was reassuring. I swung the beam round through the blackness but could see nothing so I set off down the track. By the time I was back at the tent some 15 minutes later the feeling had gone. Whatever it was had not accompanied me. When I thought about it later the only rational explanation I could come up with was that there had been deer close by. This was reassuring but not convincing. I'd never had a similar sensation when near deer. Encountered in the dark they normally snorted and trotted away.

Such experiences are not uncommon. Rennie McOwan describes many similar though generally more dramatic ones in his book *Magic Mountains*. I'm sceptical about the supernatural but have no satisfactory explanation for this experience. That there was something there I am certain. What it was I have no idea.

I reached the tent at 11 p.m. Although there were no midges outside due to the wind and rain, the porch was full of them. More concerned with invisible watchers I wasn't prepared for this and was bitten several times as I struggled with wet clothing, repellent, mosquito coils and a fading head lamp. The bites itched incredibly at first but thankfully this faded after five minutes or so. Although tired I was also hungry so I cooked a very late supper. It was nearly 1.30 a.m. when I blew out the candle.

153

The night was much cooler, a great relief. The wind had dropped but was still strong enough to keep the midges away, another relief. The sky remained overcast. My route for the day lay west to the remote mountains around the head of Loch Monar. Crossing the Monar dam I followed the road round to Monar Lodge, a clutter of buildings nestled by the loch in a cluster of trees. A couple of vehicles passed but no one stopped to ask where I was going. A sign on the lodge gate read 'Danger. Shooting in Progress Today.' It was screwed onto the gate and there was no sign it was ever covered up so I guessed it was designed to intimidate rather than inform.

From the lodge I took the path that runs along the north shore of bleak, unattractive Loch Monar with its ugly white tide mark. There were a few clumps of old pines and a fenced area that looked recently planted but overall the feeling was of empty desolation, of a land neglected. I was glad to turn away from the loch and climb the path into Toll a'Choin and into the mist.

A long, boggy ascent led to the col between Maoile Lunndaidh and Carn nam Fiaclan. I left the pack leaning against a cairn. As I started walking across the almost flat plateau to the first peak the clouds parted slightly and I could see the summit cairn ahead and, looking back, the slight rise to Carn nam Fiaclan and beyond it three dark pyramids, the peaks I'd be climbing next. The view lasted maybe ten seconds then the mist closed back in and the visibility shrank to no more than a few yards.

On the summit of Maoile Lunndaidh it started to rain. I headed back across the Cairngorm-like plateau on compass bearings. The pack didn't appear. One of my great fears was realised. I was never happy away from the pack – after all it contained warmth, shelter and food, my home in fact – though leaving it often made sense. After doing a crude sweep search and still not finding it I went all the way back to the summit and started again, trying to stay calm. This time it was there, exactly on the bearing. I hadn't gone quite far enough before. I should have checked my watch as well as the compass.

Compass bearings were needed again to find the way off Carn nam Fiaclan which went down steep slopes to a col below Bidean an Eoin Deirg. The ascent of this peak was very steep, involving nearly 1,500 feet of climbing in less than half a mile. Unable to see anything I just went straight up, on a broad buttress at first with bits of crag and some boggy ground at angles of 30° to 45°, the steepest bogs I've ever seen. Eventually the slopes converged to a narrow ridge, rocky in places but with no real exposure as the slopes either side were quite gentle. This in turn gave way to a steep face with broken crags on it, up which I scrambled on unstable rocks loosely embedded in moss and bog. Suddenly the summit cairn was right above me, perched on the edge of the ridge I'd come up. Finding it there was a satisfying finish to a climb that had been far more fun than a slog up a grassy hillside. The mist had added an air of mystery and a sense of exploration to the climb as I had no idea exactly where I was on the mountainside or what sort of terrain lay above me. I just had to think ahead the next few yards and hope that I could continue beyond them. This made for a feeling of immediacy lacking when the route was clear and the walking easy.

Still navigating by compass I went on over Sgurr a'Chaorachain and Sgurr Choinnich and then started down to the Bealach Bhearnais. Another pass, the Bealach Crudhain, lies just above this and almost caught me out in the mist and had me descending south to Loch Monar. However the altimeter showed it as being too high and on checking the compass I found the valley below ran south-east not south-west. On the actual Bealach Bhearnais I came out of the mist. The rain stopped too.

Down the Bearneas glen lay a small bothy which I decided to head for, though it would mean an extra few miles the next day, so I could have a night away from the midges and the confines of the tent. There was no path down from the bealach and the going was quite rough so getting to the bothy took longer than expected. A pair of dippers darted down the burn and there were several herds of deer, many of them hinds with fawns. At the bothy I found three walkers already settled in. They'd arrived half an hour earlier from Strathcarron. I could have squeezed in but the single room really was very small. Also, after the long day and the late night the day before I felt very tired and not that sociable so I pitched the tent down by the burn. Rain and wind kept the midges away anyway.

The folk in the bothy said the forecast was for colder, windier weather the next day. They'd been collecting Munros for the last few weeks but had only a few days left. I've been collecting them all summer, I thought, and now I've only a few weeks left. The sudden understanding that I was approaching the end of the journey made me feel sad. I realised I was enjoying the walk despite the weather, not in a superficial instant pleasure sense but in a deeper feeling of rightness and completeness, of doing what fulfilled me most. My only regret was that Denise wasn't with me. The main – the only – reason for looking forward to the end of the walk was to be with her.

The wind failed and the night became calm so copious midges and copious condensation filled the porch in the morning. I lit two coils. By the time I'd had breakfast the sun was shining and it was getting very hot in the tent. To the south-east of my camp lay three remote summits. I set off for them with sunhat and sunscreen on for the first time in 11 days but within an hour the sky was overcast. It was still a better day however with the peaks remaining below the cloud and the visibility good.

I took a direct line to Bidein a'Choire Sheasgaich, going up Coire Seasgach and then steep, boggy ledges, squelchy terraces and wet gullies to come out just west of the summit cairn which is the highest point on a narrow ridge. The climb was quite arduous but whenever I stopped for a brief rest and looked back more and more of the dramatic spiky hills to the north came into view, starting with just the tips of the peaks above Achnashellach and finishing with a great sweep round to An Teallach and the Fannichs, peaks I hadn't clearly identified before. To the south less distinct peaks faded away into Knoydart.

Lurg Mhor, the next peak, is a striking spire when viewed from the south. On the ascent it felt far less steep than it looks. Beyond the summit the narrow eastern arête out to Meall Mor was an entertaining scramble, difficult and exposed enough in parts for me to take traversing paths below some pinnacles. This impressive arête is the edge of a massive tilted series of rock strata with the steepest side on the north.

On the return to camp I traversed below the south side of Bidein a'Choire Sheasgaich to a slightly easier descent line. Before moving on I glanced in the bothy. The others had left for Lurg Mhor at 1.45 p.m., only half an hour earlier, though I hadn't seen them. On the walk back up to the Bealach Bhearnais I was able to appreciate the scenery. It seemed much less rough than when I'd stumbled down it feeling weary the evening before. The Abhainn Bhearnais, a lovely burn, rippled through wet meadows in a series of bends in the lower glen. Higher up it tumbled over rock terraces in a series of little cascades. A small cliff made up of thin layers of horizontal rock was covered with plants, an amazing profusion of mosses, ferns, flowers and even tiny trees.

The southern side of the glen is walled by the long, steep, craggy face of Beinn Tharsuinn, a big mountain though only 2,830 feet high. To the north gentler, more grassy slopes led to another long mountain, Sgurr na Feartaig, almost the same height at 2,827 feet. Near the pass there were deer again and I came within 50 yards of a group of four. They looked my way but the wind was in my face, I was below them and below the horizon, the burn masked any noise I made and the sky behind me was quite bright so they didn't appear alarmed.

From the pass there is a good path down to the Pollan Buidhe and a vehicle track. Here I wondered what to do. The time was just after 6 p.m. The next two summits, both Munros, lay directly above. I had hoped to reach Gerry's hostel at Craig in Glen Carron that evening. If I went up them now I wouldn't get there, if I didn't I would lose a day. I sat down and thought about it over a piece of flapjack and half a litre of energy drink. I decided to go up, I was here to climb hills not stay in hostels. The good zigzag path that climbs to 2,460 feet on Sgurr nan Ceannaichean helped me decide as it meant a relatively easy ascent. I put map, whistle, compass, spare film and a Jordan's Original Crunchy Bar in my windshirt pocket, tied the garment round my waist and set off. The path consisted of short, tight zigzags at first, then longer, less steep ones. Suddenly full of energy I raced up, reaching the summit of Sgurr nan Ceannaichean in just 45 minutes. I stopped there to take photographs of the view and change the film in the camera but I was still on the next peak, Moruisg, after another 37 minutes. Partly this was because these are easy, grassy hills and, free of the pack, I could run much of the time. The views were wonderful. I had a clear view of yesterday's five hills to the south with the pointed summit of Bidean an Eoin Deirg the most impressive sight. Maoile Lunndaidh looked as though it should be above Glen Shee rather than in the west, a steep-sided, flat-topped hulk of a hill. Lurg Mhor, looking amazingly steep pointed, kept coming in and out of view but the real glory was to the north and west. The Cuillin were now visible but much clearer were the Torridon hills, all bar Beinn Alligin which was hidden behind the long jagged line of Liathach which seemed to run into the equally long line of Beinn Eighe. North of a bit of Loch Maree rose Slioch, massive and magnificent. Then came A'Mhaigdean and Ruadh Stac Mor and the distant ragged skyline of An Teallach. A wonderful, wonderful view.

I could also see large cleared areas in the plantations down in Glen Carron which answered the question I had in the back of my mind about whether to walk the highway or the forest roads to Achnashellach. It would be the A890. But that was for the next day.

Huge herds of deer were high on Moruisg. I counted well over 100 beasts. They didn't seem too bothered by my presence, only moving away when I came within 50 yards or so. I ran most of the way back to the pack, reaching it 2 hours 23 minutes after setting out. I wandered down the track towards Glen Carron to the first reasonable camp-site I could see, a flat area just across the Allt a'Chonais. For the first time midges bothered me while I was walking and I had to stop to put repellent on. The site was breezy however. Just after I'd pitched the tent rain began to

157

fall. I didn't care. It had been a very long but very enjoyable day.

Strong winds and heavy rain buffeting the tent woke me twice during the night. The storm had blown away by morning however and the sky was clearing as I walked down to Glen Carron and then along the road to Achnashellach with the steep cliffs of Fuar Tholl, an excellent Corbett, rising straight ahead. This is one of the many rugged peaks, three of them Munros, lying between Glen Carron and Glen Torridon, an area that serves as an excellent introduction to the even more rocky and rough terrain to the north. Gone are the grassy ridges and long green slopes of the hills to the south. Stone dominates the landscape, the bare bones of the land jutting out through a thin covering of bog. It's exciting country and my favourite part of the Highlands.

The journey into this magic land started with a climb through the woods above Achnashellach station. This wasn't as pleasant as in the past as much of the forest had been clear felled, leaving the usual mess. Once out of the trees the scenery was magnificent. A polite estate notice said walkers were welcome, that stalking was between 15 September and 20 October and would walkers please cause minimum disturbance. There was a phone number for further information.

I walked into Coire Lair with the great buttresses of Fuar Tholl and Sgorr Ruadh rising to the west and the more gently angled scree and boulder slopes of long Beinn Liath Mhor to the east. For a short stretch the river Lair ran down a wooded gorge. A large herd of deer watched me pass. I continued on up to the Bealach Coire Lair. Here I left the pack while I clambered over rocky ground to Beinn Liath Mhor, passing a couple sitting looking at the view on the way, the only people I saw all day. The air, for once, was sharp and fresh and there were frequent bursts of sunshine giving a feeling of lightness and clarity that was welcome after all the days of humid heaviness. To the north Liathach and Beinn Eighe were close now, the first with deep gullies scoring its craggy slopes, the second with fields of grey scree covering its sides and both with jagged, exciting crests. There were clear views to the south too but the hills there were rounded and less dramatic.

Sgorr Ruadh, the red peak, its dark reddish sandstone a contrast to the pale quartzite screes of Beinn Liath Mhor, the big grey hill, is a steep block of a mountain. Stony rakes led up to the scree of the north-east ridge. I started the ascent under a suddenly darkening sky. Not far from the summit the rain began, huge drops coming down hard. I donned the windshirt I had tied round my waist. By the time I reached the top the rain was hammering down, a real cloudburst, with some soft hail mixed in. The two walkers I'd seen on Beinn Liath Mhor and whom I'd followed up here were just starting the descent, clad from head to foot in bright red waterproofs. I was soaked to the skin but not cold as there was no wind. To the west sunshine glinted on Maol Chean-dearg.

The downpour continued as I hurried back to the pack and it kept up for ten minutes more as I started along the path to the Bealach Ban and the Bealach nan Lice. Then the black clouds sped away to the north-east. The storm had lasted just 45 minutes yet the paths were inches deep in running water, and new puddles and fresh rushing rivulets were everywhere. The sun reappeared and I was mostly dry within an hour.

Below the Bealach nan Lice lay Loch an Eion, above Maol Chean-dearg. As it was now early evening and the weather was nearly perfect with an almost clear blue sky I decided to camp by the loch rather than, as I'd originally intended, go down to Torridon to the NTS camp-site, where I was to meet Denise the next day. By the time I'd climbed Maol Chean-dearg I'd have arrived very late in Torridon.

Finding a site near the loch was difficult. I'd camped here the previous year but then it had been much drier. Now much of the ground was sodden and squelched underfoot. A dryish patch of heather just above the loch would have to do, I eventually decided. As soon as I stopped, clouds of midges, the most I'd seen, assailed me. Once in the tent the coils quickly cleared them. Although the active ingredients of the new coils Denise had brought out to Glen Strathfarrar were said to be just 0.75 per cent while those of the others were 1.15 per cent they seemed to work better. They certainly made my eyes water more. I suspected that it was the amount of smoke they put out that was the real difference.

Maol Chean-dearg was a steep, rocky climb. On the way up I came on a large metal cross with 'He is risen' carved on it wedged in some rocks. Litter, I thought, is litter and whoever put it here should come and remove it. A fine sunset was in progress as I ascended. It was over by the time I reached the summit. A gibbous moon was in the sky and a ring of jagged peaks rimmed the horizon. Far below were dark lochs. Night was falling quickly as I descended and I just got down the steepest bit before the light went completely. It was absolutely calm and totally clear. The tent was soaked with dew. Far below I could see the tiny pinpricks of lights in Torridon.

The night was the coldest for over a month, just +7°C, and the pressure in the morning the lowest for nearly two months, since the day I was blown off Cairn Gorm in early July in fact. Yet there were no clouds and no wind. I must, I guessed, be in the eye of the storm. A lonely, haunting, wild cry rang round the corrie followed by another. Divers, I thought. A pair of these magnificent birds had just landed on the loch. I always think of them as symbols of the wild and their presence created a wonderful atmosphere, reason enough not to have gone down to Torridon the previous night.

With plenty of time before Denise was due to arrive I wandered slowly down to Torridon, stopping often to admire Liathach, shining in the morning light, and to take many photographs. When Denise did arrive we left almost immediately for Glen Carron to stay with an artist friend of hers at Balnacra. Vicky Stonebridge's small house, the old railway crossing keeper's cottage, was crammed with her pottery and paintings, some of which she sells under the name Balnacra Beasties. Animals and children were everywhere, a scene of amiable chaos. During the afternoon there was a huge thunderstorm. I was glad not to be high in the hills.

Chapter 11

TORRIDONIAN SANDSTONE

25 AUGUST–4 SEPTEMBER TORRIDON TO BEN WYVIS 114 MILES 41 SUMMITS

'Mountain followed mountain, and glen succeeded glen in a shimmering vista that seemed to have remained unchanged since time began.'

Mike Tomkies
A Last Wild Place

I had new boots to celebrate my 100th day, my third and last pair. Denise drove me back to Torridon where I camped on the small NTS site, a slightly damp field on the north side of the glen not far from Upper Loch Torridon. I planned to stay here for two nights and three days while I climbed Beinn Alligin, Liathach and Beinn Eighe, the three great Torridon mountains.

That evening John Manning, *TGO's* deputy editor, and two friends of his from Slovakia were due to arrive. John wanted to do Liathach the next day and I intended on backpacking over Beinn Eighe to Kinlochewe the day after that, which left Beinn Alligin for today. This splendid mountain, – the name is often translated as 'jewel' or 'jewelled' though this is disputed – rises dramatically from the shores of Upper Loch Torridon. The heart of the mountain is the great corrie, Toll a'Mhadaidh, around which the summit ridge curves.

A stroll down the road beside the loch led to the foot of the mountain. On the way I called at the store in Torridon village for a few odds and ends – chocolate bars, headlamp batteries, a tent peg to replace one lost at Loch an Eion. I also bought an NTS booklet about Torridon which I read as I continued on down the road.

From the car park the path to Beinn Alligin climbs straight up steep, boggy hillside into Coir' nan Laogh and then up to the first summit, Tom na Gruagaich. This track is very badly eroded, a wide scar of loose stones and deep channels, making it one of the worst paths I saw during the walk. Over-use is a main reason for this, of course, but I suspect the line it takes is a factor too. Stalkers' paths generally zigzag back and forth across a hillside rather than go straight up or down as they were built for ponies rather than people. This means they are less likely to act as water channels after heavy rain and also less likely to be broken down by the passage of endless boots. Stalkers' paths were built to last too. In contrast the path up Beinn Alligin is a hillwalkers' path, created by years of people walking the same route and heading directly uphill. The terrain doesn't help either. As with everywhere in this region a thin skin of muddy soil, bound together by the roots of moorland plants, covers the lower slopes. Underneath lies sandstone, an impervious rock. This means that water cannot soak away, leaving the ground soft and boggy and easily eroded. Higher up in Coir' an Laogh scree and loose rocks predominate. The path here is slippery and full of water-carved channels.

This wide blemish disfigures Beinn Alligin and destroys the wild feel. There are other ways up the mountain but this one will remain the most popular as it's the most direct and starts from the car park. The land is owned by the NTS and it is to be hoped that they will soon do some repairs to this route, perhaps building a switchbacking stone-based path to replace the current straight up and down one.

I was joined almost immediately on the ascent by another walker who announced he thought he was coming down with 'flu but would try to get to the top. Rain started about half way up, light at first then steadily increasing in strength. A dozen or more people were descending out of the mist in the upper corrie. By the time we reached Tom na Gruagaich the rain was very heavy. Surprisingly the higher summit of Sgurr Mor was clear and we caught glimpses of dark ridges and soaring peaks in the swirling clouds, patches of which were below us. A notch in the ridge just below the summit marks the top of a huge gully, the Eag Dhuibh or black cleft, which splits the face of Sgurr Mhor from top to bottom.

Beyond Sgurr Mhor lie Na Rathanan, the Horns of Alligin, three rocky towers that give a good scramble. In fine weather I'd have continued over these but as I could see nothing and was feeling cold I set off quickly back the way I had come. The path was now running with water and my new boots were soaked.

At the camp-site I found John and his friends Jan Dulla and Katarina Tomcanyova. Katarina had come to England to work as an au pair and met John while working as a volunteer ranger at Hardcastle Crags, a wooded valley near Hebden Bridge in the Yorkshire Pennines, John's home country. Jan edited a walkers' magazine in Slovakia and had just spent a month in Muddus national park in Swedish Lappland. John was cursing his tent, inevitably a test model, as it didn't have a porch so he either had to cook in the inner or with the midges which were out in force. Smoking bits of mosquito coil lined the outside of his tent door. Later in the evening a gusty wind and showers cleared the midges. Sunshine and showers was the forecast for the next few days.

The western end of Liathach lay directly above the camp-site. Running for five miles along the north side of Glen Torridon this is a superb mountain, one of the finest, if not the finest, in the Highlands. Seven summits lie on the narrow, castellated crest, of which two are classified as Munros, three as Tops. From the ridge great buttresses run down the slopes to the road with narrow gullies between them. Everywhere there is scree and rock. The north side is magnificent too with great corries lying between rocky spurs. Like many of the mountains in the area Liathach is built of thick bands of dark red Torridon sandstone capped with glittering white quartzite. The traverse of Liathach is a marvellous mountain walk. The main difficulties lie on the pinnacles of Am Fasarinen, though traversing paths, spectacularly situated, run below the hardest scrambling.

One of the Tops, Meall Dearg, isn't on the main ridge but lies at the end of the Northern Pinnacles which run north from the westernmost Munro, Mullach an Rathain. I was worried about this summit, which Irvine Butterfield says deserves 'consideration as the most difficult Top in the British Isles, challenged only by the Inaccessible Pinnacle'. Crossing the Northern Pinnacles involves rock climbing so I would have to find another way up, though I wasn't sure where this would be.

I decided to leave Meall Dearg to the end of the day. That way the others could go down and leave me to puzzle out an ascent. While I walked up Glen Torridon to the eastern end of the mountain the others drove up in John's car. We then went up the path into Coire Leith. The lower section has been extensively renovated and now consists of a stone staircase. The ascent, as everywhere on Liathach, is steep. So far the clouds were high and from the ridge we had good views of Beinn Eighe just across Coire Dubh Mor and west over Stob a'Choire Liath Mhor to Liathach's summit, Spidean a' Choire Leith, a great pyramid of pale quartzite blocks.

Mist and light rain closed in as we were clambering over the sharp-edged quartzite boulders to the summit. Because of the weather we took the traversing path below Am Fasarinen. This narrow well-worn track, running across the steep south face of the mountain and curving in and out of several gullies, is quite exposed itself in places. From the western end I scrambled back along the pinnacles to the highest point, as it's a Top. I caught up with the others on the easy ascent of Mullach an Rathain. The mist was even thicker here and they turned south to descend to Torridon. I had Meall Dearg to find.

Thinking – hoping – I might be able to skirt below the difficult sections I went out on the short arête linking Mullach an Rathain to the Northern Pinnacles. The scramble up the first one was easy but beyond it a sheer drop disappeared into dense mist. I retreated, as I did so glancing down a couple of gullies that curved down into the darkness. Steep and loose, they didn't look promising lines of descent. Back on the main ridge I walked round the head of Glas Toll a'Bathain, which lies to the west of the Pinnacles, again looking down a couple of steep 'bottomless' scree gullies. Again they didn't look inviting. I then descended the short spur west of the corrie. I came out of the mist at around 2,000 feet. To the east the steep, craggy face of Meall Dearg rose into the cloud. A couple of gullies looked as though they might provide ways up. It was now too late to find out though so I started back up to the ridge. Suddenly the cloud lifted and Meall Dearg and the Pinnacles appeared, sharp and clear. Before the mist closed back in I saw that descending the gullies from the ridge into Glas Toll a'Bathain was probably feasible but the ones down from the Pinnacles ended in crags. Once down in the corrie it looked as though it should be possible to traverse across the scree and climb either steep grassy slopes or one of the gullies to Meall Dearg. I would find out the next day.

I ran and slid back to Torridon via the mostly run-out scree gully of the Allt Slugach. I was down in 35 minutes. At the camp-site the midges were out in force and Jan and Katarina were hiding in their tent. John had gone back up the glen for his car. Other campers were standing in the smoke of a huge bonfire. I retreated to my tent too but came out again at sunset as the light was fantastic with a brilliant gold cast over the nearby trees and the hills to the south and one of the brightest rainbows I've ever seen. The intensity of the colours was breathtaking. A second paler bow curved down outside it. When John returned we escaped the midges by going to the Ben Damph Bar, a mile or so away to the south, for a meal and a few pints of beer.

Midges again ruled the camp-site at dawn. Campers were either firmly shut in their tents or wearing head nets. The others packed up and were soon saying farewell and heading back south. Company on the hills was pleasant for a change. It was only the 11th day I hadn't been alone.

After they'd gone I lay in the tent watching young robins, still in their speckled juvenile plumage, darting about the camp-site in search of food. High above there were bits of blue sky and the cloud looked a little thinner and more broken. I roused myself. It was time for another attempt on Meall Dearg.

Two hours later I was back on Mullach an Rathain in light rain, a cool northerly breeze and, unfortunately, minimal visibility. Descending one of the very loose scree and rock gullies into Glas Toll a'Bothain I set off lots of small slides and sent several rocks bouncing and echoing down the slopes. At one point a piece of faded nylon attracted my attention. I realised that it was the detachable hood of a waterproof jacket. Had it been ripped off by a gale, I wondered or, more likely, had it slipped through the numb fingers of a walker desperately trying to attach it in a storm?

Contouring across the corrie I arrived below the west face of the Northern Pinnacles and Meall Dearg ridge. I found a gully and started up but it soon became very narrow, steep and rocky and I began to worry about being able to descend again so I traversed out to the south where I found another gully that was wider and at a slightly easier angle. Although loose and greasy and quite steep at the top it wasn't very exposed and I was soon on the ridge above at the low point between the Northern Pinnacles and Meall Dearg. A path, the first sign of one since Mullach an Rathain, led along the narrow ridge to the tiny summit which I guess must be a spectacular viewpoint in clear weather. I was just pleased to reach it. The hardest Top? On the mainland maybe but there are certainly a few in the Cuillin that are harder.

I returned to camp by the same route, the round trip taking five hours. It was the only time on the walk I spent a whole day climbing one Top. On the camp-site I was astonished to see, even though there was plenty of space, a huge tent, big enough to stand up in, just a few feet in front of my door, partially blocking the view of the hills. I glowered at it but it didn't go away. Late in the afternoon the clouds cleared and a gusty wind sprang up, suppressing the midges.

I was expected in Kinlochewe the next evening where Tom and Liz Forrest, whom I knew from the *TGO* Challenge, had invited me to stay at their B&B, Cromasaig. Denise had left a supply box with them at their small outdoor shop in the centre of the village on her way home from Torridon. Although it was a long way there over the six Tops of Beinn Eighe I decided not to start that evening. I should have done. Instead I lay in the tent reading *The Highlands and Islands*, and noting how

165

prescient and valid the authors' conclusions were, especially regarding reafforestation.

Beinn Eighe is another superb peak though the best features, the great corries and high cliffs, are hidden from casual viewers as they lie on the northern side. You have to make an effort, walking into the corries or climbing to the ridge, to appreciate Beinn Eighe. A long featureless wall of scree lines the mountain on the southern side, rising directly from the road to a superb narrow rocky ridge. The walk along this is as good in my view as that on Liathach. Beinn Eighe has long been one of my favourite mountains and was the first peak in this area I climbed, long ago in 1978 on a Land's End to John O'Groats walk. At the time of the walk the mountain had five Tops but only one Munro. However, in the 1997 revision Spidean Coire nan Clach was promoted to Munro status. Even so, if Beinn Eighe were in Glen Shiel it would have six Munros!

The clouds had returned by morning and the north-west wind was bringing flurries of rain. I read my way up the four plus miles of road to the car park where the footpath into Coire Dubh Mor starts. The path had been recently repaired, very recently indeed in fact, as I soon came upon the work crew, muddy figures with mattocks and crowbars. One of them said he felt the paths they built were perhaps too smooth and not rough enough for this environment. The perils of being a path builder, he said, were that when out hillwalking for pleasure he had to stay off paths or else he spent his time examining them rather than looking at the scenery.

Higher up the coire a couple of walkers were sitting by the path. When I said I was going to Kinlochewe they recommended MORU (Mountaineering and Outdoor Recreation Unlimited), Tom Forrest's shop. I didn't tell them that's who I would be staying with.

Rounding the great buttress of Sail Mhor I reached Coire Mhic Fhearchair, one of the most spectacular corries in the Highlands with the magnificent Triple Buttress at its head. Unfortunately I was already in the mist and couldn't see a thing. The highest summit on Beinn Eighe lies on the spur to the east of the corrie. I walked round the edge of the almost invisible lochan to ascend a rough path past rocky pools and then up stony slopes to the low point on the spur. Ruadh Stac Mor was just an easy half mile to the north. I nipped out and back to it then climbed to the main ridge. On Choinneach Mhor, where there is a surprisingly large and flat area of grass, I left the pack again while I went out to the westernmost summit, Sail Mhor. A steep scramble leads down from Coinneach Mhor to an exposed and awkward step called Ceum Grannda. I avoided this by a gully to the south and then had a simple stroll round to Sail Mhor. Returning, Ceum Grannda looked quite difficult and I was glad I hadn't tried to descend it.

A couple of backpackers were on Coinneach Mhor. They'd come up from the road and were planning on going over Sail Mhor and then descending west and looking for somewhere to camp. I mentioned the gully and showed them a couple of good camp-sites on the map.

The last three peaks, Spidean Coire nan Clach, Sgurr Ban and Sgurr nan Fhir Duibhe were all in the mist although there were occasional views from the lower points on the ridge down to the road. From the last summit a rough and lengthy descent down steep, loose slopes led me into Coire Domhain and then to a good path beside the Allt a'Chuirn which I followed down the hillside and then through fenced, regenerating pine forest to the road. I reached it just as darkness fell.

I thought I remembered Denise telling me that Tom had said I would pass Cromasaig as I walked into Kinlochewe, which lay a half mile or so to the north, so I headed that way only to arrive in the middle of the village without having found the place. Puzzled, I went and looked in the window of Tom's shop, which is in the old petrol station. A notice said their B&B was three-quarters of a mile along the Torridon road, which I'd just walked down. It finally dawned on me I should check the map. Cromasaig was marked, just south of where I'd joined the road. Wearily I walked back. A headlamp shone in the dark, Tom coming to look for me. Concerned, he'd already phoned Denise who'd assured him I'd be fine.

Once in Cromasaig I was served a large, delicious plateful of sweet and sour vegetables. Then I foolishly accepted a can of Tennant's 80/- ale. It literally knocked me out. I felt very dizzy and had to lie down. I then passed out for a few seconds. I hadn't drunk anything since Coire Mhic Fhearchair early in the day and was a little dehydrated and very tired. The beer on top of a big meal was just too much for my system.

Recovering quickly from this I spent the rest of the evening talking with Liz and Tom about the walk, the mountains, the *TGO* Challenge – which Tom had done ten times and Liz had done that year – the outdoor trade, gear, mountain rescue (which Tom used to be involved in) and more. The most astonishing story I heard though wasn't an outdoor one at all but concerned the Kinlochewe Hotel. Just before Easter, said Tom, the owner simply locked the doors, loaded up a van, left the keys with the bank and left, having paid all his bills including the mortgage. It had been up for sale for three years and he'd just had enough. A good result of this was that there was now a new owner who would welcome walkers

167

when the hotel reopened. Previously the hotel had been noted for its 'No Boots, No Packs' signs. However it being shut all summer had caused problems for local B&Bs. As there was nowhere else in the village or nearby that served evening meals they'd had to do so. After a summer of this Tom and Liz said they were worn out. As they were full at the moment I slept on their front room floor, surrounded by a wonderful collection of outdoor books, especially Scottish ones. Sadly, I was too tired to stay up looking at them.

Breakfast at Cromasaig was filling, varied and very tasty. Tom went down to the shop and brought back my supplies. The box looked large and felt heavy. Coming up were six days without resupply, the longest section of the walk. Lifting my full pack I knew why I'd felt that resupplying at every possible opportunity was very important for the success of the walk.

Before departing I had a look in Tom's shop. Being an experienced hill-walker and mountaineer he had made a careful selection of gear. Although tiny by big city store standards there was everything you could need here. Both Tom and I like talking about mountains, backpacking, gear and the outdoors in general and somehow while we did so the morning slipped away. Lunchtime arrived so I finally said farewell, walked a few yards down the street and stopped at the café for a snack. I was finding it hard to leave Kinlochewe.

I'm not sure why I was procrastinating about moving on as ahead of me lay the wildest, remotest part of the walk, the vast area between Loch Maree and the Gairloch road containing Slioch (the spear), An Teallach (the forge) and a host of other untamed hills. It's often called the Last Great Wilderness though it's no more a natural wilderness than other areas of the Highlands. Most of the area is covered by the Letterewe and Fisherfield estates and is owned by Dutchman Paul van Vlissigen, one of whose concerns is to keep the area wild and undeveloped so there are no plantations or bulldozed roads sullying the region. However he also feels that reforestation is a fashion and is more interested in maintaining the deer population. (There is an interesting chapter on the estate in Auslan Cramb's *Who Owns Scotland Now?*) Much more positively Van Vlissigen agreed an access policy, the Letterewe Accord, with outdoor bodies such as the Ramblers' Association that became the model for the Concordat on Access. This accord supports the principle of freedom to roam but does ask walkers to accept limits to access during stalking. As this doesn't start until 15 September I didn't have to worry about it here. However Denise had told me that the Fannichs estate, which I would cross in four or five days' time, had been very hostile and had said they didn't want any walkers on the hills before 20 October. I'd worry about that when I got there.

There is a bridge over the Kinlochewe River east of the village but, on the advice of a local friend of Tom's who'd popped into the shop, as I was going west I walked down the road, stopping briefly at the interesting Beinn Eighe National Nature Reserve Visitor Centre, and then fording the river at Taagan where it runs, wide and shallow, over gravel beds.

Beside the river I walked through attractive, scattered woodlands of alder, birch, rowan and pine. The morning cloud had cleared and sunlight shone on the water. Soon I came to beautiful Loch Maree with the ramparts of Slioch towering above it. This magnificent block of a mountain has steep crags on three sides, defences that are breached only to the south-east where a great corrie, Tuill Bhain, lies between the encircling arms of the mountain. This corrie is reached from the cliff-walled ravine of Gleann Bianasdail which runs from Lochan Fada to Loch Maree, a deep slash in the terrain. As I turned into this imposing chasm movement high above caught my eye. Four golden eagles were soaring above the mountainsides. The sight was exciting, thrilling, a sign that these lands, although damaged, were still wild enough to support such magnificent creatures. I had probably caught sight of eagles earlier in the walk but was never sure they weren't buzzards. This time I was certain.

A little way up Gleann Bianasdail a path leads into the corrie. A walker coming down told me there was a large herd of deer near the summit. In the heart of the corrie I left the pack, with more relief than usual as the extra weight was noticeable and I was slower uphill than normal.

Unfortunately as I climbed the last slopes to the summit ridge a bank of cloud rolled in from the west and the Tops vanished. As it did so a pair of wild goats trotted in front of me and over a shallow crest. Camera in hand I crept up the slope. As I peered over the edge one of the goats suddenly raced past me. I grabbed a quick shot. A musky smell lingered in the air. A little higher I glimpsed two deer, shadowy shapes in the mist that cantered away as I passed.

Slioch has two summits of almost identical height lying at the apex of the two ridges that surround Tuill Bhain. The one with the Trig.Point is the Munro but the North Top is in much the finest situation, perched on the edge of the great buttresses of Slioch's north-west face, and has by far the finest views. This was all academic of course due to the mist and I saw nothing from either Top. Nor did I see anything as I walked east along the narrow ridge to Sgurr an Tuill Bhain from which I dropped down steep slopes back to the pack.

As it was now 8 p.m. I cast around in the corrie for a camp-site but everywhere was either bumpy and boggy or bumpy and rocky. Reaching the steep drop-off into Gleann Bianasdail I gave up and descended a rough path past some waterfalls back into that glen. In the growing dark I headed up Gleann Bianasdail, cursing the path as it climbed away from the glen floor to cross a shoulder – I wanted to find flat ground. Finally the path levelled out, then descended back down to the head of the glen and Lochan Fada where the Abhainn an Fhasaigh starts its rocky rush to Loch Maree. I crossed the stepping stones over the river in the dark, relieved the river wasn't higher. On my first visit here the river had been a swirling torrent and I'd nearly been swept away as I forded it.

Tired now I stumbled along the tussocky, hummocky banks of the lochan for a half mile or so until I found a flattish patch of dry turf by a stony beach. I pitched the tent and collapsed into it.

I woke to the sound of waves lapping on the pebbles. A cool wind was blowing along the lochan, a superb stretch of wild water surrounded by steep, craggy mountains. My plan was for a long high-level walk over the six Munros and two Tops that lay between here and Strath na Sealga to the north. I didn't quite make it, camping with two Munros still to do, partly due to the weather (strong winds, heavy showers, low cloud), partly due to rough terrain, partly due to the heavy pack and partly because I felt a little tired all day. The slow start warned me of the likelihood I wouldn't complete the day as planned. It took two hours to walk round Lochan Fada through peat bogs and over tussocks and then up to the col between Beinn Tarsuinn and A'Mhaighdean.

A'Mhaighdean is often said to be the remotest Munro as it lies nine miles from the nearest roads. Maybe so. More importantly it's a rugged, cliff-rimmed peak in a savage setting. On a clear day the views are tremendous. Today they looked like being non-existent. Tying my rain jacket round my waist I left the pack at the col and climbed the rough slopes to the cloudy summit, arriving just as two other walkers were starting down. North-east of A'Mhaighdean, across a high col above Fuar Loch Mor, is another rocky mountain, Ruadh Stac Mor. The clouds lifted as I climbed this peak, the name of which means big red peak. The sandstone crags ringing the summit really are red. They look impregnable but a path from the col makes a surprisingly easy way up scree chutes through the rock terraces to the Trig Point. A couple just leaving the Top waved to me. All around, rocky hills faded away into the grey sky. Rain began to fall and I donned my waterproof jacket, glad I had it with me. I was to keep it on for the rest of the day as there were several more heavy showers plus a cold west wind.

A traversing line below A'Mhaighdean took me back down to the pack. The round trip of the two peaks had taken two-and-a-quarter hours. To the east lay Beinn Tarsuinn, a long ridge (the name means 'transverse peak') that looks very impressive from Gleann na Muice to the north. The steep, grassy western slopes lead to a narrow, curving sandstone ridge beyond which is an unexpected flat area of large oval slabs before a last steep climb to the summit. This made for an interesting walk, despite the rain. Looking back, Ruadh Stac Mor stood out, a soaring pyramid.

Beyond Beinn Tarsuinn I was glad to find a traversing path cutting below Meall Garbh, a prominent knoll where the ridge turns north. The highest but by no means best peak of the day came next, Mullach a Choire Mhic Fhearchair, a giant mound of quartzite rubble. The cloud just beat me to the summit. There are two Tops on the south-east spur. The first, the East Top, is just an easy walk from the Munro. To reach the second, Sgurr Dubh, however involved a walk along a narrow, rocky ridge and then a scramble up steep, greasy slabs and pinnacles to the tiny summit. I'd seen the final very steep edge below the top from Beinn Tarsuinn and had wondered, with a little trepidation, how difficult it would be. Seen end on it was broader than it looked from afar and I found the scrambling easy and not very exposed except for one or two spots. Not everyone would agree. The next evening, in the Shenavall bothy book I would read comments complaining bitterly about Irvine Butterfield for describing the pinnacles on the ridge as 'easy' in his book *The High Mountains of Britain and Ireland*. The writer had clearly found it hard. However you view the scrambling, Sgurr Dubh is a great little peak, far superior in its dramatic situation to its parent.

Back at the Mullach I collected the pack and went down the very steep scree and stone path to the col with Sgurr Ban. I'd already decided it was too late in the day and I was too tired to go any further so instead of climbing Sgurr Ban I continued down east into the unnamed corrie between the two peaks in search of a camp-site. About half a mile down from the col and at a height of 2,100 feet I found a flattish, dry spot protected from the worst of the west wind by the mountain wall above me. Once I stopped moving I felt chilly so as soon as possible I was lying in my sleeping bag with my fleece sweater and warm hat on and a pan of water heating up on the stove. The temperature was just +9°C, the coldest for nearly two months. It was the penultimate day of August. I suddenly

171

remembered the woman in the Inversnaid Hotel back in June who'd told me summer was over by mid-August. What a long time ago that seemed. It was hard to connect being there and being here. Was this really the same walk? In one sense it wasn't. I was no longer the same person who'd set off grimly for Ben Lomond to return exhausted in the dark. Although three weeks into the walk that person had been tense, worried, unsure about the challenge that lay ahead, obsessed with schedules and times; now I was relaxed, confident, in touch with the mountains. As long as I kept walking the summits would come. In terms of the walk, I had then been very young, a novice, still learning about life in the wilds. I was grown-up now and much wiser and experienced in the ways of the mountains. I knew I could cope with bad weather and rough terrain. More importantly, I knew they were essential parts of the walk.

Lashing rain in the morning tested my acceptance of stormy weather. The sky was dark, the peaks in cloud. It was cold too, just +6°C. A blocked nose, sore throat and runny eyes explained the tiredness I'd felt the last few days. I appeared to be coming down with a cold, probably caught off my companion on Beinn Alligin six days earlier who, I remembered, had told me he was coming down with 'flu. I swallowed a couple of aspirin and drank more coffee than usual. A strange cry came from the slopes above, a high-pitched throaty cross between a chuckle and a horse whinnying. It must be a grouse or ptarmigan, I thought, though the call was unfamiliar.

By the time I started back up the corrie the weather had worsened. It took 40 minutes to reach Sgurr Ban but slightly longer than that to go downhill to the col to the north of the peak as the slope was a pile of wet, loose, greasy and very slippery disintegrating quartzite. Beinn a'Chlaidheimh, a greener hill with more sandstone and a narrow summit ridge, was a much more enjoyable walk. The top just reaches 3,000 feet, making it Munro number 277 and Top number 517 in the pre-1997 *Tables*. In my list it was number 477.

The very steep descent straight down to the north from the summit of Beinn a'Chlaidheimh went through little crags on a bit of path and then into heather, tussocks and bogs. Across the Abhainn Srath na Sealga lay Shenavall, a popular bothy. I had been going to camp but the weather made Shenavall attractive. The river was almost knee deep with a strong current but I was soon across.

Shenavall is a fairly roomy bothy in a wonderful situation with a superb view across Loch na Sealga to Beinn Dearg Mor and Beinn Dearg Beag, two grand Corbetts with soaring sandstone cliffs, narrow ridges and

172

deep corries that are far more mountainous than many Munros. Shenavall is popular, though, because of the hill whose slopes rise directly behind the bothy, An Teallach. This magnificent sandstone mountain, considered by some the finest in Scotland, is made up of a series of steep, rocky peaks and pinnacled ridges rising above deep corries. There are ten Tops over 3,000 feet, two of them Munros. If the weather had been fine I'd have gone up An Teallach that afternoon but I wasn't in such a hurry that I couldn't wait in the hope of good weather. Of all the mountains on the walk this was the one I most wanted to climb when it was clear. My only other traverse of the mountain was in a storm and although I'd been back to the area several times since I hadn't climbed An Teallach again because it had always been cloud-covered. The last occasion had been on a trip with Denise. We'd had an exciting night in a wild storm camped in Loch Toll an Lochain, a magnificent corrie that rivals Beinn Eighe's Coire Mhic Fhearchair, when the tent had almost been flooded, but we hadn't climbed An Teallach.

The bothy had one inhabitant, Tom McArthur from Lockerbie. He was wearing a fleece emblazoned with the words 'Ultimate Challenge' (the original name of the *TGO* Challenge). 'I've done it ten times,' he told me. We sat and chatted about the outdoors both here and in Norway. Tom's son lived there with his Norwegian wife and he had been there frequently while I had spent much of the last few winters there leading ski tours. This led on to a conversation contrasting access and land ownership in the two countries. Tom told a story of some *TGO* Challengers whose tents, with their belongings inside, were uprooted and dumped over a fence on one estate. That couldn't happen in Norway. Four more people arrived during the evening. Looking through the bothy book, it showed that six was a small number for a summer night.

By ten the next morning I was alone in the bothy and with no desire to leave as outside it was very windy with low dark clouds well down the mountainsides and steady rain, occasionally heavy. One of the couples, a Scottish pair, was away early, heading for the six Munros to the south. Earlier, while I was still in my sleeping bag in a small room in the attic, Tom had appeared with some bread and headlamp batteries. 'I got a large loaf in Dundonnell yesterday,' he said, 'and it's much more than I need.' He was leaving for Lochivraon bothy beside Loch a'Bhraoin where he'd left some supplies on the walk in. From there he would go out to the road to catch a bus home.

After he'd gone the other couple, who were from Germany, set off for Kinlochewe, planning on camping on the way and I looked round

173

Shenavall. Without people and their clutter of bright jackets, sleeping bags, cooking gear, packs and more covering the walls and the floor it looked scruffy and untidy. Empty bottles were everywhere. A small rodent, a mouse or vole, scurried across the floor. Plenty of scraps for you to eat, I thought. I considered An Teallach. But not for long. I still had a stuffed-up nose and a slight headache and the rain was torrential outside. There was a general air of lethargy about the day. Staggering over the Tops in a storm just wasn't appealing. In this wind it might well be impossible anyway. It slowly dawned on me that this was going to be a rest day, the first for eight days. It would mean altering my plans again however. My next rendezvous with Denise was at 1 p.m. in three days' time. The weather would have to improve greatly if I was to climb all the planned hills by then, especially as I'd spent two days between Lochan Fada and here instead of the one I'd intended. I was surprised to find that this didn't bother me. An extra day or two on the walk no longer seemed a problem. It never had been really, of course. I studied the maps and came up with two tentative plans. The more optimistic one left just one peak unclimbed when I met Denise, the less optimistic but, I knew, more realistic one left seven.

The first arrival of the day was an Australian walker who'd come from Carnmore bothy to the south-west. He said the wind had made crossing the pass from there difficult. Next in were two German couples, also from Carnmore, carrying huge packs. Out of them they pulled two petrol stoves which were soon roaring loudly in the porch. Soon after them the Scots couple who'd set out for the six Munros to the south returned having done only one, Beinn a'Chlaidheimh, and packed up and left for Dundonnell.

So far all the people passing through Shenavall had been well-equipped and able to cope with the severe weather. This was not so with the next group, a party of eight teenage scouts from Germany who'd walked in from Kinlochewe. They arrived soaked, most of them wearing cotton trousers and tee-shirts with inadequate rain gear on top. Much of their gear was sodden too and I watched two girls wringing out a soaked synthetic sleeping bag in the porch. A surprising amount of water was squeezed out. Their leader produced a huge pan out of his rucksack, set it up on two more noisy petrol stoves and started to boil water. Settling down inside the scouts started singing, apparently quite cheerful despite being wet.

Outside, the burn that runs past the bothy was a foaming white torrent which had burst its banks and was flooding the grass either side. Deer were grazing in the meadows by the river, indifferent to the rain. High above, a raven hung black against the cloud and wind then suddenly twisted and dived, scything through the air. A large rowan tree was growing outside the bothy. There was a note in the bothy book from the people who'd planted it 25 years ago and had come back this year.

The rain stopped sometime during the night and by morning the burns had dropped noticeably. The cloud still hung low on the mountainsides and the wind still blew though. Out of the attic window I could see the top of the rowan, dark against the pale grey sky, bending in the gusts of wind. From downstairs came German voices, the roar of petrol stoves, the clanking of the chains that act as stair rails. I lit my stove, which was standing on the floor next to my sleeping bag, and started preparing breakfast. I couldn't wait any longer. It had to be An Teallach.

A short way along the north shore of Loch na Sealga a burn runs out of the unnamed south-west corrie of An Teallach. Either side of this burn up to a height of 1,300 feet a large area has been fenced off by SNH to allow the forest to regenerate. It was a very new fence but inside it I could see tiny birches, six to eight inches high, amongst the heather along with a few small pines. I followed the fence upwards then climbed directly to Sgurr Creag an Eich, An Teallach's westernmost Top. It was misty above 2,000 feet and rain began on the summit. It kept up all day. There would be no fine day on An Teallach. From the first Top I went east to Sgurr Fiona, the first Munro, then north to Bidein a'Ghlas Thuill, the second one, meeting three walkers between them. One had been up before and assured me it was spectacular on a clear day. I believed him. Even in the mist it was impressive, all narrow, rocky ridges and steep, stony slopes with constant hints of sheer drops, mighty cliffs and soaring pinnacles.

As the next two Tops, Glas Mheall Liath and Glas Mheall Mor, lie on different spurs of Bidein a'Ghlas Thuill I ended up climbing the last three times. Reaching the first of these involved crossing some unnervingly slippery quartzite blocks, the second was just an easy stroll. The last five Tops are south of Sgurr Fiona so I had to climb that peak a second time. One of these Tops is the highest turret of the castellated ridge of the Corrag Bhuidhe, the most splendid feature of An Teallach. I had been a little concerned at traversing this but it turned out to be much easier than I expected, mainly because most difficulties can be turned on the less steep western side where myriad paths have been eroded into the soft sandstone. In fact I enjoyed the scrambling on the rough rock of the Corrag Bhuidhe. It wasn't slippery when wet unlike the quartzite blocks on Glas Mheall Liath.

The scrambling starts with Lord Berkeley's Seat, which, although I couldn't see much, felt very exposed. Immediately beyond it is the Corrag Bhuidhe. There are three main pinnacles. As I couldn't see which was the highest I climbed them all to make sure I reached the top. That done, I dropped west to skirt below a steep section then climbed back up to the Corrag Bhuidhe Buttress. After this the last two Tops, Stob Cadha Gobhlach and Sail Liath, were something of an anti-climax. From the last one I descended directly down steep rough slopes to Shenavall. I was amazed to find it empty.

Later in the evening three walkers appeared but went to camp by the river. The wind had dropped and the midges were out in their thousands so I wasn't surprised when the three burst into the bothy later carrying cooking gear and food. They'd driven up from Glasgow and said that all Scotland was basking in sunshine except for the north-west. The good weather was forecast to move this way. It hadn't by the next morning which was very dark and dull with the mist hanging in thick bands almost down to the floor of the glen. Clouds of midges were waiting outside. I could see the three campers fording the river, heading for the six Munros to the south.

My route lay south then east, into the Fannaichs, a range of smooth, grassy hills and a great contrast to the rock peaks I'd been on for almost a fortnight. I had a pleasant and uneventful walk on the path beside alder-edged Abhainn Loch an Nid to Loch an Nid itself and then round to Lochivraon bothy at the west end of Loch a'Bhraoin. About half a mile from the bothy I met a couple going to Sgurr Dubh on Mullach Coire Mhic Fhearchair. They looked familiar. Before I worked out where we'd met they recognised me. They'd been part of the group I'd met on Beinn Bheoil on 16 July, some seven weeks earlier. We had had a glass of wine on Ben Alder, they said. I remembered that one of the party had been finishing his round of the Munros there.

By the time I reached the bothy I could feel the heat of the sun through the now thin cloud. Sunshine was brightening the green slopes of A'Chailleach, westernmost of the Fannaichs. To escape the midges I had lunch inside the rather decrepit bothy, which isn't an MBA maintained one. From the writing on the walls it was mostly used by Duke of Edinburgh Award groups – or maybe they're the only ones who write on walls. A bag of food hanging from a nail and labelled 2 September – today was the third – must have been left by Tom McArthur.

It was warm enough for me to change into shorts for the climb to A'Chailleach. However as I neared the summit ridge the clouds rolled

176

back in and it began to rain. I compromised and stayed in shorts but donned my rain jacket. The next pair of Tops, Toman Coinich and Sgurr Breac, were in mist. A steep drop down to a col at 1,800 feet separates Sgurr Breac from the main cluster of Tops in the Fannaichs which contains seven Munros and three Tops. On the descent to this col I had some views of Loch Fannich, a reservoir, to the south. The scar of a new bulldozed road marred the far shore.

I climbed steeply to the low point on the ridge above, left the pack and went south to Sgurr nan Each. The summit was just out of the clouds which lay in many layers, some of them filling the glen below me. Picking up the pack again I climbed into the mist on Sgurr nan Clach Geala. There were glimpses of deep gullies running down the slopes to the east. A path ran down the narrow ridge to the north to a lochan on the col with Carn na Criche. I considered camping here but decided I could just get over the next two summits and down to Loch a'Mhadaidh before dark.

My decision was the right one, not because I reached the camp-site in daylight, I didn't, but because of the glorious light that ended the day. The low sun was just cutting above a band of thick cloud and making Carn na Criche glow gold while above the summit there hung a hazy rainbow. From the top I could see a gold and red sunset sweeping across the western sky. Above it towered some huge cumulus clouds, deep pink in the last rays of the sun. All around me lower clouds swirled, making the whole scene insubstantial and phantasmagoric.

From the summit of Carn na Criche I glanced at close-by Sgurr Mor, the highest summit in the Fannaichs. There was no time for it today though so I turned and raced in the other direction towards Meall a'Chrasgaidh. To the west the stark jagged crest of An Teallach suddenly appeared sharp and clear above the cloud.

I was back in the mist on Meall a'Chrasgaidh. As I started down the steep, craggy east side of that hill in growing darkness the clouds shrank down into the corries below me. By the time I reached Loch a'Mhadaidh it was pitch black and I was back in thick mist. I spent an hour stumbling round the boggy shores in search of a camp-site. Eventually I reached the outlet stream and camped nearby on some dry heather tussocks.

The spot where I was meeting Denise was five downhill miles away so I didn't need an early start the next day. Denise was bringing the bike with her so I could cycle east to isolated Ben Wyvis. From there I would cycle to Achnasheen to the south of the Fannaichs so I could walk back north over those summits I hadn't yet climbed.

Sitting thinking about my plans for the week ahead it sank in that there were just 23 Tops left. I'd climbed 494 hills, which seemed ridiculous. This was my 110th day, which I also found hard to grasp. I'd begun in late spring, in mid-May, and it was now early September. I'd walked through the summer and autumn was approaching. For the first time I felt that mixture of happiness and sadness that always occurs near the end of a long walk, that occurs, I guess, at the end of the successful completion of any important part of your life. I loved what I was doing, living in the wilds, moving through the hills day after day, week after week, month after month, in tune with myself and with nature, complete and fulfilled, but I also knew I would take pleasure in the achievement of finishing what I'd set out to do and in contemplating it afterwards and writing and talking about it. Only when it was over would it become whole, a unity, something I could look at as a section of my life.

My reverie fading, I reminded myself I hadn't quite finished yet. It took a couple of hours to walk down through the mist to the road. The Fannaichs were well covered with cloud but it was clearer to the west and the spiky tops of An Teallach rose above bands of cloud. I reached the road an hour before the rendezvous so set off west along it. Big clumps of yellow ragwort and white and orange ox-eye daisies along with smaller patches of devilsbit scabious lined the road.

Denise arrived and I swapped the pack for the bike. Forty-five minutes later I arrived at Garbat at the foot of Ben Wyvis. I was going no farther today however. At least not under my own power. The bike went back in the car and Denise drove me home. There seemed no point staying at Garbat. At home I planned the last stage of the walk. Chris Brasher wanted to come up the last summit, Ben Hope. He could join me in eight days' time, on 12 September, which was just right. I doubted I could finish before then anyway. I felt excited and nervous. Surely I couldn't fail now?

Chapter 12

FINAL DAYS

'The Walk had been a sprawling and untidy thing, not a neat little package you could label and stack away.'

Colin Fletcher
The Thousand-Mile Summer

Dense mist covered Slochd Summit on the A9 as we headed back north to Garbat. Once there I hid the bike in some bushes. Denise was returning home and would collect it later in the week from Ledgowan Lodge Hotel in Achnasheen, where she'd booked me in for that evening.

Ben Wyvis is a big, flat-topped, undistinguished hill with four 3,000 foot summits spread over a distance of almost five miles. Plantations, many of them recently felled, line the western slopes. A path cuts through these beside the Allt a'Bhealaich Mhoir. High up on this path I turned north-east and climbed the steep, grassy slopes to the first Top, An Cabar. I walked into the mist down in the forest. It looked like a gloomy day but to my surprise and delight I came out of it again just before the summit to see only the second cloud inversion of the walk. Only some of the highest Tops, most dramatically An Teallach, rose out of the clouds. Another walker joined me on the summit. He'd driven from Ullapool that morning and said all the western summits were clear. The walking was easy on sheep-cropped turf and I was soon over Glas Leathad Mor, the highest Top, and round to Tom a'Choinnich and Glas Leathad Beag.

Back down at the road I had a one-and-three-quarters-hour cycle ride under thick cloud to Achnasheen. Ledgowan is an old shooting lodge built in 1904 and still has much of the original character with dark wood panelling and many stags' heads decorating the walls. In the evening I sat in the bar with a pint of beer, reading. From home I'd brought books by two of the outdoor writers who've most influenced me, Edward Abbey and Colin Fletcher, American writers (though Fletcher was born in Wales) little known in Britain but whose thoughts have universal significance. During this last week I wanted to clarify and sum up, wanted to think about what the walk had involved, about how I felt about the experience, about what I'd learnt. I hoped rereading these authors would help.

A television sat in the corner of the room, the usual hotel entertainment. I switched on the news to pictures of the 120 m.p.h. winds of Hurricane Fran wreaking havoc in North Carolina. The power of nature could always make a mockery of our attempts at control.

In the morning the weather in the Highlands had a settled look with bands of mist drifting across the hillsides and more blue sky than I'd seen in a while. North of Achnasheen lay round, grassy Fionn Bheinn, an outlier of the Fannaichs and the only one of the range to lie south of Loch Fannich.

The climb up the featureless southern slopes was a hot, sweaty slog. My mind was miles away, thinking of Edward Abbey floating down the Tatshenshini river in Alaska and missing his home, the desertlands of the south-west USA. I realised, not for the first time, that my spiritual home was also in western North America, in the pristine forests and unspoilt, vast wildernesses of the Sierra Nevada, the Rockies, the Yukon, and had been since I'd walked the Pacific Crest Trail in 1982. The Highlands were where I lived but were not 'home' in a deep sense. Not yet. Home was with Denise rather than in a specific place but if I could choose where to live it would be in the mountains of North America. I thought back over all the trips I'd made in the last five years. I'd been to Nepal, Greenland, Spitsbergen, Lapland, all of them beautiful and wild but four trips stood out, ones to the Grand Canyon, the Colorado Rockies and, in both summer and winter, the Sierras.

And the Highlands? Where did they fit in now I'd spent a summer walking through them? My moods and thoughts changed. Many of the glens and the lower hillsides I found depressing now. I was too aware of how degraded they were, how bereft of both people and forests. The areas of remnant forest and those where regeneration was occurring were uplifting and beautiful but they were still pitifully small. Patches of woodland do not make a forest. The unity and harmony of nature, of everything working together, is lacking in much of the Highlands and those places where it remains are sadly small. Is there a need to restore the Great Wood of Caledon? I believe so. It is, I think, time to start the restoration of the earth, time to try to reverse the damage we have done.

And if we don't help the earth heal from our ravages there is probably no future for humanity for we are not separate from nature but part of it. Then when we are gone, the trees will return. And in the meantime we need the forest for our sanity. As Edward Abbey wrote 'we can never have enough nature'.

However my spirits rose as I climbed. Above 2,000 to 3,000 feet the hills were less changed, more natural, a reason in itself for climbing them all. Up high I felt invigorated and inspired, even in mist and rain. Up high I felt there was still much about the Highlands to be relished, to be excited about, to protect.

On the spur of Creagan nan Laogh I stopped to scribble down my thoughts. It was the first time in several weeks I'd been able to sit high on a hillside in the sunshine and think and write and stare at the view. An eagle – our greatest symbol of wilderness – soared high above. But then two jet fighters roared up the glen, shattering the calm. My peaceful rest disturbed, I continued climbing.

The summit was cloudy and windless. Within seconds of my arrival midges appeared so I quickly departed, descending north to Srath Chromhuill. This side of Fionn Bheinn was more interesting than that to the south with a rugged corrie called Toll Mor. To the west there were good views of Slioch and Lochan Fada.

In the glen a track ran beside a hydro pipeline to Loch Fannich. I walked along it, hoping there were no stalking parties about, this being the estate whose attitude Denise had described as hostile. Access restrictions made me think about the 'management' of walkers, a subject raised in the Cairngorm Partnership plan which had just been published. In national parks in North America there was overt management with visitor fees, trail permits and backcountry camp-sites. Here there was unplanned management by guidebook and the location of facilities from rights of way and footpaths to bothies, car parks, hostels, bars and cafés, all of which play a part in determining which routes walkers take. Yet walking is about being free of constraints, about going where you will when you want. At least it is for me. I don't like the idea of being 'managed'.

The track continued north-east along the loch shore to a bridge over the Abhainn a Chadh Bhuidhe. An eight-wheeled off-road vehicle was parked here. From the bootprints it looked as though the occupants had continued up the track which now ran up the glen. My route though lay across the boggy ground at the head of the reservoir to a path that led to the burnt out shell of Nest of Fannich bothy. I'd stayed here once many years ago, before it had been destroyed in an accidental fire. A vehicle track ran eastwards from the bothy ruins. A mile or so along it I dropped down to the loch to camp out of sight on dry, bumpy grass. It was a pleasant spot with spacious views over and along the bright blue loch. To the north I could see the summit of Sgurr nan Each. I sat outside the tent in bright sunshine, the easterly breeze keeping the midges away. The weird, rising and falling guttural whistling call of a diver came from far out on the water. The difference the sunshine made was enormous. It gave life, colour, brightness, a raising of the spirit.

As the sun set into a golden sky, the wind dropped and the midges appeared. I retreated into the tent but re-emerged to watch the fine light after the sun had gone. A pale purple sky faded into blue. The hills were subtle shades of grey, the water silver.

I woke to the gold of sunlight on the hills across the loch and a crescent moon high in the sky. I shivered. It was just 4°C. A low mist was creeping down the loch from the east while high above, the summits of the Fannaichs were in cloud. I lay in the tent eating breakfast and reading while I waited for the sun to bring warmth.

The sun came and dried the dew-soaked tent. I packed up, suddenly aware I would be doing this for only a few mornings more. I would be sad to lose the routine of camping, the simplicity of tent living, the concern only with the here and now, the constant presence of nature. Camping was now automatic. In the tent I lay or sat on the insulating mat, in the sleeping bag if it was cool. At my head, arranged in order across the end of the tent where I could quickly reach everything, were the stuffsack containing my 'office' – notebooks, pens, maps, paperbacks; some utilitarian essentials in plastic bags – mosquito coils, tissues, insect repellent, sunscreen; and then the plastic box containing my first aid kit and various odds and ends with matches, lighter and altimeter watch on top of it. In front of the box, where I could easily find it in the dark, lay the headlamp beside its stuffsack, which contained spare batteries and candles. At the rear of the tent stood my food bags, clothes bag and any clothes I'd taken off plus my camera and camera accessory bag. In the porch, which ran along the length of the tent, the pack lay to the right of the door with footwear and rubbish bag on top of it. The kitchen was set up in front of the inner door, every item within easy reach, so I could sit looking out at the view while I cooked. That had been my home for 81 nights out of the last 112.

To reach the last six Tops of the Fannaichs, which made up the eastern part of the range, I walked along the track beside the loch almost to

182

Fannich Lodge, turning off it to climb what appeared to be a little-used, green and mossy stalkers' path that led to a large stone shelter just below the summit of Meall Gorm. I left the pack here while I went along the south-east ridge to Meall Gorm's South-East Top and then An Coileachan. The first of these was my 500th summit though I didn't realise it at the time. Counting the Tops became less important as I neared the end. I didn't need the increase in numbers to reassure me I was making progress. The walking was easy and there were good views west to the Torridon mountains, Beinn Eighe standing out as a complex tangle of ridges and peaks. To the north I could see the road across the Dirrie More and beyond it the Beinn Dearg hills where I would be heading next.

Back on Meall Gorm I sat in the sun and admired the view. There had been too little opportunity to do this on the walk, I thought, due to storms and midges. Just beyond the summit I met another walker relaxing in the sunshine. 'There's been too much rain and wind in recent weeks,' he said, 'so I'm making the most of this.' He was camped near the Dirrie Mor where he said the midges that morning had been some of the worst he'd ever encountered. This was not welcome news as that was where I planned to camp.

I went on up Sgurr Mor, the highest of the Fannaichs. Far to the south I could see the easily identifiable bulk of Ben Nevis. Much nearer An Teallach looked superb. It had, I thought, been clear of cloud every day since I'd climbed it. To the north of An Teallach my eyes were drawn down sunny Strath More to blue Loch Broom and the whitewashed houses of Ullapool. Further round lay the fantastic peaks of Coigach, none of them Munros, all of them superb. The crenellated crest of Stac Pollaidh gave the lie to the idea that height makes a mountain. It's only 2,010 feet high, not even a Corbett. Inland I could see Ben More Assynt and, far in the distance, a small peak I thought must be Ben Klibreck, my penultimate mountain.

A midge bite distracted me from the view. More of the little beasties arrived and sent me off for Beinn Liath Mhor Fannaich. A woman and a man were sweating upwards. From a distance the woman appeared to be wearing a dark, sleeveless top over a bright, reddish orange long-sleeved one. She wasn't. At least not the second. It was her skin. Her face was the same colour. 'It's very hot,' she said. Whether the cause was the sun or the exertion or both I didn't know but I'd never seen anyone that blazing red before. It was, I thought, going to be very painful.

An easy if tussocky descent followed with bits of a path in places. I aimed for a large patch of bright green ground near the confluence of the

Allt an Loch Sgeirich and the Abhainn a'Ghiubhais Li, guessing this would be grassy and dry rather than boggy and wet like the darker areas all around. The berries on the rowans by the burns were turning red, as were the tips of the coarse moor grasses. The chosen area was dry so I camped there, selecting a slight rise in the hope it might catch any breezes that blew. As soon as I stopped though clouds of midges appeared, as forecast. By the time I zipped myself into the tent I was crawling with the little monsters. It took two smoking coils to clear them. Piles of dead midges lay everywhere and each time I picked up a bit of gear there was a wriggling mass of them underneath. Outside the tent thick clouds of midges brushed against the flysheet, sounding like gentle rain as they skittered about and then cascaded down the slick nylon in waves. A solid black writhing line formed along the length of the door zip. I was staring, fascinated, at this when I realised with horror that I hadn't got any water. Bundled up in long clothing and with hat and midge net on I made a dash for the burn. On my return I had to go through the process of clearing the tent all over again. I felt a great desire to camp without midges. In the autumn I thought I would go and sleep under the pines and the stars in Rothiemurchus Forest or Glen Feshie. The joy of being out at dusk and dawn was lost when I was cooped up in the tent.

The steady hum of midges greeted me at dawn. The flysheet was black with them. Through the thin nylon they looked like thin rods and reminded me of films of microbes squirming on glass slides under a microscope. Other than the midges the only sounds were the trickling water of the burn and the occasional harsh cry of a grouse. Mist hung round the tent.

I waited in vain for the sun to disperse mist and midges. When the humid, sweaty, mosquito coil fume-filled tent became too unpleasant I packed up and, with all my clothes on and fastened tightly, opened the tent door and crawled outside. Clouds of midges instantly covered me. I took down the tent at record speed then set off walking, still wearing the head net. After a few minutes the midges dropped away and I was free. Cautiously I raised the net. Fresh air at last! Two walkers were heading into the Fannaichs. I thought it ironic that I'd seen far more people in this area, where the estate had made it clear they wanted nobody, than in the hills to the west where at present walkers were welcome. Nobody I'd spoken too had bothered to contact the estate or, indeed, knew much about stalking.

Crossing the highway took me into the Beinn Dearg hills, a group of wild, rugged summits. I started with Am Faochagach, the least interesting of the range. In total there are six Munros and one Top in the Beinn Dearg group. Once across the bogs and streams at the head of Loch Glascarnoch I climbed steadily up the featureless slopes of this bulky hill. As I did so the sky began to clear and the sun to shine and I reached the grassy summit ridge stripped down to shorts and thin top. An Teallach again dominated the views though closer by the steep, rocky, east faces of Beinn Dearg and Cona' Mheall looked impressive. To the south a mass of hills faded away into the distance. I've climbed them all, I thought, astonished. A raven flapped off the summit cairn as I approached while nearby a flock of meadow pipits flew low over the ground. There were deer high up too, hinds with fawns.

I'd left the summit and was on the col with a bump called Meallan Ban before I realised I wasn't wearing my Tilley Hat. I checked the pack just in case I'd put it away though I knew I hadn't. I hurried back to the summit hoping it was there but suspecting it was at a col away to the south where I'd stopped briefly. I could almost see it sitting on top of the rock I'd put it on. When it wasn't on the summit I initially decided to abandon it and started to go back to the pack. But something stopped me. I paused. I felt unhappy about losing it. I like that hat, I thought. It had been the length of the Scandinavian mountains with me and now over almost all the Munros and Tops. It was battered, faded and full of memories. Reason said leave it, sentiment said don't. And sentiment won. Not that there was much of a struggle. The hat was lying exactly where I expected it to be though, as it's dark brown, I didn't see it until I was almost on top of it. I felt a ridiculous sense of relief and pleasure at finding it. Sentimental fool, I thought.

The diversion cost me almost an hour. As I went on down, the rocky faces, complex and rugged, of Beinn Dearg and Cona' Mheall above the dark blue of Loch Prille looked increasingly imposing. Once beside it I found the loch a real gem, splendidly situated. A narrow arm runs south to the outlet where the Allt Lair cascades over stone steps and then crashes steeply down a series of falls and slides, the Steall Allt Lair, for nearly 500 feet to Loch na Still in the glen below. I paused here and sat for a while watching the water tumbling down.

Above, the east ridge of Cona'Mheall led steeply to the summit. The ascent was mainly easy but just below the top the rocks steepened. I chose a poor route and almost became crag fast at the end of a narrow ledge when I couldn't climb up the wall above. To retreat I had to very carefully take my pack off and lower it down in front of me. I found an easier scramble round the corner and emerged from the rocks only yards from the summit to see two surprised walkers looking towards me.

A quick descent took me down to the col to the west where I left the pack while I went up Beinn Dearg. Again An Teallach looked magnificent as did the Coigach hills, especially Suilven. These were to dominate the views for the rest of the day. To the north there were few hills now while to the south they jostled for space. Beinn Dearg was my 508th summit. There were only nine left. I was down to single figures. It suddenly felt very close to the end.

Sitting by a little lochan back at the pack I decided to camp high just before Seana Bhraigh, the last summit of the group. The logical reason for this was that there should be fewer midges higher up. Really though it was because I wanted a last night out high in the mountains. One regret was that I'd had far fewer good mountain camps than I'd hoped and this was the last chance for one.

Not needing to hurry now I wandered over Meall nan Ceapraichean, Ceann Garbh and Eididh nan Clach Geala revelling in the complexity of the rocky landscape. I passed the spot where a few years previously I'd camped and watched a fantastic sunset (a photograph of this sunset plus an account of the walk appears in my book *Classic Hill Walks*), and went on to camp on a mat of soft thick moss and coarse grass near the lip of Cadha Dearg, the Red Pass, not far from three little lochans. It was one of the finest camp-sites of the walk, in a splendid situation looking out west to the Coigach hills. Just as I was setting up the tent the sun dipped to the horizon and there was a brilliant red sunset, well to the south of where it had been on my previous camp here as that had been in July. Two high-level camps, two wonderful sunsets. In a strange way it made up for the two ascents of An Teallach in storms .

A deer was barking very close to the tent as I went to sleep. Far out to the west on the sea tiny lights were flashing. I was due to meet Denise in Oykel Bridge the next day so I needed an early start. For once I set the alarm on my watch, for 5.30 a.m.

Waking as the day dawned was a first for the walk. Walking late into the night was always my preference rather than early starts. Advice that's often given to aspirant long distance walkers is to get the bulk of the day's walking over by midday. I've even read that you can tell serious walkers because they always get early starts. I'm quite happy not to be a serious walker if it means I can sleep in! I'm more awake in the evening than the morning so it makes sense for me to walk late in the day. (Most of this book was written between the hours of 8 p.m. and 4 a.m.) Not that I would say that's right for anyone but me. We're all different.

The strange gutteral corkscrew cries of ptarmigan were all around the tent as I ate breakfast. Clouds drifted aimlessly about the hillside. As they came and went so the world expanded and contracted, from a few yards of grey green ground to distant vistas of crags and hills. The hum of a distant engine spoilt the feeling of solitude and remoteness a little. But only a little. One delight was that there were no midges.

I started walking, certain that as on the last few days the early cloud would clear and it would become a sunny day. It was not to be. Seana Bhraigh, a crag-rimmed mountain that compares with A'Mhaighdean for remoteness, was in cloud though there were brief views of the cliffs below the summit and hints of blue above. I descended northwards towards a solid grey sky that didn't look likely to clear. I read Colin Fletcher most of the way down the track in Strath Mulzie.

Denise was waiting for me in Oykell Bridge. Over hot drinks in the hotel she passed me a list of ski tours the company I worked with, Mountain and Wildlife Ventures of Ambleside, wanted me to lead the next season. Could I do them? Yes, I said, unable to think seriously about it. Denise also produced a rather melodramatic piece from *The Sunday Post* headed 'Chris will have climbed 18 Mount Everests' according to which rain had wrecked my feet but I'd managed to soldier on. Reading the piece, which also said I would be celebrating later that week, was another jolt, another message that the walk was almost over and I would soon have to adapt to a different world, that of society and civilisation. After days alone in the hills I felt somehow outside these, which was why resupply points were sometimes so confusing, upsets that briefly cut me off from the wilds. I knew though that a few days back home and this would change and I would come back 'inside' society. The knowledge of the wilds, the awareness of the value of being alone in nature wouldn't vanish though and would make coping with the artificiality of human 'reality' easier.

Chris Brasher and Cameron McNeish, the editor of *TGO* and author of *The Munro Almanac* and *The Munros*, were coming up to Altnaharra in two days' time. There were just five more summits to climb. As the mountains drew to a close they were fairly spread out so the bike would be needed quite a bit these last few days. From Oykel Bridge I used it to reach the track that led to Loch Ailsh and Ben More Assynt. The 50 minute ride was uphill into a stiff wind under dismal skies with hints of rain and I was happy to hand the bike back to Denise. I then loaded up with supplies for the last time and set off along the track. I tried to read but heavy drizzle forced me to stop. Instead I watched the bullfinches in the trees near Benmore Lodge and the martins swooping overhead.

I camped beside the now small River Oykel in the narrow mouth of the long upper Oykel glen between the sentinels of Black Rock and Sail an Ruathair that separate the mountain world of Ben More Assynt from the moorland and plantations to the south. Here I had my first and only encounter with a stalking party. Four people, looking very Victorian in tweed jackets, plus fours and flat caps, and with two white ponies, one with a dead stag slung over its back, came down the path in the glen just as dusk was falling. The stalker came over to the tent and asked me, very politely, about my plans for the next day. I told him. 'That's fine,' he replied, 'we'll be stalking on the far hillside from where you'll be.' There was, I noticed, no mention of whether I could go or not, just where I was going.

Sitting in the tent while the rain grew heavier outside I suddenly wanted to reach the end of the walk. I felt I'd had enough of bog trotting in mist and rain. I was also beginning to make the transition back inside, back to the everyday world I'd been away from all summer. If I'd had a few more weeks I'd have felt content. Now that it was just a few days part of me was impatient to reach the end.

The gentle, musical sound of the river as it rippled over stones, a less hectic sound than other burns I'd camped by, was very soothing, a soft, rhythmic, slow trickle. I was loth to leave it the next morning but eventually did so. I followed the path up the glen then climbed east up steep grassy rakes to the south ridge of Ben More Assynt. In mist now, I followed the narrow ridge, which is mostly an easy walk though there are a few short bits of easy scrambling, over the South Top to the main summit where a cold north-west wind blew. Leaving the pack for the last time I went out along the short, stony ridge to Conival. As the mist rose and fell there were brief views of lochs far below and rocky buttresses ahead. I returned to Ben More Assynt then descended the north-east ridge to Glen Cassley. Once across the river in the glen, an easy ford, I walked along a hydro road that led across miles of bleak moorland hills to Loch Shin. I read all the way. Beyond the loch I crossed the A838 road. There was a phone box there so I rang Denise to confirm I was on schedule and to check the arrangements for the next two days. Chris and Cameron might meet me at the Crask Inn and climb Ben Klibreck with me the next day, I was told. If not, dinner was booked for 7.15 p.m. in the Altnaharra Hotel. Denise, Hazel and I were booked into a B&B, the only one in Altnaharra.

Across the road I plodded up a boggy hill then followed a deer fence beside a plantation until I found a slightly bumpy bit of grass next to a tiny trickling burn. It wasn't that scenic for the last camp of the walk but it would do. I lay in the tent and thought of the last camps of other long walks, of lying under a starry sky in the desert of southern New Mexico at the end of the Continental Divide and camping in the first blizzard of winter north of the Arctic Circle in the Yukon.

A fine morning at my last camp would have been pleasant but instead it was dismal with frequent dribbles of rain from a grey sky and a gusty wind. The nine mile or so walk to the Crask Inn was fairly dreary too as I skirted masses of little moorland mounds, mostly called Cnoc something. I reached the A836 road a little way north of the Crask Inn and walked down to it. It was closed and from the abandoned air had been for some time. There was no sign of Chris and Cameron. Or anybody else for that matter.

A track led east from the Inn. It soon became a boggy morass so I cut away north and climbed to Cnoc Sgriodain and the west ridge of Ben Klibreck. I was soon in mist and rain and saw nothing from the summit. Steep slopes led down to the Klibreck Burn and gentler, boggy terrain, which I crossed to the little fishing village of Altnaharra. It was an odd, unreal day. With no views or challenging terrain my mind wandered to the next day and beyond, too aware the walk was virtually over to pay much attention to the present.

I reached the B&B in time to have a much needed shower before Denise and Hazel arrived. Chris and Cameron turned up soon afterwards and I went over to the Altnaharra Hotel, where they were staying, for dinner. Denise and Hazel had already eaten. The hotel is a fairly formal place, used mainly by anglers. Ties were required for the dining-room. Needless to say I didn't have one. Neither did Chris or Cameron. I did have a clean shirt, which Denise had brought for me, but a tie? I hadn't worn one for years. Chris managed to persuade the management to waive their rules for once and we were able to eat. We had a table in the middle of the room. The talk over wine after the meal was quite animated. Over Chris Brasher's shoulder I kept catching sight of a man in tweed jacket and tweed tie sitting alone in the corner whose face was quite purple with rage. Not only were these people not dressed correctly but they were also noisy.

The final day came with clearing skies. I cycled north to Strath More and past the Pictish broch of Dun Dornagil to the bottom of Ben Hope. The others drove past me en route and were waiting when I arrived. Denise and Hazel came a little way up the hill with me then went back down to spend the next few hours at the coast. I continued up the steep slopes with Chris and Cameron. Ben Hope is an isolated, rugged peak with cliffs on its west and north sides, a good mountain to finish with. As we approached the summit the views opened out, a splendid panorama of spreading moorland dotted with a myriad shining lochans. There was a feeling of vast, open space.

I didn't really connect with this though, didn't really see it. My mind was running back and forth over the walk. Memories kept coming back. Ben Cruachan in that first storm; sun and warm rock on the Aonach Eagach; the otter in the woods below the Arrochar Alps; the Shelter Stone in the Cairngorms; the long glorious days over the Grey Corries, Aonachs, Ben Nevis and the Mamores; scrambling along the Cuillin ridge; golden eagles above Gleann Bianasadail and more and more and more. The inspiring high-level walks, the rocky scrambles, the slogs through miles of bogs, the bright sunshine and the heavy rains, the views of mountains vanishing into the distant horizon and the days when the mist reduced visibility to a few yards, the winds that blew me off the summits and the perfect calms when you could hear the silence, the encounters with wildlife from otters and deer to eagles and snow buntings, the wild flowers, the trees, especially the remnants of the Caledonian Forest – all of these and more combined to make the walk a memorable success, a joyous celebration of the wild land. What a wonderful mountain-packed summer it had been. Now, at the end, it was all important to me, all significant, all worthwhile. Every summit, every camp, every drop of rain, every blast of wind, even, in the euphoria of completion, every midge.

We reached the large summit cairn. I felt pleased, elated but somehow distant. I knew I'd finished but at the same time couldn't believe it. Surely I would go down, find somewhere to camp, then climb more hills the next day? Wouldn't I? Chris helped persuade me I wouldn't by producing a magnum of champagne and crystal glasses to go with it. As we were celebrating another walker arrived, who acted as though this was a normal scene to see on a mountain top. (Maybe it was, there's a lot of folk climbing the Munros these days.) We gave him some champagne, then persuaded him to take some photographs of the three of us.

Eventually it was time to descend. As we set off I turned and looked back at the summit, the last summit, the 517th summit.

Denise and Hazel were waiting at the foot of the mountain. We had more champagne. Chris and Cameron left for Inverness airport as Chris had a flight to London later that afternoon. The three of us wandered back up the hill a little way so Hazel could show me some waterfalls she'd discovered. Then it was time to go home. The walk was over.

APPENDICES

APPENDICES

Questions I'm always asked about my long-distance walks are how far did you walk each day and how far in total, how long did it take, how often did it rain and more. For those interested in these and other statistics here are some figures.

Time:	118 days
Distance:	1,770 miles (240 by bicycle)
Ascent:	575,000 feet
Daily average:	14½ miles & 4,800 feet
	15½ miles & 5,324 feet if the ten rest days are excluded

Maximum day's mileage:	25 (not including cycling days)
Maximum day's ascent:	11,000 feet (The Mamores)
Longest day:	16½ hours (The Cuillin)
Most Tops in a day:	17 (The Mamores)

Summits per day	*Days this number was climbed*
0	22
1	14
2	15
3	7
4	14
5	6
6	10
7	6
8	7

9	5
10	5
11	4
12	1
13	0
14	2
15	0
16	1
17	1

14 days had less than	1,000 feet of ascent
6	1,000+ feet of ascent
5	2,000+
6	3,000+
9	3,500+
8	4,000+
14	4,500+
8	5,000+
9	5,500+
11	6,000+
8	6,500+
6	7,000+
5	7,500+
2	8,000+
4	8,500+
2	9,500+
1	11,000+

The walk was mainly a solo one though I had company on 12 days and 64 Tops.

Nights Out

85 nights were spent camping (61 on 58 wild sites, 24 on 11 roadside camp-sites), 14 in ten bothies and 19 in ten hotels, B&Bs and private houses.

Despite my intentions, weather and logistics meant that most of my camps (46) were low-level ones, below 1,000 feet. Of the others:

19 camps were over 1,000 feet
7	1,500
8	2,000
4	2,500

1 camp was over 3,000 feet (3,100 feet on Glas Maol)

Weather

The weather was generally cool, damp, cloudy and windy. It rained at some point on 64 days. However there were some hot, sunny days. The longest sunny period was the six day one in mid-July when I walked from Ben Alder to Ben Nevis.

Summit Conditions

174 Tops were cloudy at the summit, 343 clear. However it was only raining on 115 with 402 being dry. This is surprising given the number of days on which it rained. The reasons are of course that I did far more summits when it was dry and also that on many days the rain was showery rather than constant.

People

Other walkers were met on only 54 summits. Although I did meet people on their way up and down many hills, lots of people in some places, this seems an incredibly low number. I put it down to the fact that few people climb the Tops and that most people are on summits between 11 a.m. and 3 p.m. whereas I reached many summits in the late afternoon and evening so that even popular hills like Ben Lomond were deserted when I was there.

II: EQUIPMENT

Oddly enough selecting gear for this walk proved more difficult than for the long walks I've done in much more remote areas. This was because those walks were mostly through valleys and over passes rather than summits so the weight of my gear, although important, wasn't crucial. As I was often carrying food for a week or more, plus sleeping bag and clothing to deal with below freezing temperatures, in a large (100 litres plus) and therefore heavy pack I usually ended up with around 36lb of gear before I added food and cameras. Total weights were in the 50 to 70lb range. On this walk however the prospect of many thousands of feet of ascent every day meant I needed as light a pack as possible. As Scottish summers aren't that cold (despite what some may think!) I could cut weight by carrying less clothing and a lighter sleeping bag. I was also planning on resupplying as often as possible to keep the weight of food and fuel low. My aim was to keep the weight without food or cameras down to 22 to 24lb at the most and the maximum weight carried at any time to 35 to 40lb.

At the same time my gear had to last for four months of constant use and be capable of coping with bad weather. After careful selection, which included weighing every item however small, I ended up with a basic pack weight, without food, fuel, maps or camera gear, of around 23 to 25 lb – some items not being carried all the time. My camera gear weighed 5lb, food 2½lb a day. For most of the walk I carried one 250 gram fuel cartridge (11¾oz full) and two or three maps at 3oz each (with card covers removed). Usually I only carried a few days food. Just once, in the far north, I carried six days' supplies and started a section with a pack weighing 40 to 45lb. Mostly it weighed around 30lb.

Pack

I changed packs several times during the walk! The pack is second only to footwear for comfort so my choice was important. The best packs have thick hipbelts and some form of internal frame so that most of the weight can be carried on the hips, the most efficient and comfortable way to do so. Stability was important too as I would be on rough, steep, terrain much of the time. The weight of the pack itself also mattered. Ideally a pack shouldn't weigh more than 10 per cent of the total load so I wanted one that didn't weigh more than 4lb. With less food and gear to carry than on other long walks a medium size pack, around 60–65 litres, would be adequate.

Despite the vast number of packs available I couldn't find one that fitted my requirements – they were all either too heavy or had inadequate hipbelts and frames – so when pack designer Aarn Tate asked me if I would test some prototype lightweight models I agreed. These – I used three different models – were made from a lightweight nylon but had an excellent hipbelt and back system that gave good support and stability whilst not restricting freedom of movement. Capacities were in the 65 to 75 litre range and weights around 4½lb. I found them very comfortable though there were some problems with the first one, as you would expect with a prototype. These lightweight packs are not available commercially. The nearest equivalent are Vango's Denali packs which are designed by Aarn Tate and have a similar back system. They're not very light however.

For the weeks when Aarn's packs were being shuttled back and forth between the Highlands and his base in Skelmersdale I used a couple of heavier packs, a Lowe Alpine Alpamayo 70, which was quite comfortable, and a Canadian made Arc'teryx Bora 60 pack which carried well but which I didn't find very stable on rough ground or when scrambling. None of the packs had side pockets, which add weight and can get in the way when scrambling, but they all had large lid pockets for quick access to small items. The Aarn Tate and Lowe Alpine models had two compartments, an arrangement I like as it gives better access to gear. The Bora had a single compartment with a full length side zip. Overall I prefer two compartments. A smaller, frameless, Lowe Alpine Walkabout 45 pack was used for cycling and some ascents from a base.

Footwear

I've always found lightweight, flexible, well-cushioned footwear the most comfortable, especially for high mileages and on rough terrain. Heavy, stiff boots are tiring to wear and impede a natural gait. A pound on your feet equals five on your back. After considering various models I settled on leather Brasher Hillmasters and found them ideal. My size 9½s weighed 2lb 12oz. I used three pairs in total, wearing out the soles on two of them (resoling is possible of course but not during a long walk). I was particularly impressed with the GTX model as they were still waterproof after 41 days, unlike other Gore-tex lined boots I've used which have leaked after two weeks or less. This seems to be due to the leather lining. Other Gore-tex boots have fabric inners through which tiny slivers of grit can pass and then cut the Gore-tex membrane.

I find changing my footwear at the end of the day very refreshing so I carried a pair of Reebok Amazone sports sandals (21½oz) as back-up. I also wore these for walking on 12 days when it was very hot. To the amazement, and it must be said disapproval, of many I find well-designed sports sandals like the Amazone, which is to say ones with good cushioning, a tread that grips on wet rock and straps that hold the foot and, in particular, the heel in place, the ideal footwear for hot weather walking even on rough stony terrain. At times when wet weather was forecast I also carried flexible rubber Dry Walker Bothy Boots (6oz), which were excellent for wet camp-sites as well as bothies.

Tent

There are plenty of excellent tents available. Unfortunately most of them are heavy and made to sleep two or more people. Of those designed for solo use many are so small you can't sit up inside, never mind cook or store gear. One of the few models weighing under 4lb yet having adequate room is the Swedish made Hilleberg Akto. This single hoop model weighs 3lb 12oz and was quick to pitch, rain and midge proof, very stable in high winds and had a roomy porch in which I could cook and store gear under cover.

Sleeping Bag

Despite the improvements in synthetic fills, down bags are still lighter and more compressible for the warmth. Keeping them dry is not the problem it is often thought to be. The Rab Micro 300 weighs just 23oz and was ideal for the overnight temperatures experienced, which ranged from +2° to +17°C. It was used on over 100 nights but, although grubby in places, showed no sign of wear at the end. I carried it in the bottom of the pack in a proofed Black Diamond stuffsack with taped seams inside a heavy duty plastic bag and it never got wet.

Mat

Some people can manage without a sleeping mat in summer (Hamish Brown did on his long walk) but I just can't sleep properly without one. Even with closed cell foam mats, which provide insulation from ground cold but aren't very soft, I wake several times each night with sore hips or shoulders. Because of this I've used the luxuriously soft Therm-A-Rest self-inflating mats on all my long walks, finding the comfort worth the weight. These suck in air when a valve is opened (a few puffs of breath help) making the foam filling expand so that you sleep on a springy air and foam mix. Just before this walk a new, lightest ever Therm-A-Rest appeared, the 14oz Ultralite II. It was as comfortable as earlier models and compact enough to be carried folded flat down the back of the pack.

Bivvy Bag

A bivvy bag, a waterproof bag into which I could slide for protection against the wind and rain, was carried mainly as a safety back-up for side trips away from the tent though I did use it a few times to protect my sleeping bag when sleeping in leaky bothies and under the very damp Shelter Stone in the Cairngorms. Again I searched for the lightest available and came up with the Rab Survival Zone, made from Pertex with a waterproof/breathable coating, which weighed just 8½oz, less than many plastic survival bags. It worked well with no condensation forming inside.

Cooking

On previous long walks in places like the Yukon and the Canadian Rockies I used stoves that ran on white gas (a refined form of petrol, Coleman Fuel is one type) because of the availability of the fuel. However the lightest, easiest to use stoves are ones that run off resealable butane/propane gas cartridges. As resupplying with fuel wasn't a problem I decided to use one of these. I started with a new Coleman Micro stove (5½oz) but after a few weeks I had problems with it going out unexpectedly so I reverted to using an earlier version I'd had for several years, which worked fine. (Coleman later modified the first stove in line with changes already made to later versions and it has since worked perfectly.) For the final few weeks I used a Coleman Alpine which is heavier at 13oz but much more stable because it attaches to the cartridge by way of a long hose rather than screwing into the top like the Micro. The reason for the change was that I had a number of tall 500gm cartridges I wanted to use up but which were very unsteady when used with the Micro. A 250gm (11¾oz full) cartridge lasted 4 days, a 500gm one (21½oz full), 8 days. A foil windscreen (2oz) kept off the wind.

My pans were an Evernew Titanium 0.9 litre which weighed 5.2oz and a stainless steel pint size Cascade Cup (4oz). I ate out of the first and the second doubled as a mug so no plates, bowls or cups were needed. Both pans were bought in the USA. Titanium doesn't scratch or dent easily like aluminium and is much lighter than stainless steel. Two Lexan plastic spoons weighed 1oz. I don't bother with forks on solo trips and for a knife I had a tiny Swiss Army model that lived in a trouser pocket.

Water containers were a rigid litre size Gatorade bottle (3oz) for carrying drinks while walking and a soft rollaway 4 litre Ortlieb Water Bag (2½oz) for camp use. Surprisingly the Gatorade bottle, which I'd purchased the year before at the Grand Canyon and brought home after drinking the contents because it looked useful, lasted the whole trip.

Clothing

Clothing had to be as light as possible yet still capable of dealing with the worst weather in the Highlands.

Waterproofs: Good rainwear was of course essential. For years I've preferred waterproofs with a lining laminate construction, that is two layer ones where the waterproof/breathable layer is the inner one. The lightest garments I know of with this design are the Rab Original Downpour Jacket and Overtrousers at weights of 23 and 13oz respectively. These have Permatex membrane inners and Pertex nylon outers. They are soft and comfortable to wear and proved very durable. The weather was generally cool and windy with rain on 64 days. On many days I walked for 9 to 10 hours through torrential rain and gale-force winds. The garments never leaked. The jacket was worn on 70+ days and remained waterproof throughout. The outer suffered a few minor tears on the lower pockets, caused when scrambling, but otherwise shows little sign of wear. The water repellency wore off but this can be renewed. The drying time was only slightly prolonged anyway.

Windproof: Made from ripstop Pertex the Sprayway PACS Windshell weighed a mere 7½oz. I took it instead of a shirt and, as expected, it was the garment I wore most, as a windproof shirt over a base layer on cool, breezy days, under the waterproof jacket in rain and over my fleece top for extra warmth in camp on cool evenings. It dried amazingly fast when wet and was very comfortable to wear. The design was simple, as the best designs for walking clothing usually are, just a pullover with a long front zip for ventilation, wide cuffs that enabled the sleeves to be rolled up in the heat and a high collar to keep out breezes. Finally there was a large zipped map pocket on the right chest.

Trousers: Legwear made from modern synthetic fabrics is lighter and tougher than anything else and has been my first choice for walking for several years. Buffalo Travelite trousers are made from texturised Pertex nylon and weigh only 8½oz. They were just about perfect, being windproof, breathable, quick drying, durable and comfortable. They have a good map-sized patch pocket on one thigh too. Underpants were made from wicking synthetic fabric – far better than cotton as it dries quickly. I had two pairs, one made from Coolmax polyester, one from Tactel nylon, which I swapped at supply points, the dirty pair going home to be washed. For hot weather I had various pairs of shorts, made from either synthetics or polycotton.

Warmwear: Made from Polartec 150 Microfleece the Sprayway Huggy shirt weighs only 9.75oz yet was the only warmwear I needed for most of the walk. The low weight was again due to the simple design – the only feature is a short neck zip and high collar. Other features may be nice but they add weight and aren't essential. For the first few weeks when it was very cold, with snow and sleet on the Tops at times, I also carried a

Sprayway T-Top and Pants made from Powerstretch fleece, weights 9½ and 7oz.

Base Layers: To some people's surprise I wear synthetic wicking base layers year round, finding them comfortable even in summer. Cotton, the hot weather favourite, is fine until it becomes sweat soaked, which happens very quickly when hill-walking. Then it's clammy and slow to dry. And in cool and wet weather it is cold next to the skin and potentially dangerous. By wearing a synthetic top I had no need of a spare, which I would have carried if I'd worn cotton in warm weather. Wearing synthetics in the heat isn't a new idea, Hamish Brown had found his synthetic vest 'better than a shirt in the heat' back in 1974, but it hasn't caught on.

I alternated between two long sleeved tops, sending one home to be washed at most resupply points. They were a View From nylon one, and a North Face Thermal Dynamics polyester one. Each weighed 5½oz and worked well in both cold and warm weather and also when worn for a week without being washed.

Head, Hands & Feet: I used a variety of modern high-tech socks with thick and thin padding all over the place but eventually reverted to simple knitted Ragg wool ones as I found that only these would stand up to day after day of wet weather backpacking without being washed. I usually had two pairs with me, one on my feet, one in the pack. The weight was around 4oz a pair.

Headwear consisted firstly of a fleece hat (4oz) which I lost during the third week and which was replaced by a light (2oz) acrylic hat – knitted for me by Ted Thorn, Denise's father – for cold weather and a wide-brimmed cotton Tilley Hat (5¾oz) for the sun. I needed gloves early on but as I hadn't brought any I wore socks over my hands, a trick I'd used before and which works quite well. Later I did carry a pair of windproof fleece gloves (3oz) which were more than adequate for summer storms.

Trekking Poles: I've used poles for several years, finding them very useful, particularly when descending steep, rough terrain. As well as being aids to balance they also take the strain off the knees on long descents. I also reckon I walk faster with them than without them without any increase in effort, especially uphill. For this trip I used adjustable three-section Kohla models which had curved cork grips which I found much more comfortable than ones on other poles I've used. They weighed 21oz but were only in the pack when scrambling.

Accessories

This is a dangerous area where weight can very quickly accumulate. After ruthless pruning I ended up carrying a Petzl Micro Headlamp (5.3oz), Silva 4 compass (1oz), plastic safety whistle (½oz), small first aid and repair kit (13¾oz), Mosiguard Natural midge repellent (non-DEET and works well, 2½ oz), mosquito coils with holder (6½oz), a Quantock headnet (2oz), tiny Classic model Swiss Army Knife (1oz), Avocet Vertech altimeter/watch (1½oz), Ortlieb map case (2½oz – essential!) and plastic toilet trowel (2oz).

For keeping notes I carried a couple of waterproof pens (1oz) and a series of exercise books (3½oz each) (I filled four-and-a-half of the latter). One exercise book went the whole way as it contained my route plan, lists of summits, maps and supply points, and daily recordings of which peaks I'd climbed, where I'd stayed, the weather, the height climbed and miles walked and various other data. I also used it for addresses, shopping lists and other notes.

Camera Gear

On other long walks I've carried two SLR bodies and a selection of lenses, weighing 10lb or more. Partly this was in case one of the camera bodies failed, as has happened, far from anywhere. On this trip I would never need to be without a camera for more than a few days if a problem did occur so I saved weight by only taking one body, a Nikon F50, and one lens, a 28-80 zoom, total weight 32oz. The camera was carried slung bandolier style across my chest, the most comfortable position I've found, in a padded waterproof Camera Care Systems Tusker bag with a stretch neoprene strap (13oz). After much deliberation I carried a Cullman tripod weighing 22oz. It was worth the weight. Without it I couldn't have taken many of my best photographs, including some that appear in this book. This may sound a lot of camera gear but it's the least I've ever carried on a long walk. Film was Fuji Sensia 100, a sharp, bright colour transparency film. I took 60 rolls. The only filters used were a skylight to protect the lens and, at times, a polariser.

Cycling

Saracen kindly supplied me with a Rufftrax mountain bike, my 12-year-old one (also a Saracen) having been deemed as unsafe and beyond repair by Alastair Forsyth of the Cycle Shop in Grantown-on-Spey. The new bike was a revelation – far more comfortable than my battered relic. Although I was mostly on roads rather than rough ground the 15 gears were welcome for all the hills. And when I did go off-road the knobbly tyres were appreciated. I carried a pump and tyre repair kit but never used them. Other than padded cycling shorts, which were very welcome on long rides, I didn't have any special cycling clothing though I did wear a helmet most of the time. It seemed wise on roads like the A9.

III: FOOD

Much to the astonishment of many people I've never had a problem living on dried food for months at a time. What I have learnt from my long walks is that I need plenty of calories – at least 4,000 a day – which works out at around 2½lbs of dry food per day. Variety is needed too to stave off boredom so I like to have a wide choice of foods. Because it's carbohydrates that provide immediate and ongoing energy these should make up the bulk of food, ideally in the form of complex carbohydrates rather than sugars. The latter may give a quick energy boost but this is usually then followed by a slump.

Dried food is simple and quick to prepare as well as light and low bulk to carry. On long walks I prefer specialist backpacking foods without additives rather than chemical-laden supermarket concoctions. Of those available in Britain the best I've found are from Outdoor Pantry/Be-Well Nutritional Products. These are both carefully thought out nutritionally and reasonably tasty. I approached the company to see if they would be interested in supplying any food for the walk and was delighted and surprised when they not only offered to provide all my main meals but also to make up daily breakfast and lunch packs. In return they asked me to try out some new products for them. Having packs made up in advance saved a lot of time and work and meant I was less likely to run out of items. Versions of these packs are now available in outdoor shops under the name Pack'n'Go.

Breakfast consisted of a cereal – either muesli or a hot instant porridge – and some savoury biscuits with vegetable spread or cheese. Lunch was eaten in a series of snacks – I rarely walked more than a couple of hours without eating something, a constant flow of energy being required – made up of more biscuits and cheese or spread, trail mix, chocolate bars, flapjack and Cross Bars, a high carbohydrate energy bar. For liquids I had coffee and an orange-flavoured energy drink called Turbo Pulse that

203

could be drunk hot or cold. Dinner consisted of quick cook (not instant) packet soup, freeze dried main meal and a quick cook or cold dessert. None of the meals had meat in them though one contained shrimps and I did have a few tins of tuna and sardines as lunch foods. Overall though I lived on a vegetarian diet.

The Outdoor Pantry rations provided about 3,200 kilocalories per day, which was fine for the first couple of weeks, after which my appetite grew and I had to add more. I wasn't overeating either – I still lost a stone in weight during the walk. The extra food consisted mostly of more snack items such as dried fruit, chocolate and flapjack bars as I was often walking 10 to 12 hours a day. I also carried ½lb cheese a week to add to some of the soups and main meals. Fresh garlic and various dried herbs and spices helped pep up the main meals.

I can't say that this was an exciting diet but it was adequate and although I welcomed the fresh foods Denise brought out to supply points and the meals in cafés when available I didn't grow tired of it.

IV: FURTHER READING

The literature of the Scottish hills is extensive and growing all the time. This list isn't anything like comprehensive but rather consists of books I've found useful, informative and entertaining. I've also listed other books of mine that may be of interest plus some others that I've mentioned in this book and which, although they're not about the Highlands, have influenced my thoughts on wilderness.

Abbey, Edward *Desert Solitaire*, McGraw-Hill, 1968
The Journey Home, E.P.Dutton, 1975
Abbey's Road E.P.Dutton, 1979
Down the River E.P.Dutton, 1982
Beyond the Wall Henry Holt, 1984
One Life At A Time, Please Henry Holt, 1987 – Provocative and stimulating writer on wilderness and the environment.

Allan, Elizabeth, *Burn on the Hill*, Bidean Books, 1995 – The story of the second Munroist and the first to do all the Tops as well
Bartholomew, J.C.; Bennet, D.J. & Stone, C, *Scottish Hill Tracks*, Scottish Rights of Way Society, 1995 – Useful packsize guidebook to tracks through the hills, not all of them rights of way.
Barton, Bob & Wright, Blyth, *A Chance in a Million? Scottish Avalanches* SMT, 1985 – Essential reading for the winter hillwalker.

Bearhop, D.A. (editor), *Munro's Tables* SMT, 1997 – The essential list.

Bell, J.H.B. *Bell's Scottish Climbs* Gollancz, 1988 – A selection by Hamish Brown of the Scottish sections of Bell's classic 1950 book *A Progress in Mountaineering*.

Bennet, Donald (editor), *The Munros* SMT, 1985 – Guidebook with good illustrations.

Bennet, Donald & Wallace, Bill, *Ski Mountaineering in Scotland* SMT, 1987 – Beautifully illustrated guidebook. If only all (or even most) winter days were as pictured here!

Borthwick, Alistair, *Always A Little Further* Diadem, 1983 – Classic, amusing stories of how it used to be, first published in 1939.

Brower, David, *Let the Mountains Talk, Let the Rivers Run* HarperCollins, 1996 – Inspiring reflections on restoring the environment.

Brown, Dave and Mitchell, Ian, *Mountain Days and Bothy Nights* Luath Press, 1987 – Stories of the hills.

Brown, Dave and Mitchell, Ian, *A View From The Ridge* Ernest Press, 1991 – More stories of the hills.

Brown, Hamish, *Hamish's Mountain Walk* and *Climbing the Corbetts,* Omnibus edition, Baton Wicks, 1997, – Story of the first continuous round of the Munros and an entertaining guide to the Corbetts. First published in 1978 and 1988 respectively.

Brown, Hamish, *The Last Hundred* Mainstream, 1994 – Stories of the Munros.

Brown Hamish (editor) *Poems of the Scottish Hills* AUP, 1982 – An interesting anthology.

Bull, S.P., *Black Cuillin Ridge Scrambler's Guide* SMT, 1980 – Useful guide, needs updating.

Butterfield, Irvine, *The High Mountains of Britain and Ireland* Diadem, 1986 – Detailed, well-illustrated guidebook.

Caldwell, Craig, *Climb Every Mountain* MacDonald, 1990 – Story of the author's mammoth Munros and Corbetts walk.

Cramb, Auslan, *Who Owns Scotland Now?* Mainstream, 1996 – Disturbing study of land ownership with an emphasis on the environment and detailed studies of ten estates.

Crumley, Jim, *A High and Lonely Place* Jonathan Cape, 1991 – A personal, poetic defence of the Cairngorms.

Crumley, Jim, *Among Mountains* Mainstream, 1993 – A philosophical approach.

Darling, F. Fraser and Boyd, J. Morton, *The Highlands and Islands* Collins, 1964 – Classic natural history/ecology book, still relevant.

Dempster, Andrew, *The Munro Phenomenon* Mainstream, 1995 – Fascinating facts and analysis.

Drummond, Peter and Mitchell, Ian, *The First Munroist* Ernest Press, 1993 – The story of A.E. Robertson with a selection of his photographs.

Drummond, Peter, *Scottish Hill and Mountain Names* SMT, 1991 – Fascinating.

Dufton, G.J.F., *The Ridiculous Mountains* Diadem, 1984 – Hilarious stories of the fictitious Doctor and friends.

Fletcher, Colin, *The Thousand-Mile Summer* Alfred Knopf, 1964
               The Man Who Walked Through Time Alfred Knopf, 1968
               The Complete Walker III Alfred Knopf, 1984
               The Secret Worlds of Colin Fletcher Alfred Knopf, 1989
The best writer on wilderness walking

Gilbert, Richard, *Memorable Munros* Diadem, 1983 – One man's round, interesting anecdotes.

Gordon, Seton, *Highways and Byways in the West Highlands* Birlinn, 1995 – Classic guidebook first published in 1935.

Gordon, Seton, *Highways and Byways in the Central Highlands* Birlinn, 1995 – Classic guidebook first published in 1949.

Gray, Affleck, *Legends of the Cairngorms* Mainstream, 1987 – Collection of folktales.

Gray, Muriel, *The First Fifty* Mainstream, 1991 – Irreverent and entertaining Munro stories.

Hewitt, Dave, *Walking the Watershed* Tacit Press, 1994 – Story of the first walk along the watershed of Scotland.

Johnstone, S., Brown, Hamish & Bennet, Donald (editors), *The Corbetts and Other Scottish Hills* SMT, 1990 – Well-illustrated guidebook.

Linklater, Eric, *The Prince in the Heather* Hodder & Stoughton, 1966 – Story of the Highland wanderings of Bonnie Prince Charlie.

MacInnes, Hamish, *Call Out* Hodder & Stoughton, 1973 – Mountain rescue stories.

MacNally, Lea, *Torridon* Swan Hill, 1993 – Stories from a former NTS ranger/naturalist, mostly about wildlife.

McNeish, Cameron, *The Munro Almanac* Neil Wilson Publishing, 1996 – Packsize guide.

McNeish, Cameron, *The Corbett Almanac* Neil Wilson Publishing, 1996 – Packsize guide.

McNeish, Cameron, *The Munros* Lomond Books, 1996 – Well-illustrated, well-written guide.

McNeish, Cameron, & Else, Richard, *Wilderness Walks* BBC, 1997 – Tie-in with a tv series but stands alone well with interesting routes and stories and excellent photographs.

McOwan, Rennie, *Magic Mountains* Mainstream, 1996 – Investigation into legends, ghost stories and more.

McOwan, Rennie *The Man Who Bought Mountains* NTS, 1977 – Leaflet about Percy Unna.

Moran, Martin, *The Munros in Winter,* David and Charles 1986 – The first continuous winter round.

Moran, Martin, *Scotland's Winter Mountains* David and Charles, 1988 – Detailed advice and information.

Mountaineering Council of Scotland/Scottish Landowners' Federation (compilers), *Heading for the Scottish Hills* SMT, 1988 – Contact addresses, phone numbers and maps for estates.

Muir, John *The Eight Wilderness-Discovery Books* Diadem, 1992 – Classic works by a pioneer of wilderness conservation.

Murray, W.H., *Mountaineering in Scotland/Undiscovered Scotland* Diadem, 1988 – Classic tales of climbing and exploration, first published in 1947 and 1951 respectively.

Murray, W.H, *Scotland's Mountains* SMT, 1987 – Interesting overview.

Nethersole-Thompson, Desmond and Watson, Adam, *The Cairngorms* Collins, 1974 – Classic natural history.

Oakley, Angela, *Ski Touring in Scotland* Cicerone, 1991 – Good selection of high and low level tours.

Parker, J.Wilson, *Scrambles in Skye* Cicerone, 1983 – Good guidebook to the one area where a guide is as useful as a map.

Patey, Tom, *One Man's Mountains* Canongate, 1997 – Entertaining and witty classic, first published 1971.

Ramsey, Paul *Revival of the Land – Creag Meagaidh National Nature Reserve* Scottish Natural Heritage, 1996 – Story of a great conservation success.

Scott, Sir Walter *Rob Roy* many editions – Classic adventure story.

Scottish Mountaineering Trust *District Guides* SMT – The Scottish Mountaineering Club District Guides are very detailed and contain far more information than guidebooks to walking routes. There have been several editions, all of them interesting. The guides are the *Islands* including Skye, the *Northwest Highlands*, the *Cairngorms,* the *Central Highlands,* the *Southern Highlands* and the *Southern Uplands.*

Stainforth, Gordon, *Eyes to the Hills* Constable, 1991 – Beautifully illustrated with some interesting thoughts, especially for the Munroist.

Stainforth, Gordon, *The Cuillin* Constable, 1994 – Spectacular photographs and interesting words.

Stevenson, Robert Louis, *Kidnapped* many editions – Classic tale. It's interesting to try and work out the route.

Stewart, Arthur, *Long Distance Walks in Scotland* Crowood, 1991 – A selection of multi-day treks.

Storer, Ralph, *100 Best Routes on Scottish Mountains* David and Charles, 1987 – A good selection.

Storer, Ralph, *The Joy of Hillwalking* Luath Press, 1994 – Entertaining stories and some thoughts on the reasons for hillwalking.

Stott, Louis, *The Waterfalls of Scotland* AUP, 1987 – Comprehensive.

Symonds, Hugh, *Running High* Lochar, 1991 – Story of his amazing run over all the Munros plus the 3,000 foot summits in the rest of Britain.

Tomkies, Mike, *A Last Wild Place* Jonathan Cape, 1984 – Life as a naturalist in a remote cottage in the west Highlands.

Townsend, Chris *The Great Backpacking Adventure* Oxford Illustrated Press, 1987 – Contains an account of a 500 mile Corrour to Ullapool walk over 92 Munros.
Townsend, Chris *Classic Hill Walks*, Blandford, 1996 – Illustrated hill walks, ten of them in the Highlands.
Townsend, Chris *A Guide to Hillwalking* Crowood, 1996 – How to do it.
Townsend, Chris *The Backpacker's Handbook* Second Edition, Ragged Mountain Press, 1997 – Comprehensive guide to wilderness backpacking.
Turnbull, Ronald, *Across Scotland on Foot* Grey Stone Books, 1994 – Idiosyncratic and entertaining guidebook.
Weir, Tom, *Highland Days* Gordon Wright, 1984 – Classic stories, first published in 1948.
Weir, Tom, *Tom Weir's Scotland* Gordon Wright, 1980 – A selection of essays.
Weir, Tom, *Weir's Way* Gordon Wright, 1981 – Selection of essays.
Wightman, Andy, *Who Owns Scotland*, Canongate, 1996 – Disturbing investigation into land ownership with some positive suggestions for essential reforms.

VI: USEFUL ADDRESSES

John Muir Trust, 13 Wellington Place, Edinburgh, EH6 7JD
Mountain Bothies Association, 26 Rycroft Avenue, Deeping St James, Peterborough, PE6 8NT
Mountaineering Council of Scotland, 4A St Catherine's Road, Perth, PH1 5SE
National Trust for Scotland, 5 Charlotte Square, Edinburgh, EH2 4DU
Ramblers' Association, Scotland, Crusader House, Balgonie Road, Haig Business Park, Markinch, Fife, KY7 7AQ
Royal Society for the Protection of Birds, Scottish Headquarters, 17 Regent Terrace, Edinburgh, EH7 5BH
Scottish Natural Heritage, 12 Hope Terrace, Edinburgh, EH9 2AS
Scottish Rights of Way Society, 1 Lutton Place, Edinburgh, EH10 5JR
Scottish Wild Land Group, 8 Cleveden Road, Kelvinside, Glasgow, G12 0NT